THE SHOEMAKER

AND THE

TEA PARTY

Works by Alfred F. Young

Masquerade: The Life and Times of Deborah Sampson Gannett, Continental Soldier

Beyond the American Revolution: Explorations in the History of American Radicalism (Editor)

Past Imperfect: The Essays of Lawrence W. Towner on History, Libraries and the Humanities
(Co-Editor, with Robert Karrow)

We the People: Voices and Images of the New Nation
(with Terry Fife and Mary Janzen)

American Social History Project, *Who Built America?*
(Consulting Editor)

We the People: Creating a New Nation, 1765–1815,
Chicago Historical Society (Co-Curator with Terry Fife)

The American Revolution: Explorations in the History of American Radicalism (Editor)

Dissent: Explorations in the History of American Radicalism (Editor)

The American Heritage Series
(Co–General Editor with Leonard W. Levy)

The Democratic Republicans of New York: The Origins, 1763–1797

THE SHOEMAKER

AND THE

TEA PARTY

———

Memory and the American Revolution

Alfred F. Young

Beacon Press

BOSTON

Beacon Press
25 Beacon Street
Boston, Massachusetts 02108–2892
www.beacon.org

Beacon Press books are published under the auspices of
the Unitarian Universalist Association of Congregations.

10 09   14 13 12

This book is printed on recycled acid-free paper that contains
at least 20 percent postconsumer waste and meets the uncoated paper
ANSI/NISO specifications for permanence as revised in 1992.

Book design by Boskydell Studio
Composition by Wilsted & Taylor Publishing Services

Library of Congress Cataloging-in-Publication Data
Young, Alfred Fabian, 1925–
The shoemaker and the tea party : memory and
the American Revolution / Alfred F. Young.
p. cm.
ISBN 978-0-8070-5405-5 (pbk.)
1. Boston Tea Party, 1773. 2. Hewes, George R. T. (George Robert Twelves),
1742–1840. 3. Shoemakers—Massachusetts—Boston—Biography.
4. United States—History—Revolution, 1775–1783—Social aspects.
5. Memory—Social aspects—United States. I. Title.
E215.7.Y68 1999
973.3′113—dc21 98-48922

Contents

Introduction

How does an ordinary person win a place in history? It has a lot to do with the political values of the keepers of the past—who decides whose heroes and heroines school children learn about, what statues and monuments are erected, what historic buildings are saved, and what events are commemorated. Take the few ordinary people of Boston in the Revolution about whom we have even a smattering of knowledge. Paul Revere was best known in his own time as a silversmith and a leader of the mechanics of the North End, but in Henry Wadsworth Longfellow's poem he became a legend as the horseman who warned Lexington that the "British are coming," hardly his most important accomplishment. Yet he is honored in a heroic equestrian statue. A monument to Crispus Attucks, a half-black, half-Indian sailor, and the four other victims of the Boston Massacre was erected only after a forty-year campaign by the city's African American community for recognition of their role in the Revolution and over the opposition of leading members of the Massachussetts Historical Society, who considered them "ruffians" of the "so-called Boston Massacre." Phillis Wheatley, Boston's African-born poet of the Revolutionary era, similarly (then as now) owes her place in history to advocates of equality. On the other hand, Ebenezer Mc-Intosh, the shoemaker who became the "Captain General of the Liberty Tree," a principal "mob" leader of the resistance to the Stamp Act, has never been recognized. Posterity, like patriot leaders who felt threatened at the time, has shunted him aside.

Until quite recently, professional historians have rarely opened the gates to ordinary people. How did I, a professional historian come to write about George Robert Twelves Hewes, a shoemaker, and his personal memory of the Revolution, and why, twenty years later, have I gone back to the problem of the public memory of the Revolution?[1] My answers may shed some light on why historians "do" certain kinds of history (and bypass others) and how they choose their subjects. I did not start out to write a biography of Hewes. I had no idea that "memory" would become my problem. And, more recently, I did not start out with the teasing question, "When did they start calling it the Boston Tea Party?" In fact, like everyone else, I did not think it *was* a question. I assumed the event had always been so called.

Woody Allen has said that 90 percent of life is just showing up. For historians, I would say that 90 percent of doing good history is asking the right questions, coming up with the sources that let you answer them, and reading them well. But I sometimes think an important 10 percent is serendipity—going to the library shelves, for instance, and finding not the book you set out for, but one alongside it you did not know existed, which turns out to be much more important.

You begin with questions drawn from historical scholarship, often inspired by the currents around you or sometimes by your own resistance to them. In the late 1940s and early 1950s, when I began studying American history in graduate school, it was the height of the Cold War, a time, as the historian Peter Novick writes, when "a sense of urgent crisis and impending Armageddon" permeated the academic world. The crusade against revolutions abroad—whether communist, colonial, or nationalist—and its by-product, an inquisition into political heresy at home since called McCarthyism, froze a thin layer of ice over the study of revolution, including the American Revolution. It was un-American to question "the motives" of the "founding fathers" (let alone to ask whether there might also be "founding mothers"). Professional energy and financial support poured into multivolume projects to publish the complete papers of the great men of the era: Thomas Jefferson, John Adams, George Washington, Benjamin Franklin, Alexander Hamilton, James Madison. These invaluable projects are still under way, and most will not be completed until well into the twenty-first century. Yet you could spend days touring restored Colonial Williamsburg, the political home of Jefferson, Washington, and Madison, and not know that more than half of the population of this colonial capital of Virginia were African American slaves. Urban "mobs," agrarian rebellions, slave resistance, the awakenings of religious enthusiasts—all the stuff of the radicalism of the Revolutionary era—were off-limits to those historians, who homogenized American history into "a cult of consensus."[2]

The ice did not start to melt until the heat of the American upheavals of the 1960s: the civil rights crusade, the urban uprisings, the antiwar movement, the countercultural protest of students and youth, the women's movement. These movements for equality from below demonstrated the capacity of ordinary people to change the course of contemporary history and set people looking at "history from the bottom up," a phrase popularized by the historian Jesse Lemisch, from which vantage point the publications projects, however valuable, seemed to be "the papers of Great White Men." These movements also made historians ready to challenge what the British historian E. P. Thompson called "the enormous condescension of posterity" to little-known actors on the historical stage.[3]

Current events raised questions for history rather than the other way around. For every Martin Luther King, who led the crusade for desegregation, there was a Mrs. Rosa Parks, a seamstress, who by refusing to go to the back of the bus launched the bus boycott in Montgomery, Alabama in 1955. And Rosa Parks, it turned out, was an active member of an organization, the National Association for the Advancement of Colored People (NAACP). In the 1960s there were other organizations, like the Student Nonviolent Coordinating Committee (SNCC), which conducted training sessions in nonviolent civil disobedience, and grassroots leaders who were usually ahead of and sometimes at odds with national leaders. Who, in Boston, was to Samuel Adams, the leader of the most successful campaign of civil disobedience in American history, as Rosa Parks and SNCC were to Rev. King?[4]

This was the context in the late 1960s in which I began to study the "common people" in Boston, in particular the "mechanics"—as master craftsmen, journeymen, and apprentices came to call themselves—in the making of the Revolution. I chose Boston because it was the scene of so many iconic events and a good place to test the conflicting interpretations of the Revolution. The questions that interested me were What part did the "common people"—a phrase used in the eighteenth century—play in the making of the Revolution? Did they have ideas of their own as well as ideas they shared with leaders? To what extent did they shape events, and were they changed by their experiences? Historians analyze these questions under the headings of agency, consciousness, and transformation.

But I wondered how to get a handle on ordinary people. Might it be possible to answer such questions by reconstructing the life of one rank-and-file participant? The problem is that in a society where education and literacy were unequally distributed, those of the "meaner" sort and "middling" sort, although not inarticulate, unlike the "better" sort wrote no pamphlets, spoke rarely in the town meeting (if indeed they qualified to vote), and left no massive bodies of "papers." For Boston during the period 1765 to 1775, historians know of one diary kept for two years by a twelve-year-old girl and another kept by a merchant. But life histories?

As I plowed through the conventional sources—newspapers, legal records, correspondence—George Robert Twelves Hewes, a man with a name you did not forget, kept popping up: in famous events, the Boston Massacre and the Boston Tea Party, and the not so famous tarrings and featherings and other crowd actions that won Boston a reputation as a "mobbish" town. At some point it dawned on me that two memoirs of him had been assembled by biographers when he was in his nineties and was "discovered" and celebrated in Boston as "one of the last survivors of the tea party." These memoirs told unusually full stories and were different in useful ways. At another point, when I was doing research in the library of the Bostonian Society, then located in the Old State House (for two centuries the center of government in Massachusetts), I realized that the painting with the name *The Centenarian* I passed at the top of the spiral staircase was a portrait of the same man, quite extraordinary for a shoemaker. The more I read, the more his memoirs checked out and it seemed possible to risk doing his life. Although I did not start out to do the biography of a shoemaker, once I got going I wanted to show that such a life history was possible.

Historians frown on memoirs. In the canons of historical research summed up in a much used handbook, "the value of a piece of testimony usually increased in proportion to the nearness in time and space between the witness and the events about which he testifies."[5] In other words, an eyewitness is better than a secondhand report, and an account taken down at the time better than one recalled years later. According to this scale, a memoir written late in life is flawed, and a memoir "as told to" someone else, or strained through another voice, is doubly flawed. I confess that I remained skeptical about Hewes's memory even after one independent source after another confirmed his credibility.

When I began studying Hewes, my interest in memory was focused on its accuracy. As I worked my way through Hewes's remembering, I realized that my subject was not only his experiences, what he had done and thought during the Revolution, but the *way* he remembered them, his memory, and this is the subject of the first essay in this book. In his nineties his memory was quite extraordinary, yet he could also claim that he remembered John Hancock, the wealthiest patriot merchant in Boston, at his side on a tea ship in 1773 throwing the tea overboard, something that was decidedly unlikely. In his memory of something he was convinced he had experienced—not a false memory—lay a clue to the meaning of the Revolution for him and very likely for many others of his class. There were other memories with a similar resonance. To make sense of his remembering, I had to peel his biographers away from him, unravel his memory from his experiences, and then intertwine them anew, analyzing why he was remembering the way he did. In other words, his memory itself became my subject.

Two decades ago I got little help from psychologists about how memory worked. Since that time, however, there has been a revolution in the study of *personal* memory in the field of cognitive psychology and neuroscience, and along with it an explosion in scholarship about *public* memory among scholars in history, anthropology, and literature, both producing a daunting mountain of material. "Twenty years ago, when I first entered the field of memory research," Daniel Schachter writes in the mid-1990s of his own experience as a psychologist, "it was fashionable for cognitive psychologists to compare memories to computer files that are placed in storage and pulled out when needed. Back then, nobody thought that the study of memory should include the subjective experience of remembering."[6]

The new science of personal memory offers much good news about autobiographical memory in older people. As Schachter points out, there are different memory systems, "each system depending on a particular constellation of networks in the brain." There are systems for semantic memory (general knowledge), procedural memory (how we do things), and episodic memory (about events). One system governs long-term memory, another working or temporary memory. Aging "does not produce an across-the-board decline in all memory functions." It is hard on working memory and on the recall of episodic memory, but the elderly, like everyone else, respond to cues that prime memory. Lifetime memory in the elderly is often good; older people in particular "recall more experiences from years around later adolescence and early adulthood," where there is an "enhanced memorability." Rehearsal of memory leads to its consolidation, and most important, emotion enhances memory, lending an "extraordinary power and persistence to many emotional or traumatic experiences." For all these empirical findings of the new psychology,

Schachter could have been writing about George Hewes. It is almost as if Hewes served as a laboratory model.[7]

The implications of the new understanding of memory for historians are breathtaking. As David Thelen, the editor of the *Journal of American History* writes, the first "is that memory, private and individual, as much as collective and cultural, is constructed, not reproduced. The second is that this construction is not made in isolation but in conversations with others that occur in the context of community, broader politics, and social dynamics."[8] In other words, the new psychology directs our attention to the historical context in which remembering takes place, which is precisely where it links up with historical scholarship about public memory. And this is my subject for the second essay in this book, the public memory of Hewes and the Tea Party.

If memory, personal and public, is constructed, and if historical context is crucial in understanding what impinges on the process of constructing memory, what do we have to explore in the context of the public "discovery" and "recovery" of Hewes in the 1830s?

As I thought about context, I noticed something obvious about the two biographies of Hewes that I had earlier taken for granted. Both authors used "tea party" in the title: James Hawkes called his *A Retrospect of the Boston Tea-Party*; Benjamin Bussey Thatcher called his *Traits of the Tea Party*. I quickly flipped through book titles in the card catalog of the Newberry Library, Chicago's hundred-year-old independent research library in the humanities, my base for research: before 1834 no other books included the words "tea party" in the title. Was it possible that this was the first time the phrase had been used in this way? I raced through the printed catalogs of the Library of Congress and the American history division of the New York Public Library, both more or less exhaustive. Yes, it was. I went back to the notes I had accumulated over the years in folders marked "tea party" to see what contemporaries called it. On the eve of the action in Boston, at the huge meeting of the "whole body of the people," someone cried out, "Boston harbor a teapot tonight." But as reported in print, it was referred to as "the destruction of the tea in Boston harbor."

Enter serendipity. I now stumbled on what I was *not* looking for. In my preliminary hunting I had found that the biographies of Hewes in 1834 and 1835 were not only the first books with "tea party" in the title, they also seem to have been the first books of any sort to take up the event at length and the first biographies of any actor in the event, high or low. Could it be that the event *itself* was not recognized, that it had been "forgotten" and then "remembered" sixty years later? What was at work? Was it possible that the new name and the celebration of a survivor were part of some larger process of rediscovery? When *did* they start calling it the Boston Tea Party?

Enter historical scholarship, old and new. Michael Kammen, the historian who has mapped the complex transformation of American memory over two centuries, posits the existence of "dominant memories (or mainstream collective consciousness) along with alternative (usually subordinate memories)." These correspond more or less to "official" and "popular" memory, although there is often no "sharp dichotomy" between these two. Two of Kammen's insights seem particularly relevant to the era after the Revolution: first, "that the past can be mobilized for partisan purposes," and second, "that the inventions of the past (as tradition) may occur as a means of resisting change *or* of achieving innovations."[9]

And what was it about the dates 1834 and 1835? I knew in a very general way, as I wrote in the first essay that this was a time when a new workingmen's movement appeared, but I was not prepared for the turbulence that jumped out everywhere in Boston, from the emergence of a radical labor movement and of radical abolitionism to the formation of the conservative Whig party, each claiming the heritage of the Revolution. Hewes, a mechanic, a man who had taken part in the "mob" actions of the Revolution, entered Boston in the midst of this contest for the public memory of the Revolution.

After these preliminary forays I was able to pose some questions: about Hewes, how might this contest have affected the way Hewes remembered? More important, how might it have affected the way celebrants on the Fourth of July, his portrait painter, and his Boston biographer represented him? Indeed, who were these people and what was their politics? About the Tea Party, how might the contest have affected the "recovery" of the tea action? Who, if anyone, was appropriating the Tea Party? What did it mean in the second quarter of the nineteenth century for Bostonians and other Americans to call this event "the tea party" rather than "the destruction of the tea"?

What's in a name? Does it make any difference how people name a historic event? Names are value-laden; they have political meaning. This is easy to grasp when the historic event continues to be an object of controversy, but less so for events that we have forgotten were controversial when they occurred. Take the Civil War. An entry in *The Encyclopedia of Southern History* reads "Civil War, Alternate Names of." To the United States government, it was officially the "War of the Rebellion"; Northerners commonly referred to it as "the war to save the Union," and less commonly as "the war to free the slaves." To Southerners, it was "the war of Southern independence," "the second American Revolution," and later, "the war between the states," all names that gave their cause legitimacy.[10]

The *Encyclopedia of the American Revolution* has no entry for "American Revolution, Alternate Names of," yet a similar war of names occurred at the time. In 1775, George III issued "A Proclamation for Suppressing Rebellion and Sedition," and in exile the Massachusetts Loyalist Peter Oliver wrote a book "On the Origin and Progress of the American Rebellion." Congress, on the other hand, issued a "Declaration of Independence," and Americans fought a "War for Independence" but also spoke easily of it as the "American Revolution," using the two terms interchangeably. This war of names was not sustained, probably because some seventy thousand Loyalists went into exile and those who stayed remained in disrepute. But a less recognized war of names about events during the Revolution continued. Samuel Adams patriots, for example, quickly named the occurrence of March 7, 1770, "the Boston Massacre," while to conservatives, patriot as well as Loyalist, it was "the riot on King Street." The same was true for other internal events.[11]

But more than names are at stake in what and when they called it the Tea Party. The contest over names, I discovered, is part of a larger contest for the public memory of the Revolution, a process I now think of as a willful forgetting and a purposeful remembering of American history. What does it mean for an event to be "lost," then "found" and given a new name? What does it mean for a person to be plucked from obscurity, made into a celebrity, and then more or less forgotten? This contest for the memory of the Revolution jogs us to think anew about the larger historical process of forgetting and remembering.

THE SHOEMAKER

AND THE

TEA PARTY

PART ONE

George Robert Twelves Hewes
(1742–1840)

*A Boston Shoemaker and the Memory
of the American Revolution*

Late in 1762 or early in 1763, George Robert Twelves Hewes, a Boston shoemaker in the last year or so of his apprenticeship, repaired a shoe for John Hancock and delivered it to him at his uncle Thomas Hancock's store in Dock Square. Hancock was pleased and invited the young man to "come and see him on New Year's day, and bid him a happy New-Year," according to the custom of the day, a ritual of noblesse oblige on the part of the gentry. We know of the episode through Benjamin Bussey Thatcher, who interviewed Hewes and wrote it up for his *Memoir* of Hewes in 1835. On New Year's Day, as Thatcher tells the story, after some urging by his master,

> George washed his face, and put his best jacket on, and proceeded straightaway to the Hancock House (as it is still called). His heart was in his mouth, but assuming a cheerful courage, he knocked at the front door, and took his hat off. The servant came:
> "Is 'Squire Hancock at home, Sir?" enquired Hewes, making a bow.
> He was introduced directly to the *kitchen*, and requested to seat himself, while report should be made above stairs. The man came down directly, with a new varnish of civility suddenly spread over his face. He ushered him into the 'Squire's sitting-room, and left

him to make his obeisance. Hancock remembered him, and addressed him kindly. George was anxious to get through, and he commenced a desperate speech—"as pretty a one," he says, "as he any way knew how,"—intended to announce the purpose of his visit, and to accomplish it, in the same breath.

"Very well, my lad," said the 'Squire"—now take a chair, my lad."

He sat down, scared all the while (as he now confesses) "almost to death," while Hancock put his hand into his breeches-pocket and pulled out a crown-piece, which he placed softly in his hand, thanking him at the same time for his punctual attendance, and his compliments. He then invited his young friend to drink his health—called for wine—poured it out for him—and ticked glasses with him,—a feat in which Hewes, though he had never seen it performed before, having acquitted himself with a creditable dexterity, hastened to make his bow again, and secure his retreat, though not till the 'Squire had extorted a sort of half promise from him to come the next New-Year's—which, for a rarity, he never discharged.[1]

The episode is a demonstration of what the eighteenth century called deference.

Another episode catches the point at which Hewes had arrived a decade and a half later. In 1778 or 1779, after one stint in the war on board a privateer and another in the militia, he was ready to ship out again, from Boston. As Thatcher tells the story: "Here he enlisted, or engaged to enlist, on board the *Hancock*, a twenty-gun ship, but not liking the manners of the Lieutenant very well, who ordered him one day in the streets to take his hat off to him—which he refused to do for any man,—he went aboard the '*Defence*,' Captain Smedley, of Fairfield Connecticut."[2] This, with a vengeance, is the casting off of deference.

What had happened in the intervening years? What had turned the young shoemaker tongue-tied in the face of his betters into the defiant person who would not take his hat off for any man? And why should stories like this have stayed in his memory sixty and seventy years later?

George Robert Twelves Hewes was born in Boston in 1742 and died in Richfield Springs, New York, in 1840. He participated in several of the principal political events of the American Revolution in Boston, among them the Massacre and the Tea Party, and during the war he served as a privateersman and militiaman. A shoemaker all his life, and intermittently or concurrently a fisherman, sailor, and farmer, he remained a poor man. He never made it, not before the war in Boston, not at sea, not after the war in Wrentham and Attleborough, Massachusetts, not in Otsego County, New York. He was a nobody who briefly became a somebody in the Revolution and, for a moment near the end of his life, a hero.

Hewes might have been unknown to posterity save for his longevity and a shift in the historical mood that rekindled the "spirit of '76." To Americans of the 1830s the Boston Tea Party had become a leading symbol of the Revolution, and Hewes lived long enough to be thought of as one of the last surviving participants, perhaps the very last. In 1833, when James Hawkes "discovered" him in the "obscurity" of upstate New York, Hewes was ninety-one but thought he was ninety-eight, a claim Hawkes accepted when he published the first memoir of Hewes in 1834.[3] Thus in 1835 when Hewes was invited to Boston, people thought that this survivor of one of the greatest moments of the Revolution was approaching his one hundredth birthday and on "the verge of eternity," as a Fourth of July orator put it.[4] He became a celebrity, the guest of honor on Independence Day, the subject of a second biography by Thatcher and of an oil portrait by Joseph Cole, which hangs today in Boston's Old State House.

To Thatcher, Hewes was one of the "humble classes" that made the success of the Revolution possible. How typical he was we can only suggest at this point in our limited knowledge of the "humble classes." Probably he was as representative a member of the "lower trades" of the cities and as much a rank-and-file participant in the political events and the war as historians have found. The two biographies, which come close to being oral histories (and give us clues to track down Hewes in other ways), provide an unusually rich cumulative record, over a very long period of time, of his thoughts, attitudes, and values. Consequently, we can answer, with varying degrees of satisfaction, a number of questions about one man of the "humble classes." About the "lower trades": why did a boy enter a craft with such bleak prospects as shoemaking? what was the life of an apprentice? what did it mean to be a shoemaker and a poor man in Boston? About the Revolution: what moved such a rank-and-file person to action? what action did he take? may we speak of his "ideology"? does the evidence of his loss of deference permit us to speak of change in his consciousness? About the war: how did a poor man, an older man, a man with a family, exercise his patriotism? what choices did he make? About the results of the Revolution: how did the war affect him? to what extent did he achieve his life goals? why did he go west? what did it mean to be an aged veteran of the Revolution? What, in sum, after more than half a century had passed, was the meaning of the Revolution to someone still in the "humble classes"?

1

A Man in His Nineties

A wide variety of sources can be used to check Hewes's rec-ollections, fill in what is missing in the biographies, and supply context. But to get at Hewes, the historian has essentially a ma-jor double task: separating him from his two biographers, James Hawkes and Benjamin Bussey Thatcher, and sifting the memo-ries of a man in his nineties to recover actions and feelings from sixty to eighty years before. The problem is familiar to scholars who have used the rich body of WPA narratives of former slaves taken down by interviewers in the 1930s and who have had to ask: who recorded these recollections, under what circumstances, and with what degree of skill? how does memory function in the aged? what is remembered best and least? how do subsequent emotions and values color or overlie the memory of events in the distant past?[1]

The two biographies of Hewes were part of "a spate" of narra-tives of the Revolution by ordinary soldiers and sailors that ap-peared in print, especially from the 1820s on.[2] Together with the autobiographies, diaries, and journals, unpublished at the time, we know of at least 500 such first-person accounts of men who saw military service.[3] Much of this remembering was stimulated

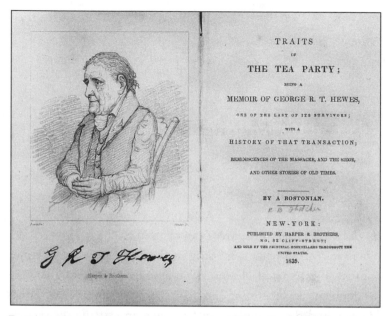

Benjamin Bussey Thatcher's 1835 memoir of Hewes, written "By a Bostonian," was one of the first books to use the term "Tea Party" and write about the event at length. *Courtesy American Antiquarian Society.*

by the pension laws of 1818 and especially of 1832, which required veterans to submit, in lieu of written records, "a very full account" of their military service. These laws produced no less than eighty thousand personal narratives—Hewes's among them—which are finally coming under the scrutiny of historians.[4]

Hawkes and Thatcher had different strengths and weaknesses. We know hardly anything about James Hawkes; he took the pseudonym "A Citizen of New York" and published in New York City. He may have been a journalist.[5] He discovered Hewes by an "accidental concurrence of events" and interviewed him in his familiar surroundings in Richfield Springs over several days in 1833 around the Fourth of July. Hawkes's virtue was that he tried to take down Hewes in the first person, although more often than not he lapsed into the third person or interrupted Hewes's narrative with long digressions, padding the story. He did not know enough about either the Revolution or Boston to question Hewes or follow up his leads, and he had a tendency to use Hewes as an exemplar of the virtues of Benjamin Franklin and selfless patriotism. But in his ignorance he allowed Hewes to structure his own story and convey his own feelings. Thus the book at times has an "as told to" flavor, and when Hawkes allows Hewes to speak, we can agree that "his language is remarkable for its grammatical simplicity and correctness."[6]

Benjamin Bussey Thatcher, on the other hand, intruded, as the language of his account of the visit to John Hancock suggests. He could not resist embellishing Hewes's stories or inventing dialogue. He brought to Hewes the same compassion for the lowly and sense of the uses of history that he brought to other historical subjects. A Boston gentleman, reformer, abolitionist, Bowdoin graduate, and lawyer, at the age of twenty-six he had written a short biography of Phillis Wheatley, Boston's black poet of the eighteenth century, a memoir of a Liberian missionary, and four volumes on American Indians, two of them collections of biographies.[7] Thatcher talked to Hewes on the latter's "triumphal" return to Boston in 1835, walked him around town, primed his memory. He lifted almost everything in Hawkes (without attribution) but also extracted a good many new anecdotes, especially about Hewes's youth, and expanded others about the Revolution. Occasionally he was skeptical; he read old newspapers and talked to other survivors to check the background. Thatcher thus added to the record, although in a form and tone that often seem more his own than Hewes's. And while his interests as a reformer led him to inquire, for example, about schools and slavery in Hewes's

Boston, they also led him to dissociate Hewes from the "mob," probably with some distortion. Thus Thatcher's portrayal, while fuller than Hawkes's, is also more flawed.[8]

Hewes's remembering, once distinguished from the overlay of these biographies, also had strengths and weaknesses. He was, to begin with, in remarkable physical condition. In 1833 Hawkes found his "physical and intellectual" powers "of no ordinary character." "I have generally enjoyed sound health," Hewes said. He showed few signs of his advanced age. His hair was light brown, salted with gray, and he had most of it. He was not bent down by his years but was "so perfectly erect" and moved "with so much agility and firmness . . . that he might be taken for a man in all the vigour of youth." He regularly walked two or three miles each day, and for his sessions with Hawkes he walked five miles back and forth to Hawkes's lodgings. He was of such an "active disposition" that Hawkes found he would hardly stay put long enough to be interviewed. When Hewes became excited, his "dark blue eyes," which Hawkes called "an index to an intelligent and vigorous mind," would "sparkle with a glow of lustre."[9] Thatcher was impressed with "a strength and clearness in his faculties" often not present in men twenty years younger. "Both his mental and bodily faculties are wonderfully hale. He converses with almost the promptness of middle life." His mind did not wander. He answered questions directly, and "he can seldom be detected in any redundancy or deficiency of expression." He was not garrulous.[10]

Both men were amazed at Hewes's memory. Thatcher found it "so extraordinary" that at times it "absolutely astonished" him.[11] Hewes recounted details from many stages of his life: from his childhood, youth, and young adulthood, from the years leading up to the Revolution, from seven years of war. While he told next to nothing about the next half-century of his life, his memory of recent events was clear. He graphically recalled a trip to Boston in 1821. He remembered names, a remarkable array of them that Thatcher checked.[12] He remembered how things looked; he even seemed to recall how things tasted. Most important, he remembered his own emotions, evoking them once again. He seems to have kept no diary or journal, and by his own claim, which Hawkes accepted, he had not read any accounts of the Tea Party or by implication any other events of the Revolution.[13]

His mind worked in ways that are familiar to students of the processes of memory.[14] Thus he remembered more for Thatcher in Boston in 1835 than for Hawkes in Richfield Springs in 1833. This is not surprising; he was warmed up and was responding to cues as he returned to familiar scenes and Thatcher asked him pointed questions. Having told many episodes of his life before—to his children and grandchildren, and to children and adults in Richfield Springs—he thus had rehearsed them and they came out as adventure stories.

His memory also displayed common weaknesses. He had trouble with his age, which may not have been unusual at a time when birthdays were not much celebrated and birth certificates not issued.[15] He had trouble with sequences of events and with the intervals of time between events. He was somewhat confused, for example, about his military tours of duty, something common in other veterans' narratives.[16] He also got political events in Boston somewhat out of order, telescoping what for him had become one emotionally. Or he told his good stories first, following up with the less interesting ones. All this is harmless enough. He remembered, understandably, experiences that were pleasant, and while he did well with painful experiences that had been seared into him—like childhood punishments and the Boston Massacre—

he "forgot" other experiences that were humiliating. There are also many silences in his life story, and where these cannot be attributed to his biographers' lack of interest (as in his humdrum life from 1783 to 1833), because his memory is so good we are tempted to see significance in these silences.

All in all, we are the beneficiaries in Hewes of a phenomenon psychologists recognize in "the final stage of memory" as "life review," characterized by a "sudden emergence of memories and a desire to remember, and a special candour which goes with a feeling that active life is over, achievement is completed." A British historian who has taken oral history from the aged notes that "in this final stage there is a major compensation for the longer interval and the selectivity of the memory process, in an increased willingness to remember, and commonly too a diminished concern for fitting the story to the social norms of the audience. Thus bias from both repression and distortion becomes a less inhibiting difficulty, for both teller and historian."[17]

On balance, Hewes's memory was strong, yet what he remembered, as well as the meaning he attached to it, inevitably was shaped by his values, attitudes, and temperament. There was an overlay from Hewes as well as his biographers. First, he had a stake, both monetary and psychic, in his contribution to the Revolution. He had applied for a pension in October 1832; by the summer of 1833, when he talked to Hawkes, it had been granted. He had also become a personage of sorts in his own locale, at least on the Fourth of July. And when he talked with Thatcher he was bathed in Boston's recognition. Thus though he did not have to prove himself (as did thousands of other veterans waiting for action on their applications), he had spent many years trying to do just that. Moreover, he had to live up to his reputation and had the possibility of enhancing it.

Second, he may have imposed an overlay of his current religious values on the younger man. He had generally been "of a cheerful mind," he told Hawkes, and Thatcher spoke of the "cheerfulness and evenness of his temper."[18] There is evidence for such traits earlier in his life. In his old age, however, he became a practicing Methodist—composed in the assurance of his own salvation, confident of his record of good deeds, and forgiving to his enemies. As a consequence he may well have blotted out some contrary feelings he had once held. One suspects he had been a much more angry and aggressive younger man than he or his biographers convey.

Finally, in the 1830s he lived in a society that no longer bestowed the deference once reserved for old age and had never granted much respect to poor old shoemakers.[19] In the Revolution for a time it had been different; the shoemaker won recognition as a citizen; his betters sought his support and seemingly deferred to him. This contributed to a tendency, as he remembered the Revolution, not so much to exaggerate what he had done—he was consistently modest in his claims for himself—as to place himself closer to some of the great men of the time than is susceptible to proof. For a moment he was on a level with his betters. So he thought at the time, and so it grew in his memory as it disappeared in his life. And in this memory of an awakening to citizenship and recognition from his betters we shall argue—a memory with both substance and shadow—lay the meaning of the Revolution to George Hewes.

2

A Boston Childhood

In 1756, when Hewes was fourteen, he was apprenticed to a shoemaker. Why did a boy become a shoemaker in mid-eighteenth-century Boston? The town's shoemakers were generally poor and their prospects were worsening. From 1756 to 1775, eight out of thirteen shoemakers who died and left wills at probate did not even own their own homes.[1] In 1790, shoemakers ranked thirty-eighth among forty-four occupations in mean tax assessments.[2]

It was not a trade in which boys were eager to be apprentices. Few sons continued in their father's footsteps, as they did, for example, in prosperous trades like silversmithing or shipbuilding.[3] Leatherworkers, after mariners, headed the list of artisans who got their apprentices from the orphans, illegitimate children, and boys put out to apprenticeship by Boston's Overseers of the Poor.[4] In England, shoemaking was a trade with proud traditions symbolized by St. Crispin's Day, a shoemakers' holiday, a trade with a reputation for producing poets, philosophers, and politicians, celebrated by Elizabethan playwrights as "the gentle craft."[5] But there were few signs of a flourishing shoemaker culture in Boston before the Revolution. In children's lore shoemakers were prover-

In this Revolution-era view of the crowded North End of Boston, ships are at anchor in the harbor, a shipyard is at the water's edge, and churches are the highest buildings on the skyline. From an engraving by William Burgis, revised by William Price about 1769. *Courtesy American Antiquarian Society.*

bially poor, like the cobbler in a Boston chapbook who "labored hard and took a great deal of pains for a small livelihood."[6] Shoemakers, moreover, were low in status. John Adams spoke of shoemaking as "too mean and dimi[nu]tive an Occupation" to hold a client of his who wanted to "rise in the World."[7]

Where one ended up in life depended very much on where one started out. George was born under the sign of the Bulls Head and Horns on Water Street near the docks in the South End. His father—also named George—was a tallow chandler and erstwhile tanner. Hewes drew the connections between his class origins and his life chances as he began his narrative for Hawkes:

My father, said he, was born in Wrentham in the state of Massachusetts, about twenty-eight miles from Boston. My grandfather having made no provision for his support, and being unable
to give him an education, apprenticed him at Boston to learn a
mechanical trade. . . .

In my childhood, my advantages for education were very limited, much more so than children enjoy at the present time in my
native state. My whole education which my opportunities permit-
ted me to acquire, consisted only of a moderate knowledge of
reading and writing; my father's circumstances being confined to
such humble means as he was enabled to acquire by his mechanical
employment, I was kept running of errands, and exposed of course
to all the mischiefs to which children are liable in populous cities.[8]

Hewes's family on his father's side was "no better off than what
is called in New England *moderate*, and probably not as good."[9]
The American progenitor of the line seems to have come from
Wales and was in Salisbury, near Newburyport, in 1677, doing
what we do not know. Solomon Hewes, George Robert's grandfather, was born in Portsmouth, New Hampshire, in 1674, became a joiner, and moved with collateral members of his family
to Wrentham, originally part of Dedham, near Rhode Island.
There he became a landholder; most of his brothers were farmers;
two became doctors, one of whom prospered in nearby Providence. His son—our George's father—was born in 1701.[10] On the
side of his mother, Abigail Seaver, Hewes's family was a shade
different. They had lived for four generations in Roxbury, a small
farming town immediately south of Boston across the Neck. Abigail's ancestors seem to have been farmers, but one was a minister.[11] Her father, Shubael, was a country cordwainer who owned
a house, barn, and two acres. She was born in 1711 and married
in 1728.[12]

George Robert Twelves Hewes, born August 25, 1742, was the

sixth of nine children, the fourth of seven sons. Five of the nine survived childhood—his three older brothers, Samuel, Shubael, and Solomon, and a younger brother, Daniel. He was named George after his father, Robert after a paternal uncle, and the unlikely Twelves, he thought, for his mother's great uncle, "whose Christian name was Twelve, for whom she appeared to have great admiration. Why he was called by that singular name I never knew." More likely, his mother was honoring her own mother, also Abigail, whose maiden name was Twelves.[13]

The family heritage to George, it might be argued, was more genetic than economic. He inherited a chance to live long: the men in the Seaver line were all long-lived. And he inherited his size. He was unusually short—five feet, one inch. "I have never acquired the ordinary weight or size of other men," Hewes told Hawkes, who wrote that "his whole person is of a slight and slender texture." In old age he was known as "the little old man."[14] Anatomy is not destiny, but Hewes's short size and long name helped shape his personality. It was a big name for a small boy to carry. He was the butt of endless teasing jibes—George Robert what?—that Thatcher turned into anecdotes whose humor may have masked the pain Hewes may have felt.[15]

"Moderate" as it was, Hewes had a sense of family. Wrentham, town of his grandfather and uncles, was a place he would be sent as a boy, a place of refuge in the war, and after the war his home. He would receive an inheritance three times in his life, each one a reminder of the importance or potential importance of relatives. And he was quite aware of any relative of status, like Dr. Joseph Warren, a distant kinsman on his mother's side.[16]

His father's life in Boston had been an endless, futile struggle to succeed as a tanner. Capital was the problem. In 1729 he bought a one-third ownership in a tannery for £600 in bills of credit.

Two years later, he sold half of his third to his brother Robert, who became a working partner. The two brothers turned to a rich merchant, Nathaniel Cunningham, who put up £3500 in return for half the profits. The investment was huge: pits, a yard, workshops, hides, bark, two horses, four slaves, journeymen. For a time the tannery flourished. Then there was a disastrous falling out with Cunningham: furious fights, a raid on the yards, debtors' jail twice for George, suits and countersuits that dragged on in the courts for years. The Hewes brothers saw themselves as "very laborious" artisans who "managed their trade with good skill," only to be ruined by a wealthy, arrogant merchant. To Cunningham, they were incompetent and defaulters. Several years before George Robert was born, his father had fallen back to "butchering, tallow chandlering, hog killing, soap boiling &c."[17]

The family was not impoverished. George had a memory as a little boy of boarding a ship with his mother to buy a small slave girl "at the rate of two dollars a pound."[18] And there was enough money to pay the fees for his early schooling. But beginning in 1748, when he was six, there was a series of family tragedies. In 1748 an infant brother, Joseph, died, followed later in the year by his sister Abigail, age thirteen, and brother Ebenezer, age two. In 1749 his father died suddenly of a stroke, leaving the family nothing it would seem, his estate tangled in debt and litigation.[19] George's mother would have joined the more than one thousand widows in Boston, most of whom were on poor relief.[20] Sometime before 1755 she died. In 1756 Grandfather Seaver died, leaving less than £15 to be divided among George and his four surviving brothers. Thus in 1756, at the age of fourteen, when boys were customarily put out to apprenticeship, George was an orphan, the ward of his uncle Robert, as was his brother Daniel, age twelve, each with a legacy of £2 17s. 4d. Uncle Robert, though warmly recollected by Hewes, could not do much to help him: a glue-maker, he was struggling to set up his own manufactory.[21] Nor could George's three older brothers, whom he also remembered fondly. In 1756 they were all in the "lower" trades. Samuel, age twenty-six, and Solomon, twenty-two, were fishermen; Shubael, twenty-four, was a butcher.

The reason why George was put to shoemaking becomes clearer: no one in the family had the indenture fee to enable him to enter one of the more lucrative "higher" trades. Josiah Franklin, also a tallow chandler, could not make his son Benjamin a cutler because he lacked the fee.[22] But in shoemaking the prospects were so poor that some masters would pay to get an apprentice. In addition, George was too small to enter trades that demanded brawn; he could hardly have become a ropewalk worker, a housewright, or a shipwright. Ebenezer McIntosh, the Boston shoemaker who led the annual Pope's Day festivities and the Stamp Act demonstrations, was a small man.[23] The trade was a sort of dumping ground for poor boys who could not handle heavy work. Boston's Overseers of the Poor acted on this assumption in 1770,[24] as did recruiting officers for the American navy forty years later.[25] The same was true in Europe.[26] Getting into a good trade required "connections"; the family connections were in the leather trades, through Uncle Robert, the gluemaker, or brother Shubael, the butcher. Finally, there was a family tradition. Grandfather Shubael had been a cordwainer, and on his death in 1756 there might even have been a prospect of acquiring his tools and lasts. In any case, the capital that would be needed to set up a shop of one's own was relatively small. And so the boy became a shoemaker—because he had very little choice.

[3]

The Apprentice

Josiah Franklin had known how important it was to place a boy in a trade that was to his liking. Otherwise there was the threat that Benjamin made explicit: he would run away to sea. Hawkes saw the same thrust in Hewes's life: shoemaking "was never an occupation of his choice," he "being inclined to more active pursuits."[1] George was the wrong boy to put in a sedentary trade that was not to his liking. He was what Bostonians called "saucy"; he was always in Dutch. The memories of his childhood and youth that Thatcher elicited were almost all of defying authority—his mother, his teachers at dame school, his schoolmaster, his aunt, his shoemaker master, a farmer, a doctor.

Hewes spoke of his mother only as a figure who inflicted punishment for disobedience. The earliest incident he remembered could have happened only to a poor family living near the waterfront. When George was about six, Abigail Hewes sent him off to the nearby shipyards with a basket to gather chips for the fire. At the water's edge George put the basket aside, straddled some floating planks to watch the fish, fell in, and sank to the bottom. He was saved only when some ship carpenters saw the basket without the boy, "found him motionless on the bottom, hooked

In this crude broadside engraving of Pope's Day held every November 5 in Boston, an effigy of the devil prompts the Pope (who prompts the Stuart pretender to the throne whose effigy is not shown). The North End and South End Pope's Day companies united in 1765 under Ebenezer McIntosh, "Captain General of the Liberty Tree." *Courtesy Library of Congress.*

him out with a boat hook, and rolled him on a tar barrel until signs of life were discovered." His mother nursed him back to health. Then she flogged him.[2]

The lesson did not take, nor did others in school. First there was a dame school with Miss Tinkum, wife of the town crier. He ran away. She put him in a dark closet. He dug his way out. The next day she put him in again. This time he discovered a jar of quince marmalade and devoured it. A new dame school with "mother McLeod" followed. Then school with "our famous Master Holyoke," which Hewes remembered as "little more than a series of escapes made or attempted from the reign of the birch."[3]

Abigail Hewes must have been desperate to control George. She sent him back after one truancy with a note requesting Holyoke to give him a good whipping. Uncle Robert took pity and sent a substitute note. Abigail threatened, "If you run away again I shall go to school with you myself."[4] When George was about ten, she took the final step: she sent him to Wrentham to live with one of his paternal uncles. Here, George recalled, "he spent several years of his boyhood . . . in the monotonous routine of his Uncle's farm." The only incident he recounted was of defying his aunt. His five-year-old cousin hit him in the face with a stick "without any provocation." George cursed the boy out, for which his aunt whipped him, and when she refused to do the same with her son, George undertook to "chastise" him himself. "I caught my cousin at the barn" and applied the rod. The aunt locked him up but his uncle let him go, responsive to his plea for "equal justice."[5]

Thus when George entered his apprenticeship, if he was not quite the young Whig his biographers made him out to be, he was not a youth who would suffer arbitrary authority easily. His master, Downing, had an irascible side and was willing to use a cowhide. Hewes lived in Downing's attic with a fellow apprentice, John Gilbert. All the incidents Hewes recalled from this period had two motifs: petty defiance and a quest for food. There was an escapade on a Saturday night when the two apprentices made off for Gilbert's house and bought a loaf of bread, a pound of butter, and some coffee. They returned after curfew to encounter an enraged Downing, whom they foiled by setting pans and tubs for him to trip over when he came to the door. There was an excursion to Roxbury on Training Day, the traditional apprentices' holiday in Boston, with fellow apprentices and his younger brother. Caught stealing apples, they were taken before the farmer, who was also justice of the peace and who laughed uproariously at Hewes's name and let him go. There was an incident with a doctor who inoculated Hewes and a fellow worker for smallpox and warned them to abstain from food. Sick, fearful of death, Hewes and his friend consumed a dish of venison in melted butter and a mug of flip—and lived to tell the tale.[6]

These memories of youthful defiance and youthful hunger lingered on for seventy years: a loaf of bread and a pound of butter, a parcel of apples, a dish of venison. This shoemaker's apprentice could hardly have been well fed or treated with affection.

The proof is that Hewes tried to end his apprenticeship by the only way he saw possible: escape to the military. "After finding that my depressed condition would probably render it impracticable for me to acquire that education requisite for civil employments," he told Hawkes, "I had resolved to engage in the military service of my country, should an opportunity present." Late in the 1750s, possibly in 1760, as the fourth and last of England's great colonial wars with France ground on and His Majesty's army recruiters beat their drums through Boston's streets, Hewes and Gilbert tried to enlist. Gilbert was accepted, but Hewes was not. Recruiting captains were under orders to "enlist no Roman-Catholic, nor any under five feet two inches high without their shoes." "I could not pass muster," Hewes told Hawkes, "because I was not tall enough."[7] As Thatcher embroiders Hawkes's story, Hewes then "went to the shoe shop of several of his acquaintances and heightened his heels by several taps [;] then stuffing his stocking with paper and rags," he returned. The examining captain saw through the trick and rejected him again. Frustrated, humiliated, vowing he would never return to Downing, he took an even more desperate step: he went down to the wharf and tried to enlist on a British ship of war. "His brothers, however, soon heard of it and interfered," and, in Thatcher's words, "he was compelled to abandon that plan." Bostonians like Solomon and Samuel Hewes, who made their living on the waterfront, did not need long memories to remember the city's massive resistance to the impressment sweeps of 1747 and to know that the British navy would be, not escape, but another prison.[8]

About this time, shoemaker Downing failed after fire swept his shop (possibly the Great Fire of 1760).[9] This would have freed Hewes of his indenture, but he was not qualified to be a shoemaker until he had completed apprenticeship. As Hewes told it, he therefore apprenticed himself "for the remainder of his minority," that is, until he turned twenty-one, to Harry Rhoades, who paid him $40. In 1835 he could tell Thatcher how much time he then had left to serve, down to the month and day. Of the rest of his "time" he had no bad memories.[10]

Apprenticeship had a lighter side. Hewes's anecdotes give tantalizing glimpses into an embryonic apprentice culture in Boston to which other sources attest—glimpses of pranks played on masters, of revelry after curfew, of Training Day, when the militia displayed its maneuvers and there was drink, food, and "frolicking" on the Common. One may speculate that George also took part in the annual Pope's Day festival, November 5, when apprentices, servants, artisans in the lower trades, and young people of all classes took over the town, parading effigies of Pope, Devil, and Pretender, exacting tribute from the better sort, and engaging in a battle royal between North End and South End Pope's Day "companies."[11]

Hewes's stories of his youth, strained as they are through Thatcher's condescension, hint at his winning a place for himself as the small schoolboy who got the better of his elders, the apprentice who defied his master, perhaps even a leader among his peers. There are also hints of the adult personality. Hewes was punished often, but if childhood punishment inured some to pain, it made Hewes reluctant to inflict pain on others. He developed a generous streak that led him to reach out to others in trouble. When Downing, a broken man, was on the verge of leaving for Nova Scotia to start anew, Hewes went down to his ship and gave him half of the $40 fee Rhoades had paid him. Downing broke into tears. The story smacks of the Good Samaritan, of the Methodist of the 1830s counting his good deeds; and yet the memory was so vivid, wrote Thatcher, that "his features light up even now with a gleam of rejoicing pride." Hewes spoke later of the "tender sympathies of my nature."[12] He did not want to be, but he was a fit candidate for the "gentle craft" he was about to enter.

[4]

The Shoemaker

In Boston from 1763, when he entered his majority, until 1775, when he went off to war, Hewes never made a go of it as a shoemaker. He remembered these years more fondly than he had lived them. As Hawkes took down his story, shifting from the third to the first person:

> Hewes said he cheerfully submitted to the course of life to which his destinies directed.
>
> He built him a shop and pursued the private avocation of his trade for a considerable length of time, until on the application of his brother he was induced to go with him on two fishing voyages to the banks of New Foundland, which occupied his time for two years.
>
> After the conclusion of the French war . . . he continued at Boston, except the two years absence with his brother.
>
> During that period, said Hewes, when I was at the age of twenty-six, I married the daughter of Benjamin Sumner, of Boston. At the time of our intermarriage, the age of my wife was seventeen. We lived together very happily seventy years. She died at the age of eighty-seven.
>
> At the time when the British troops were first stationed at

Boston, we had several children, the exact number I do not recollect. By our industry and mutual efforts we were improving our condition.[1]

Thatcher added a few bits to this narrative, some illuminating. The "little shop was at the head of Griffin's Wharf," later the site of the Tea Party. Benjamin Sumner, "if we mistake not," was a "sexton of one of the principal churches in town." His wife was a "washer-woman" near the Mill Pond, assisted by her five daughters. Hewes courted one of the girls when he "used to go to the house regularly every Saturday night to pay Sally for the week's washing." The father was stern, the swain persistent, and after a couple of years George and Sally were married. "The business was good, and growing better," Thatcher wrote, "especially as it became more and more fashionable to encourage our own manufactures."[2]

The reality was more harsh. What kind of shoemaker was Hewes? He had his own shop—this much is clear, but the rest is surmise. There were at that time in Boston about sixty to seventy shoemakers, most of whom seem to have catered to the local market.[3] If Hewes was typical, he would have made shoes to order, "bespoke" work; this would have made him a cordwainer. And he would have repaired shoes; this would have made him a cobbler. Who were his customers? No business records survive. A shoemaker probably drew his customers from his immediate neighborhood. Located as he was near the waterfront and the ropewalks, Hewes might well have had customers of the "meaner" sort. In a ward inhabited by the "middling" sort he may also have drawn on them. When the British troops occupied Boston, he did some work for them. Nothing suggests that he catered to the "carriage trade."[4]

Was his business "improving" or "growing better"? Probably it was never very good and grew worse. From his own words we know that he took off two years on fishing voyages with his brothers. He did not mention that during this period he lived for a short time in Roxbury.[5] His prospects were thus not good enough to keep him in Boston. His marriage is another clue to his low fortune. Sally (or Sarah) Sumner's father was a sexton so poor that his wife and daughters had to take in washing. The couple was married by the Reverend Samuel Stillman of the First Baptist Church, which suggests that this was the church that Benjamin Sumner served.[6] Though Stillman was respected, First Baptist was not "one of the principal churches in town," as Thatcher guessed, but one of the poorest and smallest, with a congregation heavy with laboring people, sailors, and blacks.[7] Marriage, one of the few potential sources of capital for an aspiring tradesman, as Benjamin Franklin made clear in his autobiography, did not lift Hewes up.

Other sources fill in what Hewes forgot. He married in January 1768. In September 1770 he landed in debtors' prison. In 1767 he had contracted a debt of £6 8s. 3d. to Thomas Courtney, a merchant-tailor, for "making a sappled coat & breeches of fine cloth." The shoemaker bought this extravagant outfit when he was courting. What other way was there to persuade Sally's parents that he had good prospects? Over the three years since, he had neither earned enough to pay the debt nor accumulated £9 property that might be confiscated to satisfy it. "For want of Goods or Estate of the within named George Robt Twelve Hewes, I have taken his bodey & committed him to his majesty's goal [sic] in Boston," wrote Constable Thomas Rice on the back of the writ. There may have been a touch of political vindictiveness in the action: Courtney was a rich Tory later banished by the state.[8] Who got Hewes out of jail? Perhaps his uncle Robert, perhaps a brother.

Once out of jail, Hewes stayed poor. The Boston tax records of 1771, the only ones that have survived for these years, show him living as a lodger in the house of Christopher Ranks, a watchmaker, in the old North End. He was not taxed for any property.[9] In 1773 he and his family, which now included three children, were apparently living with his uncle Robert in the South End; at some time during these years before the war they also lived with a brother.[10] After almost a decade on his own, Hewes could not afford his own place. In January 1774 he inadvertently summed up his condition and reputation in the course of a violent street encounter. Damned as "a rascal" and "a vagabond" who had no right to "speak to a gentleman in the street," Hewes retorted that he was neither "and though a poor man, in as good credit in town" as his well-to-do antagonist.[11]

The economic odds were against a Boston shoemaker thriving in these years. Even the movement "to encourage our manufactures" may have worked against him, contrary to Thatcher. The patriot boycott would have raised his hopes; the Boston town meeting of 1767 put men's and women's shoes on the list of items Bostonians were encouraged to buy from American craftsmen.[12] But if this meant shoes made in Lynn—the manufacturing town ten miles to the north that produced eighty thousand shoes in 1767 alone—it might well have put Hewes at a competitive disadvantage, certainly for the ladies' shoes for which Lynn already had a reputation. And if Hewes was caught up in the system whereby Lynn masters were already "putting out" shoes in Boston, he would have made even less.[13] Whatever the reason, the early 1770s were hard times for shoemakers; Ebenezer McIntosh also landed in debtors' jail in 1770.[14]

As a struggling shoemaker, what would have been Hewes's aspirations? He does not tell us in so many words, but "the course of his life," Hawkes was convinced, was marked "by habits of industry, integrity, temperance and economy"; in other words, he practiced the virtues set down by "another soap boiler and tallow chandler's son" (Thatcher's phrase for Benjamin Franklin). "From childhood," Hewes told Hawkes, "he has been accustomed to rise very early and expose himself to the morning air; that his father compelled him to do this from his infancy." ("Early to bed, Early to rise, makes a man healthy, wealthy and wise.") "I was often . . . admonished," said Hewes, "of the importance of faithfulness in executing the commands of my parents, or others who had a right to my services." Thatcher also reported that "he makes it a rule to rise from the table with an appetite, and another to partake of but a single dish at a meal." ("A Fat kitchen makes a lean will, as Poor Richard says.")[15]

Poor Richard spoke to and for artisans at every level—masters, journeymen, and apprentices—whose goal was "independence" or "a competency" in their trade. What he advocated, we need remind ourselves, "was not unlimited acquisition but rather prosperity, which was the mid-point between the ruin of extravagance and the want of poverty. The living he envisaged was a decent middling wealth, which could only be attained through unremitting labor and self-control."[16] Hewes's likely goal, then, was to keep his shop so that his shop would keep him.

But he could no more live by Poor Richard's precepts than could Franklin. "Industry" must have come hard. He was in an occupation "never of his choice." How could he "stick to his last" when he was "inclined towards more active pursuits"? "Avoid, above all else, debt," counseled Poor Richard, warning that "fond pride of dress is sure a very curse; E'er Fancy you consult, consult your purse." But Hewes surrendered to pride and as a consequence to the warden of the debtors' jail. "Economy"—that is, saving—produced no surplus. And so he would succumb, when war presented the opportunity, to the gamble for sudden wealth. He was as much the object as the exemplar of Poor Richard's advice, as indeed was Franklin himself.

If Hewes's memories softened such realities, in other ways his silences spoke. He said nothing about being part of any of Boston's traditional institutions—church, town meeting, or private associations. He was baptized in Old South, a Congregational church, and married by the minister of the First Baptist Church; there is no evidence that he took part in either.[17] In his old age a convert to Methodism, a churchgoer, and Bible reader, he reminisced to neither biographer about the religion of youth.

Nor does he seem to have taken part in town government. He was not a taxpayer in 1771. He probably did not own enough property to qualify as a voter for either provincial offices (£40 sterling) or town offices (£20 sterling).[18] Recollecting the political events of the Revolution, he did not speak of attending town meetings until they became what patriots called meetings of "the whole body of the people," without regard to property. The town had to fill some two hundred minor positions; it was customary to stick artisans with the menial jobs. Hewes's father was hogreeve (responsible for dealing with stray swine) and measurer of boards. Harry Rhoades held town offices. McIntosh was made a sealer of leather. Hewes was appointed to nothing.[19]

He does not seem to have belonged to any associations. McIntosh was in a fire company. So was Hewes's brother Shubael. Hewes was not. Shubael and a handful of prosperous artisans became Masons. Hewes did not.[20] It was not that he was a loner. There was simply not much for a poor artisan to belong to.[21]

There was no shoemakers' society or general society of mechanics. Shoemakers had a long tradition of taking ad hoc collective action, as did other Boston craftsmen, and Hewes may have participated in such occasional informal activities of the trade.[22] Very likely he drilled in the militia with other artisans on Training Day (size would not have barred him). He seems to have known many artisans and recalled their names in describing events. So it is not hard to imagine him at a South End tavern enjoying a mug of flip with Adam Colson, leatherworker, or Patrick Carr, breechesmaker. Nor is it difficult to imagine him in the streets on November 5, in the South End Pope's Day company captained by McIntosh. After all, what else was there in respectable Boston for him to belong to? All this is conjecture, but it is clear that, though he lived in Boston proper, he was not part of proper Boston—not until the events of the Revolution.

The Massacre

Between 1768 and 1775, the shoemaker became a citizen—an active participant in the events that led to the Revolution, an angry, assertive man who won recognition as a patriot. What explains the transformation? We have enough evidence to take stock of Hewes's role in three major events of the decade: the Massacre (1770), the Tea Party (1773), and the tarring and feathering of John Malcolm (1774).

Thatcher began the story of Hewes in the Revolution at the Stamp Act but based his account on other sources and even then claimed no more than that Hewes was a bystander at the famous effigy-hanging at the Liberty Tree, August 14, 1765, that launched Boston's protest. "The town's-people left their work—and Hewes, his hammer among the rest—to swell the multitude." The only episode for which Thatcher seems to have drawn on Hewes's personal recollection was the celebration of the repeal of the act in May 1766, at which Hewes remembered drinking from the pipe of madeira that John Hancock set out on the Common. "Such a day has not been seen in Boston before or since," wrote Thatcher.[1]

It is possible that Thatcher's bias against mobs led him to draw

The murder of Christopher Seider in February 1770 is depicted in this crude engraving on a broadside. The eleven-year-old boy who joined the picketing of the shop of importer T. Lilly lies dying, shot by a customs official from a second-story window. The boy's mother looks on aghast. *Courtesy Historical Society of Pennsylvania.*

a curtain over Hewes's role. It is reasonable to suppose that if Hewes was a member of the South End Pope's Day company, he followed McIntosh, who was a major leader of the crowd actions of August 14 and 26, the massive processions of the united North and South End companies on November 1 and 5, and the forced resignation of stampmaster Andrew Oliver in December. But it is not likely; in fact, he may well have been off on fishing voyages in 1765. Perhaps the proof is negative: when Hewes told Hawkes the story of his role in the Revolution, he began not at the Stamp Act but at the Massacre, five years later. On the night of the Mas-

The patriot newspaper *Boston Gazette* reported the Boston Massacre March 12, 1770, a week after the event, on a page lined with mourner's black, featuring Paul Revere's engraving and five coffins representing the victims. *Courtesy Library of Congress.*

sacre, March 5, Hewes was in the thick of the action. What he tells us about what brought him to King Street, what brought others there, and what he did during and after this tumultuous event gives us the perspective of a man in the street.

The presence of British troops in Boston beginning in the summer of 1768—four thousand soldiers in a town of fewer than sixteen thousand inhabitants—touched Hewes personally. Anecdotes about soldiers flowed from him. He had seen them march off the transports at Long Wharf; he had seen them every day occupying civilian buildings on Griffin's Wharf near his shop. He knew how irritating it was to be challenged by British sentries after curfew (his solution was to offer a swig of rum from the bottle he carried).

More important, he was personally cheated by a soldier. Sergeant Mark Burk ordered shoes allegedly for Captain Thomas Preston, picked them up, but never paid for them. Hewes complained to Preston, who made good and suggested he bring a complaint. A military hearing ensued, at which Hewes testified. The soldier, to Hewes's horror, was sentenced to three hundred fifty lashes. He "remarked to the court that if he had thought the fellow was to be punished so severely for such an offense, bad as he was, he would have said nothing about it." And he saw others victimized by soldiers. He witnessed an incident in which a soldier sneaked up behind a woman, felled her with his fist, and "stripped her of her bonnet, cardinal muff and tippet." He followed the man to his barracks, identified him (Hewes remembered him as Private Kilroy, who would appear later at the Massacre), and got him to give up the stolen goods, but decided this time not to press charges.[2] Hewes was also keenly aware of grievances felt by the laboring men and youths who formed the bulk of the crowd—and the principal victims—at the Massacre.[3] From Hawkes and Thatcher three causes can be pieced together.

First in time, and vividly recalled by Hewes, was the murder of eleven-year-old Christopher Seider on February 23, ten days before the Massacre. Seider was one of a large crowd of schoolboys and apprentices picketing the shop of Theophilus Lilly, a merchant violating the anti-import resolutions. Ebenezer Richardson, a paid customs informer, shot into the throng and killed Seider. Richardson would have been tarred and feathered, or worse, had not Whig leaders intervened to hustle him off to jail. At Seider's funeral, only a week before the Massacre, five hundred boys marched two by two behind the coffin, followed by two thousand or more adults, "the largest [funeral] perhaps ever known in America," Thomas Hutchinson thought.[4]

Second, Hewes emphasized the bitter fight two days before the Massacre between soldiers and workers at Gray's ropewalk down the block from Hewes's shop. Off-duty soldiers were allowed to moonlight, taking work from civilians. On Friday, March 3, when one of them asked for work at Gray's, a battle ensued between a few score soldiers and ropewalk workers joined by others in the maritime trades. The soldiers were beaten and sought revenge. Consequently, in Thatcher's words, "quite a number of soldiers, in a word, were determined to have a row on the night of the 5th."[5]

Third, the precipitating events on the night of the Massacre, by Hewes's account, were an attempt by a barber's apprentice to collect an overdue bill from a British officer, the sentry's abuse of the boy, and the subsequent harassment of the sentry by a small band of boys that led to the calling of the guard commanded by Captain Preston. Thatcher found this hard to swallow—"a dun from a greasy barber's boy is rather an extraordinary explanation of the origin, or one of the occasions, of the massacre of the 5th of March"—but at the trial the lawyers did not. They battled over defining "boys" and over the age, size, and degree of aggressiveness of the numerous apprentices on the scene.[6]

Hewes viewed the civilians as essentially defensive. On the evening of the Massacre he appeared early on the scene at King Street, attracted by the clamor over the apprentice. "I was soon on the ground among them," he said, as if it were only natural that he should turn out in defense of fellow townsmen against what was assumed to be the danger of aggressive action by soldiers. He was not part of a conspiracy; neither was he there out of curiosity. He was unarmed, carrying neither club nor stave as some others did. He saw snow, ice, and "missiles" thrown at the soldiers. When the main guard rushed out in support of the sentry, Private Kilroy dealt Hewes a blow on his shoulder with his gun. Preston ordered the townspeople to disperse. Hewes believed they had a legal basis to refuse: "they were in the king's highway, and had as good a right to be there" as Preston.[7]

The five men killed were all workingmen. Hewes claimed to know four: Samuel Gray, a ropewalk worker; Samuel Maverick, age seventeen, an apprentice to an ivory turner; Patrick Carr, an apprentice to a leather-breeches worker; and James Caldwell, second mate on a ship—all but Christopher Attucks. Caldwell, "who was shot in the back was standing by the side of Hewes, and the latter caught him in his arms as he fell," helped carry him to Dr. Thomas Young in Prison Lane, then ran to Caldwell's ship captain on Cold Lane.[8]

More than horror was burned into Hewes's memory. He remembered the political confrontation that followed the slaughter, when thousands of angry townspeople faced hundreds of British troops massed with ready rifles. "The people," Hewes recounted, "then immediately chose a committee to report to the governor the result of Captain Preston's conduct, and to demand of him satisfaction."[9] Actually the "people" did not choose a committee "immediately." In the dark hours after the Massacre a self-appointed group of patriot leaders met with officials and forced Hutchinson to commit Preston and the soldiers to jail. Hewes was remembering the town meeting the next day, so huge that it had to adjourn from Faneuil Hall, the traditional meeting place that held only twelve hundred, to Old South Church, which had room for five to six thousand. This meeting approved a committee to wait on the officials and then adjourned, but met again the same day, received and voted down an offer to remove one regiment, then accepted another to remove two. This was one of the meetings at which property bars were let down.[10]

What Hewes did not recount, but what he had promptly put down in a deposition the next day, was how militant he was after the Massacre. At 1:00 A.M., like many other enraged Bostonians, he went home to arm himself. On his way back to the Town House with a cane he had a defiant exchange with Sergeant Chambers of the Twenty-Ninth Regiment and eight or nine soldiers, "all with very large clubs or cutlasses." A soldier, Dobson, "ask'd him how he far'd; he told him very badly to see his townsmen shot in such a manner, and asked him if he did not think it was a dreadful thing." Dobson swore "it was a fine thing" and "you shall see more of it." Chambers "seized and forced" the cane from Hewes, "saying I had no right to carry it. I told him I had as good a right to carry a cane as they had to carry clubs."[11]

The Massacre had stirred Hewes to political action. He was one of ninety-nine Bostonians who gave depositions for the prosecution that were published by the town in a pamphlet. Undoubtedly, he marched in the great funeral procession for the victims that brought the city to a standstill. He attended the tempestuous trial of Ebenezer Richardson, Seider's slayer, which was linked politically with the Massacre. ("He remembers to this moment, even the precise words of the Judge's sentence," wrote Thatcher.)[12] He seems to have attended the trial of the soldiers or Preston or both.

It was in this context that he remembered something for which there is no corroborating evidence, namely, testifying at Preston's trial on a crucial point. He told Hawkes:

> When Preston, their captain, was tried, I was called as one of the witnesses, on the part of the government, and testified, that I believed it was the same man, Captain Preston, that ordered his soldiers to make ready, who also ordered them to fire. Mr. John Adams, former president of the United States, was advocate for the prisoners, and denied the fact, that Captain Preston gave orders to his men to fire; and on his cross examination of me asked whether my position was such, that I could see the captain's lips in motion when the order to fire was given; to which I answered, that I could not.[13]

Perhaps so: Hewes's account is particular and precise, and there are many lacunae in the record of the trial (we have no verbatim transcript) that modern editors have assiduously assembled. Perhaps not: Hewes may have "remembered" his brother Shubael on the stand at the trial of the soldiers (although Shubael was a defense witness) or his uncle Robert testifying at Richardson's trial. Or he may have given pretrial testimony but not have been called to the stand.[14]

In one sense, it does not matter. What he was remembering was that he had become involved. He turned out because of a sense of kinship with "his townsmen" in danger; he stood his ground in defense of his "rights"; he was among the "people" who delegated a committee to act on their behalf; he took part in the legal process by giving a deposition, by attending the trials, and, as he remembered it, by testifying. In sum, he had become a citizen, a political man.

[6]

The Tea Party

Four years later, at the Tea Party on the night of December 16, 1773, Hewes the citizen "volunteered" and became the kind of leader for whom most historians have never found a place. The Tea Party, unlike the Massacre, was organized by the radical Whig leaders of Boston. They mapped the strategy, organized the public meetings, appointed the companies to guard the tea ships at Griffin's Wharf (among them Daniel Hewes, George's brother), and planned the official boarding parties. As in 1770, they converted the town meetings into meetings of "the whole body of the people," one of which Hutchinson found "consisted principally of the Lower ranks of the People & even Journeymen Tradesmen were brought in to increase the number & the Rabble were not excluded yet there were divers Gentlemen of Good Fortunes among them."[1]

The boarding parties showed this same combination of "ranks." Hawkes wrote:

> On my inquiring of Hewes if he knew who first proposed the project of destroying the tea, to prevent its being landed, he replied that he did not; neither did he know who or what number were to volunteer their services for that purpose. But from the significant

allusion of some persons in whom I had confidence, together with the knowledge I had of the spirit of those times, I had no doubt but that a sufficient number of associates would accompany me in that enterprise.[2]

The recollection of Joshua Wyeth, a journeyman blacksmith, verified Hewes's story in explicit detail: "It was proposed that young men, not much known in town and not liable to be easily recognized should lead in the business." Wyeth believed that "most of the persons selected for the occasion were apprentices and journeymen, as was the case with myself, living with tory masters." Wyeth "had but a few hours warning of what was intended to be done."[3] Those in the officially designated parties, about thirty men better known, appeared in well-prepared Indian disguises. As nobodies, the volunteers—anywhere from fifty to one hundred men—could get away with hastily improvised disguises. Hewes said he got himself up as an Indian and daubed his "face and hands with coal dust in the shop of blacksmith." In the streets "I fell in with many who were dressed, equipped and painted as I was, and who fell in with me and marched in order to the place of our destination."

At Griffin's Wharf the volunteers were orderly, self-disciplined, and ready to accept leadership.

When we arrived at the wharf, there were three of our number who assumed an authority to direct our operations, to which we readily submitted. They divided us into three parties, for the purpose of boarding the three ships which contained the tea at the same time. The name of him who commanded the division to which I was assigned was Leonard Pitt [Lendell Pitts]. The names of the other commanders I never knew. We were immediately ordered by the respective commanders to board all the ships at the same time, which we promptly obeyed.

But for Hewes there was something new: he was singled out of the rank and file and made an officer in the field.

> The commander of the division to which I belonged, as soon as we were on board the ship, appointed me boatswain, and ordered me to go to the captain and demand of him the keys to the hatches and a dozen candles. I made the demand accordingly, and the captain promptly replied, and delivered the articles; but requested me at the same time to do no damage to the ship or rigging. We then were ordered by our commander to open the hatches, and take out all the chests of tea and throw them overboard, and we immediately proceeded to execute his orders; first cutting and splitting the chests with our tomahawks, so as thoroughly to expose them to the effects of the water. In about three hours from the time we went on board, we had thus broken and thrown overboard every tea chest to be found in the ship; while those in the other ships were disposing of the tea in the same way, at the same time. We were surrounded by British armed ships, but no attempt was made to resist us. We then quietly retired to our several places of residence, without having any conversation with each other, or taking any measures to discover who were our associates.[4]

This was Hewes's story, via Hawkes. Thatcher, who knew a good deal more about the Tea Party from other sources, accepted it in its essentials as an accurate account. He also reported a new anecdote, which he treated with skepticism, namely, that Hewes worked alongside John Hancock throwing tea overboard. And he added that Hewes, "whose whistling talent was a matter of public notoriety, acted as a boatswain," that is, as the officer whose duty it was to summon men with a whistle. That Hewes was a leader is confirmed by the reminiscence of Thompson Maxwell, a teamster from a neighboring town who was making a delivery to Hancock the day of the event. Hancock asked him to go to Griffin's Wharf. "I went accordingly, joined the band under one Captain

Hewes; we mounted the ships and made tea in a trice; this done I took my team and went home as any honest man should."[5] "Captain" Hewes—it was not impossible.

As the Tea Party ended, Hewes was stirred to further action on his own initiative, just as he had been in the hours after the Massacre. While the crews were throwing the tea overboard, a few other men tried to smuggle off some of the tea scattered on the decks. "One Captain O'Connor whom I well knew," said Hewes, "came on board for that purpose, and when he supposed he was not noticed, filled his pockets, and also the lining of his coat. But I had detected him, and gave information to the captain of what he was doing. We were ordered to take him into custody, and just as he was stepping from the vessel, I seized him by the skirt of his coat, and in attempting to pull him back, I tore it off." They scuffled. O'Connor recognized him and "threatened to 'complain to the Governor.' 'You had better make your will first,' quoth Hewes, doubling his fist expressively," and O'Connor escaped, running the gauntlet of the crowd on the wharf. "The next day we nailed the skirt of his coat, which I had pulled off, to the whipping post in Charlestown, the place of his residence, with a label upon it," to shame O'Connor by "popular indignation."[6]

[7]

Tar and Feathers

A month later, at the third event for which we have full evidence, Hewes won public recognition for an act of courage that almost cost his life and precipitated the most publicized tarring and feathering of the Revolution. The incident that set it off would have been trivial at any other time. On Tuesday, January 25, 1774, at about two in the afternoon, the shoemaker was making his way back to his shop after his dinner. According to the very full account in the *Massachusetts Gazette*,

> Mr. George-Robert-Twelves Hewes was coming along Fore-Street, near Captain Ridgway's, and found the redoubted John Malcolm, standing over a small boy, who was pushing a little sled before him, cursing, damning, threatening and shaking a very large cane with a very heavy ferril on it over his head. The boy at that time was perfectly quiet, notwithstanding which Malcolm continued his threats of striking him, which Mr. Hewes conceiving if he struck him with that weapon he must have killed him out-right, came up to him, and said to him, Mr. Malcolm I hope you are not going to strike this boy with that stick.[1]

Malcolm had already acquired an odious reputation with patriots of the lower sort. A Bostonian, he had been a sea captain, an army officer, and recently an employee of the customs service.

In this caricature a London engraver has telescoped the tarring and feathering of John Malcolm in Boston, January 1774, with the Tea Party seen in the background. Sailors, wearing striped trousers, are prominent in the crowd about to cart Malcolm through town. *Courtesy Carnegie Museum of Art.*

He was so strong a supporter of royal authority that he had traveled to North Carolina to fight the Regulators, a rebellion of back-country farmers, and boasted of having a horse shot out from under him. He had a fiery temper. As a customs informer he was known to have turned in a vessel to punish sailors for petty smuggling, a custom of the sea. In November 1773, near Portsmouth, New Hampshire, a crowd of thirty sailors had "genteely tarr'd and feather'd" him, as the *Boston Gazette* put it: they did the job over his clothes. Back in Boston he made "frequent complaints" to Hutchinson of "being hooted at in the streets" for this by "tradesmen"; and the lieutenant governor cautioned him, "being a passionate man," not to reply in kind.[2]

The exchange between Malcolm and Hewes resonated with class as well as political differences:

Malcolm returned, you are an impertinent rascal, it is none of your business. Mr. Hewes then asked him, what had the child done to him. Malcolm damned him and asked him if he was going to take his part? Mr. Hewes answered no further than this, that he thought it was a shame for him to strike the child with such a club as that, if he intended to strike him. Malcolm on that damned Mr. Hewes, called him a vagabond, and said he would let him know he should not speak to a gentleman in the street. Mr. Hewes returned to that, he was neither a rascal nor vagabond, and though a poor man was in as good credit in town as he was. Malcolm called him a liar, and said he was not, nor ever would be. Mr. Hewes retorted, be that as it will, I never was tarred nor feathered any how. On this Malcolm struck him, and wounded him deeply on the forehead, so that Mr. Hewes for some time lost his senses. Capt. Godfrey, then present, interposed, and after some altercation, Malcolm went home.[3]

Hewes was rushed to Joseph Warren, the patriot doctor, his distant relative. Malcolm's cane had almost penetrated his skull. Thatcher found "the indentation as plainly perceptible as it was sixty years ago." So did Hawkes. Warren dressed the wound, and Hewes was able to make his way to a magistrate to swear out a warrant for Malcolm's arrest "which he carried to a constable named Justice Hale."[4] Malcolm, meanwhile, had retreated to his house, where he responded in white heat to taunts about the halfway tarring and feathering in Portsmouth with "damn you let me see the man that dare do it better."

In the evening a crowd took Malcolm from his house and dragged him on a sled into King Street "amidst the huzzas of thousands." At this point "several gentlemen endeavoured to divert the populace from their intention." The ensuing dialogue laid bare the clash of conceptions of justice between the sailors and laboring people heading the action and Sons of Liberty leaders. The "gentlemen" argued that Malcolm was "open to the laws of the land which would undoubtedly award a reasonable satisfaction to the parties he had abused," that is, the child and Hewes. The answer was political. Malcolm "had been an old impudent and mischievous [*sic*] offender—he had joined in the murders at North Carolina—he had seized vessels on account of sailors having a bottle or two of gin on board—he had in other words behaved in the most capricious, insulting and daringly abusive manner." He could not be trusted to justice. "When they were told the law would have its course with him, they asked what course had the law taken with Preston or his soldiers, with Capt. Wilson or Richardson? And for their parts they had seen so much partiality to the soldiers and customhouse officers by the present Judges, that while things remained as they were, they would, on all such occasions, take satisfaction their own way, and let them take it off."[5] The references were to Captain Preston, who had been tried and found innocent of the Massacre, the soldiers who had been let off with token punishment, Captain John Wilson, who had been indicted for inciting slaves to murder their masters but never tried,[6] and Ebenezer Richardson, who had been tried and found guilty of killing Seider, sentenced, and then pardoned by the Crown.

The crowd won and proceeded to a ritualized tarring and feathering, the purpose of which was to punish Malcolm, force a recantation, and ostracize him.

> With these and such like arguments, together with a gentle crouding of persons not of their way of thinking out of the ring they proceeded to elevate Mr. Malcolm from his sled into a cart, and stripping him to buff and breeches, gave him a modern jacket [a coat of tar and feathers] and hied him away to liberty-tree, where they proposed to him to renounce his present commission, and swear that he would never hold another inconsistent with the liberties of his country; but this he obstinately refusing, they then

carted him to the gallows, passed a rope round his neck, and threw the other end over the beam as if they intended to hang him: But this manoeuvre he set at defiance. They then basted him for some time with a rope's end, and threatened to cut his ears off, and on this he complied, and they then brought him home.[7]

Hewes had precipitated an electrifying event. It was part of the upsurge of spontaneous action in the wake of the Tea Party that prompted the Whig leaders to promote a "Committee for Tarring and Feathering" as an instrument of crowd control. The "Committee" made its appearance in broadsides signed by "Captain Joyce, Jun.," a sobriquet meant to invoke the bold cornet who had captured King Charles in 1647.[8] The event was reported in the English newspapers, popularized in three or four satirical prints, and dramatized still further when Malcolm went to England, where he campaigned for a pension and ran for Parliament (without success) against John Wilkes, the leading champion of America. The event confirmed the British ministry in its punitive effort to bring rebellious Boston to heel.[9]

What was lost to the public was that Hewes was at odds with the crowd. He wanted justice from the courts, not a mob; after all, he had sworn out a warrant against Malcolm. And he could not bear to see cruel punishment inflicted on a man, any more than on a boy. As he told the story to Thatcher, when he returned and saw Malcolm being carted away in tar and feathers, "his instant impulse was to push after the procession as fast as he could, with a blanket to put over his shoulders. He overtook them [the crowd] at his brother's [Shubael's] house and made an effort to relieve him; but the ruffians who now had the charge of him about the cart, pushed him aside, and warned him to keep off." This may have been the Good Samaritan of 1835, but the story rings true. While "the very excitement which the affront must have wrought upon him began to rekindle," Hewes conveyed no hatred for Malcolm.[10]

The denouement of the affair was an incident several weeks later. "Malcolm recovered from his wounds and went about as usual. 'How do you do, Mr. Malcolm?' said Hewes, very civilly, the next time he met him. 'Your humble servant, Mr. George Robert Twelves Hewes,' quoth he,—touching his hat genteelly as he passed by. 'Thank ye,' thought Hewes, 'and I am glad you have learned *better manners at last.*'"[11] Hewes's mood was one of triumph. Malcolm had been taught a lesson. The issue was respect for Hewes, a patriot, a poor man, an honest citizen, a decent man standing up for a child against an unspeakably arrogant "gentleman" who was an enemy of his country.

[8]

The Patriot

Hewes's role in these three events fits few of the categories that historians have applied to the participation of ordinary men in the Revolution. He was not a member of any organized committee, caucus, or club. He did not attend the expensive public dinners of the Sons of Liberty. He was capable of acting on his own volition without being summoned by any leaders (as in the Massacre). He could volunteer and assume leadership (as in the Tea Party). He was at home on the streets in crowds but he could also reject a crowd (as in the tarring and feathering of Malcolm). He was at home in the other places where ordinary Bostonians turned out to express their convictions: at funeral processions, at meetings of the "whole body of the people," in courtrooms at public trials. He recoiled from violence to persons if not to property. The man who could remember the whippings of his own boyhood did not want to be the source of pain to others, whether Sergeant Burk, who tried to cheat him over a pair of shoes, or John Malcolm, who almost killed him. It is in keeping with his character that he should have come to the aid of a little boy facing a beating.

Nevertheless, Hewes was more of a militant than he conveyed

or his biographers recognized in 1834 and 1835. He was capable of acting on his own initiative in the wake of collective action at both the Massacre and the Tea Party. He had "public notoriety," Thatcher tells us for his "whistling talent"; whistling was the customary way of assembling a crowd.[1] According to Malcolm, Hewes was among the "tradesmen" who had "several times before affronted him" by "hooting" at him in the streets.[2] And the patriots whose names stayed with him included Dr. Thomas Young and William Molineaux, the two Sons of Liberty who replaced Ebenezer McIntosh as "mob" leaders.[3]

What moved Hewes to action? It was not the written word; indeed there is no sign he was much of a reader until old age, and then it was the Bible he read. "My whole education," he told Hawkes, "consisted of only a moderate knowledge of reading and writing."[4] He seems to have read one of the most sensational pamphlets of 1773, very likely Thomas Hutchinson's letters to Great Britain exposing the machinations of the colony's high Tories, which he prized enough to hold onto for more than fifty years, but he was certainly not like Harbottle Dorr, the Boston shopkeeper who pored over every issue of every Boston newspaper, annotating Britain's crimes for posterity.[5]

Hewes was moved to act by personal experiences that he shared with large numbers of other plebeian Bostonians. He seems to have been politicized, not by the Stamp Act, but by the coming of the troops after 1768, and then by things that happened to him, that he saw, or that happened to people he knew. Once aroused, he took action with others of his own rank and condition—the laboring classes who formed the bulk of the actors at the Massacre, the Tea Party, and the Malcolm affair—and with other members of his family: his uncle Robert, "known for a staunch Liberty Boy," and his brother Daniel, a guard at the tea ship. Shubael, alone among his brothers, became a Tory.[6] These shared experiences were interpreted and focused more likely by the spoken than the written word and as much by his peers at taverns and crowd actions as by leaders in huge public meetings.

As he became active politically he may have had a growing awareness of his worth as a shoemaker. McIntosh was clearly the man of the year in 1765; indeed, Whigs were no less fearful than Loyalists that "the Captain General of the Liberty Tree" might become the Masaniello of Boston.[7] After a shoemaker made the boot to hang in the Liberty Tree as an effigy of Lord Bute, "Jack Cobler" served notice that "whenever the Public Good requires my services, I shall be ready to distinguish myself." In 1772 "Crispin" began an anti-Loyalist diatribe by saying, "I am a shoemaker, a citizen, a free man and a freeholder." The editor added a postscript justifying "Crispin's performance" and explaining that "it should be known what common people, even *coblers* think and feel under the present administration."[8] In city after city, "cobblers" were singled out for derision by conservatives for leaving their lasts to engage in the body politic.[9] Hewes could not have been unaware of all this; he was part of it.

He may also have responded to the rising demand among artisans for support of American manufacturers, whether or not it brought him immediate benefit. He most certainly subscribed to the secularized Puritan ethic—self-denial, industry, frugality—that made artisans take to the nonimportation agreement with its crusade against foreign luxury and its vision of American manufactures. And he could easily have identified with the appeal of the Massachusetts Provincial Congress of 1774 that equated the political need "to encourage agriculture, manufacturers and economy so as to render this state as independent of every other state as the nature of our country will admit" with the "happiness of particular families" in being "independent."[10]

But what ideas did Hewes articulate? He spoke of what he did but very little of what he thought. In the brief statement he offered Hawkes about why he went off to war in 1776, he expressed a commitment to general principles as they had been brought home to him by his experiences. "I was continually reflecting upon the unwarrantable sufferings inflicted on the citizens of Boston by the usurpation and tyranny of Great Britain, and my mind was excited with an unextinguishable desire to aid in chastising them." When Hawkes expressed a doubt "as to the correctness of his conduct in absenting himself from his family," Hewes "emphatically reiterated" the same phrases, adding to a "desire to aid in chastising them" the phrase "and securing our independence."[11] This was clearly not an afterthought; it probably reflected the way many others moved toward the goal of independence, not as a matter of original intent, but as a step made necessary when all other resorts failed. Ideology thus did not set George Hewes apart from Samuel Adams or John Hancock. The difference lies in what the Revolution did to him as a person. His experiences transformed him, giving him a sense of citizenship and personal worth. Adams and Hancock began with both; Hewes had to arrive there, and in arriving he cast off the constraints of deference.

The two incidents with which I introduced Hewes's life measure the distance he had come: from the young man tongue-tied in the presence of John Hancock to the man who would not take his hat off to the officer of the ship named *Hancock*. Did he cast off his deference to Hancock? Hewes's affirmation of his worth as a human being was a form of class consciousness. Implicit in the idea "I am as good as any man regardless of rank or wealth" was the idea that any poor man might be as good as any rich man. This did not mean that all rich men were bad. On the contrary, in Boston, more than any other major colonial seaport, a majority of the merchants were part of the patriot coalition; "divers Gentlemen of Good Fortunes," as Hutchinson put it, were with the "Rabble." This blunted class consciousness. Boston's mechanics, unlike New York's or Philadelphia's, did not develop mechanic committees or a mechanic consciousness before the Revolution. Yet in Boston the rich were forced to defer to the people in order to obtain or retain their support. Indeed, the entire public career of Hancock from 1765 on—distributing largesse, buying uniforms for Pope's Day marchers, building ships to employ artisans—can be understood as an exercise of this kind of deference, proving his civic virtue and patriotism.[12]

This gives meaning to Hewes's tale of working beside Hancock at the Tea Party—"a curious reminiscence," Thatcher called it, "but we believe it a mistake."

> Mr. Hewes, however, positively affirms, as of his own observation, that *Samuel Adams and John Hancock were both actively engaged in the process of destruction.* Of the latter he speaks more particularly, being entirely confident that he was himself at one time engaged with him in the demolition of the same chest of tea. He recognized him not only by his *ruffles* making their appearance in the heat of the work, from under the disguise which pretty thoroughly covered him,—and by his figure, and gait;—but by his features, which neither his paint nor his loosened club of hair behind wholly concealed from a close view;—and by his voice also, for he exchanged with him an Indian *grunt*, and the expression "*me know you*," which was a good deal used on that occasion for a countersign.[13]

Thatcher was justifiably skeptical; it is very unlikely that Hancock was there. Participants swore themselves to secrecy; their identity was one of the best-kept secrets of the Revolution. In fact, in 1835 Thatcher published in an appendix the first list of those "more or less actively engaged" in the Tea Party as furnished by "an aged Bostonian," clearly not Hewes.[14] Hancock was not named. More important, it was not part of the patriot plan for the well-known leaders to be present. When the all-day meeting that sanctioned the action adjourned, the leaders, including Hancock, stayed behind conspicuously in Old South.[15] Still, there can be little question that Hewes was convinced at the time that Hancock was on the ship: some gentlemen were indeed present; it was reasonable to assume that Hancock, who had been so conspicuous on the tea issue, was there; Hewes knew what Hancock looked like; he was too insistent about details for his testimony to be dismissed as made up. And the way he recorded it in his mind at the time was the way he stored it in his memory.

Hewes in effect had brought Hancock down to his own level. The poor shoemaker had not toppled the wealthy merchant; he was no "leveler." But the rich and powerful—the men in "ruffles"—had become, in his revealing word, his "associates." John Hancock and George Hewes breaking open the same chest at the Tea Party remained for Hewes a symbol of a moment of equality. To the shoemaker, one suspects, this above all was what the Revolutionary events of Boston meant, as did the war that followed.

[9]

Soldier and Sailor

Hewes's decisions from 1775 to 1783—his choice of services and the timing and sequence of his military activities—suggest a pattern of patriotism mingled with a hope to strike it rich and a pressing need to provide for his family.

After the outbreak of hostilities at Lexington and Concord in April 1775, Boston became a garrison town; patriot civilians streamed out—perhaps ten thousand of them—Tory refugees moved in, and the number of British troops grew to 13,500 by July. Hewes sent his wife and children to Wrentham—his father's native town—where they would be safe with relatives. His brother Daniel did the same; Solomon went elsewhere; Shubael alone stayed with the British, as butcher-general to General Gage. George himself remained—"imprisoned," as he remembered it —prevented like other able-bodied men from leaving the city. He made a living as a fisherman; the British allowed him to pass in and out of the harbor in exchange for the pick of the day's catch. He was in Boston nine weeks, was harassed by soldiers on the street, witnessed the Battle of Bunker Hill from a neck of land far out in the bay (he "saw [Joseph Warren] fall"), and saw the corpses of British soldiers "chucked" into an open pit at one end

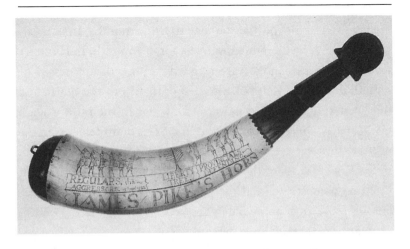

James Pike, a New England militia man who fought at the Battle of Bunker Hill, carved the dramatic symbolism of the Liberty Tree on his powderhorn: British "Regulars, the Aggressors" and "Provincials, Defending" the tree. *Courtesy Chicago Historical Society.*

of the Common. One morning he bade good-bye to Shubael, hid his shoemaker's tools under the deck of a small boat borrowed from a Tory, and, after a narrow scrape with British guards, made good an escape with two friends to nearby Lynn. The Committee of Safety took him to Cambridge, where General Washington plied him with questions about conditions in Boston—an interview we shall return to. Then he made his way south to Wrentham.[1]

Hewes's record of service thereafter can be reconstructed with reasonable accuracy by matching what he claimed in his pension application in 1832 and told his biographers against information from official records and other contemporary sources.[2] After some months, very likely in the fall of 1776, he enlisted on a privateer at Providence on a voyage north that lasted about three months. He returned to Wrentham and a year later, in the fall of

1777, served in the militia from one to three months. In late August 1778 he served again, most likely for one month. In February 1779 he made a second privateering voyage, this time out of Boston, an eventful seven-and-a-half-month trip to the South and the West Indies. In 1780 he very likely was in the militia again from late July to late October, and in 1781 he definitely was in the militia at the same time of year. That was his final tour of duty: in the closing years of the war, to avoid the Massachusetts draft, he hired a substitute. All these enlistments were out of Attleborough, the town immediately south of Wrentham.[3] All were as a private; he did not rise in the ranks.

Several things stand out in this record. Hewes did not go at once, not until he provided for his family. He remembered that he did not make his first enlistment until "about two years after the battle of Bunker Hill," although actually it was closer to a year or fifteen months.[4] He served often, twice at sea, at least four and possibly five times in the militia, but not at all in the Continental army, which would have meant longer periods away from home. For almost all of these stints he volunteered; once he was drafted; once he sent a substitute; he drew these distinctions carefully.[5]

This record, put alongside what we know about other Massachusetts men in the war, places Hewes a good cut above the average. He served at least nine months in the militia and ten-and-a-half months at sea—about twenty months in all. In Concord, most men "were credited with under a half a year's time";[6] in Peterborough, New Hampshire, only a third did "extensive service" of over a year.[7] Hewes served less than the thirty-three months of the average man in the Continental army.[8] He was not one of the men whom John Shy has called the "hard core" of Revolutionary fighters, like the shoemaker "Long Bill" Scott of Peterborough. But neither was he one of the sunshine patriots Robert

Gross found in Concord who came out for no more than a few militia stints early in the war. He served over the length of the fighting. Like others who put in this much time, he was poor; even in Concord after 1778, soldiers in the militia as well as the army "were men with little or nothing to lose."[9] Hewes was in his mid-thirties; he and Sarah had four children by 1776, six by 1781. He spent most of the years of war at home providing for them, doing what, he did not say, but possibly making shoes for the army like other country cordwainers.[10] His patriotism was thus tempered by the need for survival.

Going to war was a wrenching experience. When Hewes told his wife he intended to "take a privateering cruise," she "was greatly afflicted at the prospect of our separation, and my absence from a numerous family of children, who needed a father's parental care." Taught from boyhood to repress his emotions ("I cannot cry," Thatcher reported him saying when punishment loomed), Hewes cut the pain of parting by a ruse.

> On the day which I had appointed to take my departure, I came into the room where my wife was, and inquired if all was ready? She pointed in silence to my knapsack. I observed, that I would put it on and walk with it a few rods, to see if it was rightly fitted to carry with ease. I went out, to return no more until the end of my cruise. The manly fortitude which becomes the soldier, could not overcome the tender sympathies of my nature. I had not courage to encounter the trial of taking a formal leave. When I had arrived at a solitary place on my way, I sat down for a few moments, and sought to allay the keenness of my grief by giving vent to a profusion of tears.[11]

Why was privateering Hewes's first choice? Privateering, as Jesse Lemisch has put it, was legalized piracy with a share of the booty for each pirate.[12] Under a state or Continental letter of marque, a privately owned ship was authorized to take enemy vessels as prizes. The government received a share, as did the owners and crew, prorated by rank. During the seven years of war, the United States commissioned 2,000 privateers, 626 in Massachusetts alone, which itself issued 1,524 commissions. In 1776, when Hewes made his decision, Abigail Adams spoke of "the rage for privateering" in Boston, and James Warren told Samuel Adams that "a whole country" was "privateering mad."[13]

War for Hewes meant opportunity: a chance to escape from a humdrum occupation never to his liking; to be at thirty-five what had been denied at sixteen—a fighting man; above all, a chance to accumulate the capital that could mean a house, a new shop, apprentices and journeymen, perhaps a start in something altogether new. He was following a path trod by tens of thousands of poor New Englanders ever since the wars against the French in the 1740s and 1750s.[14] As an economic flyer, however, privateering ultimately proved disastrous for Hewes.

His first voyage went well. He sailed on the *Diamond* out of Providence, attracted possibly by an advertisement that promised fortune and adventure. They captured three vessels, the last of which Hewes brought back to Providence as a member of the prize crew. He said nothing about his share; by inference he got enough to whet his appetite but not enough to boast about. He also nearly drowned off Newfoundland when a line he and two shipmates were standing on broke.[15]

His second voyage was shattering. He went on the Connecticut ship of war *Defence*, commanded by Captain Samuel Smedley and sailing from Boston with the *Oliver Cromwell*. The *Defence* and the *Cromwell* captured two richly laden vessels and later, after a layover in Charleston, South Carolina, two British privateers; on the way home, the *Defence* stopped a ship and relieved the Tory

passengers of their money. The prize money from the two privateers alone was $80,000.[16] But Hewes got nothing. His share was
supposed to be $250, "but some pretext was always offered for
withholding my share from me; so that I have never received one
cent of it." When he asked for his wages, Captain Smedley "told
me he was about fitting out an expedition to the West Indies, and
could not, without great inconvenience, spare the money then;
but said he would call on his way to Providence . . . and would pay
me; but I never saw him afterwards. Neither have I, at any time
since, received a farthing, either of my share of prize money or
wages."[17]

There was an adventurous side to privateering. His stories
stress the thrill of the chase, the intrepid maneuvering of his ship
in battle, the excitement of a boarding party. They also deal with
the prosaic. He remembered manning the pumps on the leaking
Defence "for eight days and eight nights to keep us from sinking."
He remembered before battle that "we sat up all night . . . we
made bandages, scraped lint, so that we might be prepared to
dress wounds as we expected to have a hard time of it."[18] The man
of tender sympathies did not become a bloodthirsty buccaneer.

Most important of all was the memory that at sea he had participated in making decisions and that the captains had shown
deference to their crews. On his first voyage, the initial agreement
was for a cruise of seven weeks. "When that term had expired,"
said Hewes, "and we had seen no enemy during the time, we were
discouraged, and threatened to mutiny, unless he would return."
Captain Stacey asked for one more week, after which he promised to sail home if they saw nothing, "to which we assented."
On the second voyage, when the *Defence* sighted enemy ships and
Captain Smedley "asked us if we were willing to give chase to
them, we assented, we were all ready to go and risk our lives with

him." In Charleston, their tour of duty legally over, Smedley proposed a five-day extension when the British privateers were sighted. "Our Captain put it to a vote, and it was found we were unanimously agreed to make the cruise."[19] One hesitates to call this process democratic: even the captain of a pirate ship could not function without the support of his crew. What Hewes remembered was that the captains deferred to him and his mates, not the other way around.

This is the motif of his encounter with George Washington in 1775. When Hewes and his fellow escapees from Boston were taken to Washington's headquarters at Craigie House in Cambridge, the Reverend Peter Thatcher recognized him as the nephew of the "staunch Liberty Man" Robert Hewes. Washington invited Hewes into his parlor—"with him, alone. There he told him his story, every word of it, from beginning to end, and answered all his questions besides." Washington, in Hewes's words, "didn't *laugh*, to be sure, but *looked amazing good-natured* you may depend." Washington then treated him and his companions to punch and invited them and Thatcher to a meal. All this is entirely possible. Washington was considering an invasion of Boston; he would have welcomed intelligence from a street-wise man just out of the town, and as a Virginia planter he knew the importance of the gesture of hospitality. Hewes also claimed that "Madam Washington waited upon them at table all dinnertime," but this is improbable, and Thatcher the biographer erred in stating that she was "known to have been with her husband at the date of the adventure."[20]

In military duty on land there was no recognition of this sort from his betters, though he was in the militia, by reputation the most democratic branch of service. Even his adventures were humdrum. The "general destination" of his units, he told

Hawkes, was "to guard the coasts." He saw action at the Battle of Newport Island in August 1778 under General John Sullivan. He remembered "an engagement" at Cobblehill, "in which we beat them with a considerable slaughter of their men." He remembered rowing through the darkness in silence in an attack on a British fort that had to be aborted when one of the rowers talked. He remembered the grim retreat from Newport Island, crossing the waters at Howland's Ferry. On duty at West Point in 1781 he went out on forays against the "cowboys," lawless bands pillaging Westchester County. In all this activity he claimed no moment of glory; there was a lot of marching; a lot of sentry duty; much drudgery.[21] If he mended shoes for soldiers, as did other shoemakers in the ranks, he did not speak of it. And military service did not kindle in him an ambition to rise, as it did in a number of other shoemakers who became officers.[22]

After all this service it hurt to be subjected to an inequitable draft. As Hewes explained to Hawkes with considerable accuracy, Massachusetts required all men of military age to serve "or to form themselves into classes of nine men, and each class to hire an able bodied man, on such terms as they could, and pay him for his services, while they were to receive their pay of the state." Attleborough instituted such a procedure early in 1781. Why did Hewes refuse to go? He was frank with Hawkes: the "extreme exigencies" of his family and the "pressure of his circumstances" forced him to "withdraw his services from the army." The decision was painful, and it was costly. Hewes's substitute "demanded . . . specie while we received nothing of the government but paper money, of very little value, and continually depreciating."[23]

Thatcher was right: his service was "poorly rewarded." Hewes was one of "the mass of people, at large; such as had little property to fight for, or to lose, on one hand, and could reasonably expect to gain still less, either in the way of emolument or distinction on the other."[24] Instead, the inequities of civilian life were repeated on an even crasser scale. The rich could easily afford a substitute; the men who had already fought paid through the nose for one. The ship's officers got their share of the prize; the poor sailor got neither prize money nor wages.

But the war meant more than this to Hewes. It left a memory of rights asserted (by a threat of mutiny) and rights respected by captains who put decisions to a vote of the crew, and of the crew giving assent. It was a memory, above all, of respect from his betters: from General Washington at Cambridge, from captains Stacey and Smedley at sea, as from John Hancock in Boston. For a moment, it had been a world that marched to the tune of the old English nursery rhyme supposedly played at Cornwallis's surrender, "The World Turned Upside Down." Then "in a trice" Hewes's world came right side up—but little if any better than before.

Family Man

For thirty-three years, from 1783 to about 1815, George Hewes almost eludes us. We know that at the end of the war he did not return to Boston but stayed in Wrentham; that he produced a large family; that after the War of 1812 he moved to Otsego County, New York. But we hardly know what he did during these years. His biographers were uninterested. Hawkes said he was in "laborious pursuits either in some agricultural or mechanical employment." Later lore had it that he returned to the sea and "for many years" was "a mate on merchant vessels in the West Indies trade," lore that has been impossible to verify.[1] Legal documents refer to him in 1796–97 as a "yeoman" and in 1810 as a "cordwainer."[2] These clues are not inconsistent. Wrentham in those years was a small inland farming town of about two thousand people, no more than a good day's walk to the port of Providence.[3] If Hewes was a cordwainer, he would have had to be a farmer too, as were most country shoemakers. If he went to sea, he would have had to fall back on landlubber pursuits, especially in his later years. There were few "old salts" in their fifties or sixties.

All we may say with certainty is that he came out of the war poor and stayed poor. By 1783, he had turned forty and had very little to show for it. That he did not go back to Boston, that he did not visit there more than a few times until 1821, tells us how small a stake he had in his native city. In this he was like at least a thousand other Bostonians—for the most part "the poorest and least successful"—who migrated elsewhere.[4] "The shop which I had built in Boston, I lost," he told Hawkes. British troops "appropriated it for the purpose of a wash and lumber house, and eventually pulled it down and burnt it up."[5] He owned no real estate. After seven years of war he could hardly count on customers waiting at his door. There was really nothing to go back to. Uncle Robert had died. His brothers were still there: Solomon was a fisherman and Daniel a mason, but Shubael could list himself as gentleman. Hewes bore his Loyalist brother no ill will; he named a son Shubael in 1781. But his own low estate, compared to his brother's success, must have rankled.

There is no evidence that he acquired land in Wrentham. The census names him; the records of real estate bought and sold do not.[6] The town's tax records of the 1790s list him only as a "poll rateable," owning neither real nor personal taxable property. In 1796, at the age of fifty-four, he was assessed thirty-three cents for his Massachusetts poll tax, seven cents for his county tax, fifty cents for his town tax.[7] He may possibly have been joint owner of property listed in someone else's name; more likely he rented or lived on a relative's land.[8] His uncle Joseph, a Providence physician who died in 1796, willed George and Sarah one thirty-sixth share of the estate—$580.25. The windfall helped keep him going. In 1810 he finally became a property holder in Attleborough: a co-owner, with eighteen others, of "a burying yard."[9]

That Hewes stayed poor is also suggested by what little we know about his children. Sarah Hewes gave birth to fifteen, it would seem, of whom we have the names of eleven, three girls and eight boys, possibly all who survived birth. Six were born by 1781, the rest by 1796 at the latest. The naming pattern suggests the strength of family attachments: Sally for her mother; Mary and Elizabeth for aunts, Hewes's father's sisters; Solomon, Daniel, and Shubael after his brothers (and Solomon also for his grandfather, Shubael also for Sally's relative). One son was named Eleven, and the last-born, George Robert Twelves Fifteen.[10] What can we make of this? A mischievous sense of humor? His own long name, the subject of teasing in his youth, after all had been a way of getting attention. Perhaps the only inheritance a poor shoemaker-farmer-seaman could guarantee—especially to his eleventh and fifteenth children—was a name that would be a badge of distinction as his had been.

Hewes could do little for this brood. Solomon, the firstborn, became a shoemaker—undoubtedly trained by his father. Robert became a blacksmith. For the other sons we know no occupations. Of the daughters, two of the three married late—Elizabeth at twenty-two but Sarah (also Sally) in her mid-thirties and Mary at thirty-two—understandable when a father could not provide a suitor with dowry, position, or a sought-after craft skill.[11]

For a while the Heweses lived in Attleborough, but the only trace they left is the share of the "burying yard."[12] Attleborough was not much different from Wrentham; a farming town closer to Providence, it also had a few of the mills that dotted southern New England these years. For opportunity the family would have to move much farther away. And so they did, like tens of thousands of families who left New England in the 1790s and early 1800s, and like a large number of New England veterans.[13] Robert, Sally who married William Morrison, and Elizabeth who married Preserved Whipple moved to Otsego County, New

York. George Fifteen went first to Connecticut, then to Richfield Springs, finally to Michigan. Solomon also moved to Otsego County for a while, then went down east to Union, Maine, where he acquired twenty-eight acres. Eleven went to Kentucky.[14]

What had become these years of George Hewes, the citizen? We have only one thing to go on. According to family tradition, during the War of 1812 he tried to enlist in the navy as a boatswain but was turned down; tried to ship out on the frigate *Constitution;* then tried to join Commodore Perry's fleet on Lake Erie. There is even a story that he walked to Braintree to enlist ex-President John Adams's support.[15] Two sons we know saw service, Eleven in the Kentucky militia, under General Henry Clay, and George Fifteen in Connecticut. Such patriotism in Wrentham, where there was "no rush of men" to arms, would have been extraordinary.[16] It meant that the War of 1812 was a second War of Independence to Hewes; and to have sons who responded meant that the father had passed on well the heritage of the Revolution.

At the end of the war, perhaps before, George and Sarah Hewes went west to Richfield Springs. George was seventy-four, Sarah sixty-five. His family was dispersed, but three or four children were already in Otsego County or accompanied him there. Did he mean to spend his declining years in retirement with his family? He was still vigorous. One suspects he went in search of the "living," the "independence," that had eluded the artisan and the recognition that had eluded the citizen. He had gone from city to sea to small town; now he would try again in a place where at the least he would be with sons and daughters. And so he left Wrentham about 1815, as he had left Boston in 1775, probably with not much more than the tools of his trade. Only this time he had an old soldier's uniform as well.

[11]

Veteran

In New York, Hewes did not find independence either for himself or through his children. For the last decade of his life he did not even have the haven of family. He did, however, find recognition. Richfield Springs, sixty-five miles west of Albany and eighteen north of Cooperstown, was no longer frontier country after 1815. Otsego County had been opened up in the 1790s by Judge William Cooper, the novelist's father, who boasted of settling fifty thousand families. The pioneers were already moving away to find more fertile land on better terms in western New York or the Old Northwest. Richfield Springs was located in a beautiful area of rolling hills and low mountain peaks, of streams and lakes. In the 1820s, after mineral waters were discovered, it became a resort town. But its prosperity was uneven. It did not get a post office until 1829.[1]

What did Hewes do during these years? We have more to go on for the last twenty-five years of his life than for the three decades before: Hawkes's account is supplemented by some fascinating reminiscences by Hewes's contemporaries collected in 1896 by the historian James Grant Wilson. According to "an old jesting rhyme attributed to James Fenimore Cooper who knew honest Hewes,"

Old Father Hewes, he makes good shoes,
And sews them well together
It has no heels but those he steals
And begs his upper leather.[2]

Hewes, then, was once again a shoemaker.

He and Sally lived in "a small house which his son Robert had built for him" on Robert's land.[3] Sarah Morrison was nine miles away in German Flats and Elizabeth Whipple was also in the area, each with a large and growing family. Fifteen lived nearby for a time, a property holder; so did Solomon. As before, their father had no house or land of his own.[4]

He can hardly have prospered. The clue is that when Daniel, his last surviving brother, died in 1821, Hewes traveled with Robert to Boston for five days in a one-horse wagon to secure their legacy. For the third time in his life a will loomed—Grampa Shubael left £2 17s. 6d. in 1756, and Uncle Joseph, $580.25 in 1796— a windfall so important when there were no other prospects of accumulation. George's brother Solomon had died in 1816, Shubael in 1813. Daniel left an estate that came to $2,900 after expenses; he willed a third to Hewes and his children. Hewes considered his share "a considerable sum," but it could not have stretched very far. "For some years," Hawkes wrote in 1833, Robert had "contributed what was necessary" to support his father and mother.[5]

Sarah died in 1828, aged eighty-seven years and nine months, the tombstone said. Actually she was seventy-seven. It is difficult to bring Sarah out from her husband's shadow. He spoke of her with affection: "we lived together very happily," he told Hawkes; he expected to see her in heaven. He had hardly married her for money; he had courted her for two years. He was grief-stricken when he left her in wartime. He called her Sally, not Sarah, certainly not Mrs. Hewes. What was her role? A washerwoman before she was married, she labored a lifetime as a housewife, without servants. She bore, it seems, fifteen children and raised eleven of them. She was illiterate; unlike her husband, she signed her name with a mark. A daughter of a sexton, she may well have been religious. Certainly, she was apolitical; had she been a "Daughter of Liberty," Thatcher, who dwelt on the subject, would have caught it. When George got home from the Tea Party and told her his story, " 'Well George,' said she, at the end of it, *did you bring me home a lot of it?* " "We shouldn't wonder," Thatcher added, "if Mrs. Hewes was more of a tea-drinker than a Whig." Or, we might add, more of a woman struggling to make ends meet on a shoemaker's income.[6]

After she died, it was all downhill. George moved from one child to another, each so poor they could not long provide for him. At first, he lived with Robert, who soon after, "having met with some misfortune, was obliged to sell his house" and move farther west. For a while he was "a sojourner among friends." Then he moved in with his daughter and son-in-law, the Morrisons, but stayed only a year. "Morrison and his wife had several children," wrote Hawkes, "and were, as they are now very poor . . . Morrison not being able by his manuel [*sic*] services to provide for his family but a mere subsistence." Hewes had a "severe sickness." Next he took up "a short residence with a son who resides near Richfield Springs," very likely George, Jr. Soon after, he "fell down a stairway on some iron ware," severely lacerating both legs. He healed with remarkable speed for a man his age, but a son with eight children to feed could not provide "for his comfortable support." Finally, a "worthy gentleman" in the neighborhood took the old man in, and it was there that Hawkes found him in 1833, "pressed down by the iron hand of poverty" and "supported by the charity of his friends." His children had failed and, in the classic style of poor pioneers, were moving on to greener fields. They and his grandchildren would scatter, most to the Midwest, some to California, some still in mechanic trades in Boston.[7]

In the fall of 1832 Hewes applied successfully for a veteran's pension. He may have applied earlier, for Hawkes spoke of a "long and expensive process" begun about fifteen or twenty years before. If true, Hewes must have been frustrated: he would not have been eligible until the 1832 law required no more than six months' service in any branch.[8] Hewes's application, in the hand of the county clerk to which a local judge and county official attested, gives minute details of his service. A clerk in Washington disallowed three of the months he claimed at sea, listing him for seven months', fifteen days' service as a seaman and nine months in the militia. It added up to sixteen months, fifteen days, or less than the two years required for a full pension; he was therefore prorated down to $60 a year, with $150 in arrears retroactive to 1831. It was, Hawkes thought, a "miserable pittance of a soldier's pension."[9]

Meanwhile, Hewes was winning recognition of a sort. A "venerable lady" whom James Grant Wilson spoke to in 1896 said she first met Hewes in 1820 at a "house raising" where she saw "an alert and little old man with the cocked hat and faded uniform of a continental soldier, who charmed the young people with the account of the destruction of the tea in Boston in December 1773, and his stories of battles on land and sea." Another woman, who attended school in Richfield Springs with one of Hewes's granddaughters, said she was always delighted to listen to the old soldier's stories and to see him on the Fourth of July, "when he would put on his ancient uniform, shoulder his crutch, like Goldsmith's veteran, and show how fields were won."[10] By the late 1820s, possibly earlier, Hewes had become a figure at Fourth of July observances. In 1829 the local paper reported that he "walked three miles on foot to join in the festivities," and "after mingling in the enjoyments of the occasion, with a fine flow of spirits returned in the same manner thro' the wet to home." In 1833 the celebrants toasted him as "the last survivor of the tea party," and he toasted them in turn.[11]

The "venerable lady" also claimed to have seen "the old soldier in conversation with James Fenimore Cooper who invited Hewes to his home in Cooperstown where he was quite a lion at the author's table." This is entirely possible. The novelist, who returned to his family home at intervals, was always mining old-timers for the lore of the sea and the Revolution. Later he would invite Ned Meyers, an old salt, to spend five months at Cooperstown while he took down his life. Hewes's tales of the "cowboys and skinners" of Westchester could have added to Cooper's store of information for *The Spy;* his adventures at sea would have confirmed Cooper in his idealization of American privateersmen, a theme in several of his sea novels and his naval history.[12]

This recognition, it can be argued, had a price. The old man had to dress up in his uniform and tell stories. He was trotted out once a year on Independence Day. He had to play a role; perhaps this may have contributed to his "remembering" himself almost ten years older than he was. And the already-quoted "jesting rhyme," whether Cooper's or not, suggests that if children sat at his feet to hear his tales, they also poked fun at "Old Father Hewes."

Hawkes captured a mood in Hewes that bordered on alienation, especially as he talked about his reactions to Boston in 1821, when he went there to receive his legacy. Hewes spoke of the experience in haunting, poetic language. As he walked around town, he looked for old friends.

> But, alas! I looked in vain. They were gone. Neither were those who once knew them as I did, to be found. The place where I drew my first breath and formed my most endearing attachments, had to me become a land of strangers.

He looked for familiar places.

> Not only had my former companions and friends disappeared, but the places of their habitations were occupied by those who could give no account of them. The house in which I was born was not to be found, and the spot where it stood could not be ascertained by any visible object.

The physical city of 1775 was gone.

> The whole scenery about me seemed like the work of enchantment. Beacon hill was levelled, and a pond on which had stood three mills, was filled up with its contents; over which two spacious streets had been laid and many elegant fabrics erected. The whole street, from Boston Neck to the Long Wharf, had been built up. It was to me almost as a new town, a strange city; I could hardly realize that I was in the place of my nativity.

As he stood in the market, an "aged man" stared at him, then asked,

> Was you not a citizen of Boston at the time the British tea was destroyed in Boston harbour? I replied that I was, and was one of those who aided in throwing it into the water. He then inquired who commanded the division to which I belonged in that affair; I told him one Leonard Pitt. So he did mine, said he; and I had believed there was a man by the name of Hewes aboard the same ship with me, and I think you must be that man.[13]

They had a "social glass," reminisced, parted. "I found he as well as myself had outlived the associates of his youthful days." Hewes did his legal business, saw his nephews and nieces, and after three days headed home.[14]

Sometime in his declining years Hewes became a Methodist. He was known to the children of the village as "The Old Saturday Man," Wilson reported, because "every Saturday for several years he walked into Richfield Springs for the purpose of being present at the services of the Methodist Church of which he was a member."[15] This lore seems trustworthy. He had become a Bible reader ("he can still read his Bible without glasses," a grandson wrote in 1836), and Hawkes found that he "often expresses his gratitude to a kind providence, for the many favours with which he has been indulged." He was also known for his temperance, a badge of Methodists. It stuck in the memory of the "venerable lady" that at the house-raising Hewes was "perhaps the only man present who did not drink the blackstrap (a mixture of whiskey and molasses) provided for the occasion."[16]

Hewes had not been a member of any other church in Richfield Springs and could hardly have been a Methodist before moving there.[17] But it is not surprising that he became one. Methodism had a growing appeal to poor, hard-working people low in status, whether among shoemakers in Lynn, Massachusetts (a center of Methodist missionaries), textile workers in Samuel Slater's mill in Webster, Massachusetts, or rural folk in the west.[18] Richfield Springs had no fewer than three Methodist chapels scattered around the township, none of which could sustain a minister; circuit riders or laymen served them. Many things about the Methodists would have attracted Hewes: a warm atmosphere of Christian fellowship; a stress on sobriety and industriousness, the Franklinian virtues he had been raised on; the promise of salvation without regard to rank or wealth.[19] This was also a church that stressed lay leadership; shoemakers could serve as stewards, "class" leaders, and lay preachers. Hewes's Methodism seems late blooming; he may have found in the fellowship of the chapel the wholehearted acceptance of himself as a person that was missing in the Fourth of July kind of recognition from the village.

[12]

Hero

For Hewes, the publication of James Hawkes's *A Retrospect of the Boston Tea-Party* in 1834 led to recognition in New England. There is no sign that the book caused a ripple in Richfield Springs or Otsego County, but in Boston it paved the way for the return of one of the "last surviving members" of the Tea Party. Hewes's attraction was his age, supposedly almost one hundred, combined with his role in a symbolic moment of the Revolution. In 1821 Hewes had been ignored. By 1835 a change in historical mood made Boston ready for him. Angry veterans forced from the pension lists in the 1820s helped bring old soldiers into the public eye, leading to the more liberal act of 1832. At the laying of the cornerstone of the Bunker Hill Monument in 1825, Daniel Webster and Lafayette shared the honors with forty veterans of the battle and two hundred other veterans of the Revolution. In the 1830s Ralph Waldo Emerson interviewed survivors of the fight at Concord Bridge, and in 1831 Oliver Wendell Holmes wrote "The Last Leaf," a poem about an aged survivor of the Tea Party.[1]

Workingmen demonstrated a special identification with the artisan republicanism of the Revolution. The Massachusetts Charitable Mechanics Association—masters all—toasted "our

79

revolutionary mechanics" in 1825. On the Fourth of July, 1826, a shoemaker offered a toast to "the *Shoemakers* of *the Revolution*— they risked their little *all* upon the great *end* and gave *short quarters* to the foe, in 'the times that tried men's soles.'" Meanwhile Seth Luther, asserting the right of journeymen and factory operatives to combine against masters, asked "was there no *combination* when Bostonians . . . made a dish of tea . . . using Boston harbor for a tea pot?" In May 1835, when Boston journeymen house carpenters, masons, and stone cutters went on strike, they claimed "by the blood of our fathers shed on our battle fields on the War of the Revolution, the rights of American Freeman."[2]

In 1835 Hewes returned to New England on a triumphal tour of sorts accompanied by his youngest son, Fifteen. At Providence he was interviewed by the local newspaper, and the merchant patriarch Moses Brown called on him. On the way to Boston he stopped at Wrentham, perhaps to visit, perhaps to crow a bit. In Boston the papers noted his arrival, printing an excerpt from Hawkes's book. He was a celebrity. He stayed with his nephew Richard Brooke Hewes, Shubael's son, a politician who doubtless made the arrangements for his uncle's visit. Thatcher interviewed him for his biography, reliving his life in Boston. He sat for a portrait by Joseph G. Cole, Boston's rising young painter, which, entitled *The Centenarian*, would be on display at the Athenaeum Gallery within a month. A group of ladies presented him with a snuffbox.[3]

The highlight, of course, was the Fourth of July. He was the featured guest at South Boston's observance. "In a conspicuous part of the procession," according to the newspaper, "was the venerable Mr. Hewes, in a barouche, drawn by four splendid greys," accompanied by the lieutenant governor and his entourage. There was a church service and a dinner. When the orator of the day reached the Tea Party and "alluded to the venerable patriot," Hewes "arose and received the united and enthusiastic congratulations of the audience." He was supported on one side by Major Benjamin Russell, for forty years a leader of the mechanic interest as printer and publisher, and on the other by Colonel Henry Purkitt, who had been a cooper's apprentice and, like Hewes, a Tea Party volunteer. The orator was effusive in his tribute to Hewes, "formerly a citizen of Boston," now "on the verge of eternity": "Though you come to the land of your childhood, leaning upon a staff and feeling your dependence on the charities of a selfish world, you are surrounded by friends who feel that their prosperity is referable to the privations sacrifices and personal labors of you and your brave associates in arms." At the dinner after the toasts it was Hewes's turn. "Under the influence of strong emotion he gave the following toast, 'Those I leave behind me, May God Bless them.'"[4]

When the celebrations ended, Hewes made his way to Augusta, Maine. Solomon, his eldest, had died there the year before, and his wife had just died, but there were grandchildren to visit. He also went to Portland, perhaps for more family. From Maine, back to Boston, and thence home to Richfield Springs.

Several things struck those who saw Hewes. The first, of course, was his age. Not surprisingly, people came forward from all around—Wrentham, Attleborough, Boston, Maine—to testify, as they had in Richfield Springs, that he was indeed one hundred, if not more. The second was his remarkable physical condition. The third was his wonderful mood. A correspondent of the *Boston Courier* who rode the stagecoach to Augusta was astonished that "he bore the ride of fifty-eight miles with very little apparent fatigue, amusing himself and his fellow passengers occasionally upon the route, with snatches of revolutionary songs, and by the recital of anecdotes of the days which tried mens souls." He was in his glory. And lastly, there was his demeanor. Hewes's Providence interviewer found him "even at this age, a brave, high spirited, warm hearted man, whose tongue was never controlled by ceremony, and whose manners have not been moulded by the fashion of any day. His etiquette may be tea party etiquette, but it was not acquired at tea parties in Beacon Street or Broadway."[5] Hewes, in short, was still not taking his hat off for any man.

The remaining five years in Richfield Springs were no different than the previous twenty. Thatcher's biography appeared late in 1835, but there is no sign that it was read any more than Hawkes's. "The Old Saturday Man" continued to walk to church. The veteran continued to be a guest on the Fourth of July. His family was dispersed; there were more than fifty grandchildren, and occasionally one visited him. In 1836 George Whipple, Elizabeth's son, found him "pretty well, and very jovial. He sang for me many old songs and told over all the incidents of the 'scrape' in Boston Harbor. His memory is uncommonly good for one of his age. He jumped about so when I made myself known to him he liked to have lost his drumsticks." The old man clearly was starved for company. A visit from a grandchild only underscored his isolation. In 1836 he sat for a portrait by a local artist, commissioned by a grandson. He looked smaller, shrunken.[6]

On July 4, 1840, as Hewes was getting into a carriage to go to the annual observance, the horses bolted and he was seriously injured. He died on November 5, Pope's Day, once the "grand gala day" of Boston's apprentices. He was buried in what became the Presbyterian cemetery, where his wife already lay. There seem to have been no obituary notices, no public memorial services.

From mid-century on, Hewes began to make an occasional appearance in histories of the nation, the Revolution, Boston, or the Tea Party.[7] Descendants also kept his memory alive. Children and grandchildren named sons after him; one great-grandson bore the distinctive George Twelves Hewes (1861–1921). The generation that matured late in the nineteenth century rediscovered him as some compiled a mammoth genealogy and others applied to patriotic societies.[8] In 1896 his remains were exhumed and reinterred ceremoniously in the Grand Army of the Republic plot in Lakeview Cemetery, Richfield Springs. The inscription on the tombstone reads "George R. T. Hewes, one who helped drown the tea in Boston, 1770, died November 5, 1840, aged 109 years 2 months."[9] If anyone in town knew the truth, no one wanted to destroy the myth. The next year James Grant Wilson published the first article devoted to Hewes, perpetuating the notion that Hewes was the last survivor of the Tea Party.[10]

In 1885 a great-grandson gave the Cole painting to the Bostonian Society, which has displayed it ever since at the Old State House. In the opinion of contemporaries, it was "an admirable likeness."[11] It shows a happy man of ninety-three in his moment of triumph in Boston. He wears Sunday clothes, nineteenth-century style, and leans forward in a chair, his hands firmly gripping a cane. His face is wrinkled but not ravaged; his features are full, his eyes alert. He has most of his hair. There is a twinkle in his eyes, a slightly bemused smile on his lips. The mood is one of pride. It is not a picture of a man as a shoemaker, but we can understand it only if we know the man was a shoemaker. It shows the pride of a man the world had counted as a nobody at a moment in his life when he was a somebody, when he had won recognition from a town that had never granted it before. It is the pride of a citizen, of one who "would not take his hat off to any man." The apprentice who had once deferred to John Hancock lived with the memory that Hancock had toiled side by side with him, throwing tea chests into Boston harbor. The man who'd had to defer to British officers, royal officials, and colonial gentry had lived to see General Washington, ship captains, and now lieutenant governors, educated lawyers, and writers defer to him.

It is the pride of a survivor. His enemies had all passed on. His "associates," the patriots, had all gone to their graves. He had outlived them all. Fortified by his religion, the old man could rejoice that he would soon join them, but as their equal. "May we meet hereafter," he told his Independence Day well-wishers, "where the wicked will cease from troubling and the true sons of Liberty be forever at rest."[12]

PART TWO

When Did They Start Calling It the Boston Tea Party?

The Contest for the Memory of the American Revolution

People did not call it the Tea Party after it happened in Boston the night of December 16, 1773, at least not in print. "Tea Destroyed by Indians" was the heading on one broadside song. "The destruction of the tea in Boston harbor" was the way contemporaries, friend and foe alike, referred to this serious political event in public accounts and private letters. How ordinary Bostonians spoke of it in their workplaces, on the street, or in the taverns is another matter. "Boston harbor a teapot" is what someone had cried out near the end of the overflow meeting at Old South meetinghouse on December 16. This coded language, tinged with dry Yankee humor, would have been on everyone's lips from the time of the first giant meeting of "the whole body of the people" late in November until it became clear that the royal governor was not going to allow the undutied tea to be sent back to England and the patriots were not going to allow it to land. So they "made tea" in Boston harbor.

This essay is an exploration of the public memory of the American Revolution and of the contest for that memory. It has its origins in the discoveries I describe at the beginning of this book about three things I had always taken for granted. The first discovery was that Americans have not always called this iconic event the "tea party." At some point in history this term entered the spoken and the written language, but just when is something of a mystery. As surprising as it may seem, the two biographies of George Robert Twelves Hewes, *A Retrospect of the Tea-Party* (1834) and *Traits of the Tea Party* (1835), were not only the first books to feature "tea party" in the title, they were also the first of any sort to focus on the event itself and the first biographies of any participant, high or low. Thus Hewes and the term "tea party" emerge in print culture at the same time—or so it seems.

The second discovery was that the use of the term "tea party" coincided with the recovery of a public memory of the event. In the half-century or so afterwards, the "action against the tea" did not leave a strong imprint on public memory, although it obviously lived on in private memory, as the reminiscences of Hewes and others attest. *Private memory* is what an individual remembers about an event he or she has experienced or observed. *Public memory,* on the other hand, is what a society remembers collectively or, after most private memories have faded or disappeared, the way it constructs the past from many sources. Public memory flows from private memory as well as from the official memory promoted by those we might call the "keepers of the past."

From the 1770s into the 1820s, the first half-century or so after the Revolution, the "action against the tea" was not passed on in public memory in the ways important events usually are. It was not celebrated, the day was not set aside, there were no designated Tea Party orations (as there had been Boston Massacre orations); the places associated with it were not sanctified, the participants were not honored (indeed, they remained largely unknown), the songs about it went unsung; books did not catechize children

about it, and no American artist depicted the event until the
1830s. Why should this happen?

In the 1820s and 1830s, the American Revolution entered what
C. Vann Woodward has in another context called a "twilight
zone that lies between living memory and written history . . . one
of the favorite breeding places of mythology." In this spirit, Michael Kammen subtitled his pathbreaking book laying out what
Americans have made of the Revolution over two hundred years
The Revolution in the American Imagination. Eric Hobsbawm
used the arresting term "the invention of tradition" to direct attention to the conscious process in almost all countries, especially
during the nineteenth century, through which elites and popular
movements created the rituals, symbols, and texts of a politically
usable history. The half-century after the Revolution was such a
time: a public memory was created, imagined, and invented by
the generations who had not lived through it. By the 1830s the
events of that time were not remembered history, save among a
surviving remnant, and their remembering—and the appropriation of their memories—took place in the context of this politicized construction of public memory.[1]

My third epiphany was about the years 1834 and 1835. In 1834
Hewes was "discovered" when the first biography was published;
he was rediscovered in 1835 on his return to Boston for the Fourth
of July celebrations when he became hero for the day and the subject of a portrait intended for public exhibition and a second biography. What could have created a context for this unusual reception? Among historians, these years are most familiar as the point
at which the fierce war between Andrew Jackson and the Bank of
the United States produced a new opposition party, the Whigs,
whose name attempted to seize the mantle of the patriot leaders

of the Revolution. In Boston, as I soon realized, these were times of ardent labor radicalism among journeymen mechanics and radical abolitionism led by William Lloyd Garrison, both of which claimed the heritage of the Revolution. It was a moment of extraordinary turbulence, of strikes for a ten-hour day and "mob" violence: a Catholic convent in Charlestown was burned in 1834, and Garrison nearly lynched in 1835.

Hewes entered Boston in July 1835 at the height of these struggles over public memory. Several questions, as I have noted, began to jell in my mind: how might this contest have affected the way Hewes remembered, the way he constructed his own memory. More important, how might it have affected the way the celebrants on the Fourth of July, his portrait painter, and his biographer represented him? who were these people and what was their politics? how might the larger contest for the memory of the Revolution have affected the "recovery" of the Tea Party, and who, if anyone, had claimed it? what did it mean in the second quarter of the nineteenth century to say "the tea party" rather than "the destruction of the tea"?

In pursuit of these questions I have sometimes felt like an archeologist who, to find evidence of ancient civilizations, has to sift through layers of geologic strata, in this case, the silt of public memory deposited by successive generations of Bostonians. At the lowest level, from 1765 to 1775, the leaders of the Whig Sons of Liberty began their attempt to control the memory of events. In the next layer, which spans the years from about 1783 to the early 1820s, prewar events, including the Tea Party, leave few traces. By 1825, however, I come upon a mound of evidence registering a massive shift to public commemoration of the battles and veterans of the war. And in the 1835 layer, I uncover signs of radical claims and conservative counterclaims to the Revolution.

This sets the stage for exploring the recovery of the Tea Party and Hewes. Finally, in the layer of public memory from the latter part of the nineteenth century, I try to see how the Tea Party and Hewes "entered history." We seem to be present at the creation of an American icon and an unsung hero. How did it happen?

[1]

Taming the Revolution, 1765–1775

In Boston, the process of controlling the memory of the Revolution began even as the events were taking place, indeed, almost before they were over. The tea action, unlike those events the leaders of the Sons of Liberty neither willed nor controlled and those they lost control over, was in their hands from beginning to end. Yet shaping public memory of the event presented a challenge they were unable to meet.

To grasp the situation we must return to the principal Whig problem of the era: the "mob." The Tory interpretation of the popular side of the Revolution—"the people were like the Mobility of all countries, perfect Machines, wound up by any Hand who might first take the Winch"—epitomized in the history written by the arch Loyalist Peter Oliver, Chief Justice of the Supreme Court of the colony in exile in England, was a caricature of the reality in Boston. In the long decade of conflict leading up to the break with Britain, as the Whig leadership around Samuel Adams—men for the most part of the "middling" sort—confronted the British establishment, its Loyalist allies, and a divided merchant community, they struggled to control the popular movement. Such admonitions as "No violence or you'll hurt the cause" and "No mobs, no confusions, no tumults" in the patriot press can be taken as their motto for the decade. By 1775 they had established a coalition that included all but a minority of the merchant class.[1]

In the eighteenth century, long before the imperial crisis, Boston had a tradition of crowd action and a reputation as a "mobbish" town. Crowd action was often "quasi-institutional," as the historian Pauline Maier has put it: crowds used "extralegal means to implement official demands" or to "enforce laws otherwise not enforceable" or "to extend the law in urgent situations beyond its technical limits." Crowds of laboring people also acted in their own interests, most strikingly against impressment, dragnet sweeps of the port to press men into the much hated British navy. In the Knowles Riot of 1747, rioters held the city for three days to force the return of impressed dockside workers. Over the decades, however, elites developed a pattern of disavowing mobs not of their own making, claiming that they were composed, as in the Knowles Riot, of "Foreign Seaman, Servants, Negroes, and other persons of mean and vile condition."[2]

In the 1740s one mob became an institution in Boston. On Pope's Day, November 5 (in England, Guy Fawkes Day), the city was taken over for the day and night by apprentices, journeymen, young people of all sorts, seamen, and sometimes blacks to celebrate their holiday. During the day, children begged for money, and rival companies from North End and South End neighborhoods paraded giant effigies of the devil prompting the Pope in turn prompting the Stuart Pretender to the throne; at night, they engaged in bone-breaking battles to capture and burn each other's effigies. Minister and magistrate tolerated the festival as an expression of a political Protestant anti-Popery but could do no more than regulate its "excesses."[3]

In their resistance to British policies, Whig leaders were preoc-
cupied with harnessing, mobilizing, or suppressing the energies
of the crowd. What they could not fully manage in the making,
they attempted to control in the commemoration. Reaction to the
Stamp Act set the pattern. Resistance in 1765–66 was built on the
scaffolding, symbolism, and leadership of the Pope's Day companies in collaboration with the leader of the Sons of Liberty. The
rival companies coalesced, Ebenezer McIntosh, a shoemaker and
leader of the South End company, became the leader of the
united group whose officers were outfitted, wined, and dined by
John Hancock and other patriot merchants. From 1765 until 1773,
Pope's Day was tamed, the gang warfare channeled into unified
patriotic processions against detested British symbols.

To protest the Stamp Act there were five major actions in 1765,
two in August, two in November, and one in December. The
first, on August 14, was organized by the leadership to intimi-
date Andrew Oliver, the Stamp Act commissioner designate, by
hanging effigies on what became the Liberty Tree, holding a formal procession, pulling down Oliver's office, damaging his house,
and making personal threats against him. The second, on August
26, in which a crowd gutted the house of Lieutenant Governor
Thomas Hutchinson, likely rose out of "private resentments" but
all the same delighted a wide range of Boston patriots. Then, on
November 1, the day the Stamp Act was to go into effect, McIntosh, "sensible & manly" who "dressed genteelly," as Judge Oliver
told the story, "paraded the Town with a Mob of 2000 men in two
files. If a whisper was heard among his followers, the holding up
of his finger hushed it in a moment." On November 5, the united
companies marched again, and on December 17, McIntosh es-
corted Andrew Oliver to the Liberty Tree to force another resig-

nation. McIntosh was dubbed "Captain General of the Liberty Tree."[4]

The Sons of Liberty were highly selective. They claimed August 14, disavowed August 26, and ignored November 1, November 5, and December 17, thus setting a pattern of dissociating themselves from what, either through their own making or that of others, was politically embarrassing. From 1766 to 1769, they commemorated August 14 at an elaborate subscription dinner attended by several hundred men who traveled out to a suburb in chaises and carriages, while suppressing the memory of "the detestable" August 26. McIntosh, feared by some as a possible "Masaniello," the leader of a seventeenth-century proletarian rebellion in Naples, was shunted aside, replaced as crowd leader by Dr. Thomas Young and William Molineux, who were members of the Whig inner circle.

There was no single "mob" and "no single pattern" to Boston's crowd actions, as Dirk Hoerder's analysis has established. At one pole were crowd actions organized by Whig leaders in their campaign to boycott those merchants who violated agreements not to import British goods. The Whig pattern is recognizable through written records: a town meeting, public notices warning the targets to desist, articles in the papers, a formal delegation or committee, and recognizable leaders, all an effort to clothe the action in legitimacy. At the other pole were tarring-and-feathering crowds, lower class and led from within, and usually organized on the spur of the moment against a target of opportunity, which in Boston invariably meant customs officers or informers against whom the laboring classes had their own grievances.[5]

Whig leaders were quick to memorialize self-initiated street actions that got out of hand as well as actions they did not initiate that yet served their purposes. An example of the first was the picketing of T. Lilly's shop by boys in February 1770, which turned sour when a customs official shot into the crowd, killing eleven-year-old Christopher Seider. Whig leaders organized a funeral procession of five hundred boys and two thousand men and women for Seider "the martyr." The famous example of the second is the confrontation of townspeople with British troops several weeks later, on March 5. Whig leaders were engaged in a campaign to remove the troops, but the clash on March 5 was a chaotic event not willed by any party, the result of friction between troops and townspeople, especially the laboring classes. Angry citizens confronted angry soldiers. After soldiers shot into the crowd, Whig leaders arrived to cool down the enraged populace and take over negotiations with British officials. The next day they led the town meeting protest to remove the troops, then organized a second massive funeral procession for the victims, five young workers, in which fifteen thousand people marched through the streets.[6]

The memory of the event of March 5—complex, experienced from multiple vantage points, producing multiple memories— was immediately politicized. To patriots it was "The Bloody Massacre Perpetrated on King Street," the title of Paul Revere's lurid engraving, out within the week: British soldiers, on the command of Captain Thomas Preston, mercilessly shooting down defenseless, passive civilians whose clothing suggested that they were drawn from the respectable classes. To the British it was "the riot on King street," a plot hatched by patriot leaders. To John Adams and Josiah Quincy, conservative patriot lawyers acting as defense attorneys for Preston and the soldiers in the trials, the townspeople were the aggressors and the soldiers acted in self-defense. In characterizing the crowd as "a motley rabble of saucy boys, negroes and molottoes, Irish teagues, and outlandish jack tarrs"—all outsiders to the body politic—Adams continued the patriot pattern of dissociation, thereby establishing that proper Bostonians were law abiding. Bostonians then, and later, oscillated between these two constructs of events.[7]

Whig leaders now swallowed up one commemoration with another. Every March 5 from 1771 through 1775, the town sponsored an overflowing meeting at Old South meetinghouse, at which orators perpetuated the memory of the Massacre as proof of the danger of standing armies. The Massacre oration replaced the commemoration of the Stamp Act protest and was intended to replace Pope's Day.[8]

Whig leaders were able to appropriate the public memory of events in part because there were no rival groups strong enough to sustain alternative memories. Whigs dominated the town meeting and the newspapers, and they had the support of the clergy in the dissenting churches. Even with their own newspaper and the support of the Anglican clergy, Loyalists were no match for them and went into exile after 1776.[9] In all the political actions of the decade, "mechanics" were indispensable, both the "respectable mechanics and tradesmen" of the "middling" sort, as master artisans liked to call themselves, and the apprentices, journeymen, and artisans of the "inferior" sort (like Hewes), unskilled laborers, and seamen, all lumped together by "the better sort" as "the lower sort." The Sons of Liberty leaders were dependent on masters as qualified voters in the town meeting, as members of their caucuses, and as stabilizing elements in crowd actions. Paul Revere, a prosperous silversmith, was recognized not only for his talents as an engraver in the patriot cause but also as a trusted leader in the North End, the heart of the maritime trades. But in Boston, masters did not organize a Committee of Mechanics, as did their counterparts in New York City, or write broadsides to "The Tradesmen, Mechanics and Manufacturers" on the right of "leather aprons" to run for public office, as in Philadelphia. The Adams leadership, by treating mechanics with a condescending respect, frustrated the growth of self-consciousness and self-organization. As a result, they failed to develop institutions that might perpetuate their own memories of the era.[10]

Comfortable with masters, the Whig leaders were on edge among the "lower sort." They shouldered McIntosh aside, replacing him with their own "mob" leaders. In 1774, as an instrument of crowd control, they created, "Captain Joyce, Jun.," the chairman of a fictitious Committee on Tarring and Feathering, and eventually banned Pope's Day. They were more comfortable seeing the laboring classes as "victims" who could be canonized as passive martyrs to British aggression, than as aggressive opponents of troops and customs officers who had a tendency to express their class resentments in attacks on the houses, and other symbols of wealth, of upper-class Loyalists.[11]

The forms of opposition popularized during the era—effigy burning, tarring and feathering, massive processions, Liberty Trees and Liberty Poles—would survive without recognition in official memory or print culture, passed on by oral tradition in the personal memories of ordinary people, to emerge in the popular protest of later generations. The events themselves—political, complex, many sided—would require the support of other means to sustain public memory.

[2]

The Destruction of the Tea, 1773

The action against the tea occurred sui generis and presented extraordinary problems to its leaders in both the doing and the remembering. It had its beginnings in late October 1773, gained momentum in two massive meetings in late November, and reached a climax in meetings on December 14 and 16, the second of which ended with the destruction of the tea. This event was unique in ways that later generations have not always been willing to recognize.[1]

It was the largest mass action of the decade. Attendance at these meetings of "the whole body of the people," at which the property qualifications of official town meetings were abandoned, easily reached five thousand. The final meeting at Old South, attended by many supporters from the surrounding towns and overflowing into the streets, was the largest Boston had ever seen. The numbers involved in direct action at Griffin's Wharf were relatively small, perhaps thirty to fifty men in the designated boarding parties (the invited), joined by volunteers who had been forewarned like Hewes (the semi-invited) and young men swept up in the excitement of the day (the self-invited), in all, around one hundred fifty men. Given the size of the three vessels, it is hard to envision many more than that. The spectators, from one to two thousand people, stood silently on the docks during the three-hour action. The leaders' achievement was to mobilize the entire spectrum of social classes for the meetings as well as the master mechanics, journeymen, and apprentices who predominated in the boarding parties. The support of the traditional Pope's Day constituency was all the more remarkable because on November 5, 1773, the customary warfare between the North End and South End, pent up since the truce of 1765, had broken out in full fury. Ebenezer McIntosh, the acknowledged unity leader in limbo since 1766, could boast about the tea party years later that "it's my chickens that did the job."[2]

It was a quasi-military action, the boldest and most dangerous in Boston up to that time. The first "body" meetings authorized military action: an armed watch on Griffin's Wharf to prevent the tea from being landed. When Samuel Adams told the meeting he had armed himself, townspeople followed suit; there was not a pistol to be bought anywhere in town. The boarding parties risked arrest and prosecution. The leaders stayed behind in Old South to give themselves what today would be called "plausible deniability." The "invited" took a pledge of secrecy. All participants risked life and limb. Several British naval vessels, marines aboard, rode in the harbor, and more troops were stationed at Castle William on one of the harbor islands. No one knew whether Governor Hutchinson would ask for troops. As it turned out, he was unwilling to risk it, lest it produce a bloodbath. The crowd on the wharf thus served as insurance against military intervention. But the boarding parties had to work in tense circumstances and at high speed; the period of grace for clearing custom expired at midnight on December 16, and the owners would be required by law to land the tea. The parties began at about six in the evening and finished the job in about three hours.

All in all, the tea action was the most revolutionary act of the decade in Boston. Leaders came close to articulating in public the classical Lockean justification for revolution. The meetings of "the whole body of the people" were palpably illegal. Thomas Young, Samuel Adams's lieutenant, said he had "read in Judge Blackstone that when the Laws and Constitution do not give the subject redress in any Grievance, that then he is in a state of nature and he declared that they (the People assembled) were in such a state—in such a state (he added) as were the Commonality of England at Runny Mead under King John when Magna Charta was first framed."

Young was a radical by any usage of the term and later one of the shapers of Pennsylvania's democratic constitution. Yet conservative, lawyerly John Adams went through the same political reasoning to justify civil disobedience as the last resort after all other remedies have been exhausted. The question was "whether the Destruction of the Tea was necessary" and his answer was that "it was absolutely and indispensably so." Why? "They could not send it [the tea] back" because the Governor and other officials "would not suffer it." But "to let it be landed would be giving up the principle of Taxation by Parliamentary Authority against which the Continent have struggled for 10 years." And so he was beside himself the morning after the event. "This is the most magnificent Moment of all," he wrote in his diary. "There is a Dignity, a Majesty, a Sublimity, in this effort of the Patriots that I greatly admire. The People should never rise, without doing something to be remembered—something notable and striking. This destruction of the Tea is so bold, so daring, so firm, intrepid and inflexible, and it must have so important Consequences, and so lasting, that I can't but consider it as an Epocha in History."[3]

The tea action was the most carnivalesque event of the era. Planned, deliberate, controlled, the action was also a wild reversal of the traditional order. Mockery suffused the major events of the decade. Pope's Day, with its grotesque effigies, was nothing if not wild parody. The first demonstration against the Stamp Act was a mock hanging and a mock funeral procession. At the Liberty Tree the organizers also halted every farmer's cart coming into town, mock "stamping" everything in sight, street theater worthy of a Marx brothers movie. Tarring and feathering, in which the crowd ceremoniously carted the accused to the gallows, mocked the legal system. But the action against the tea ships—destroying £9,659 of private property belonging to the powerful East India Tea Company, defying Parliament, defying the whole array of British officials and military might in the colony—this was truly turning the world upside down.[4]

The action was carnivalesque in two respects. First, it was a mock enactment of the making of tea. The cry in Old South, "Boston harbor a teapot tonight," set the tone. The spirit of the day and night, after two weeks of suspense, was one of festive euphoria. After the boarding party had left the church, Dr. Young, to hold the crowd, was "very merry (the people often shouting and clapping him)" making a ridiculous speech on "the ill effects of tea on the [physical] constitution," as if they were destroying something dangerous to personal health. At the wharf, Joshua Wyeth, a journeyman blacksmith, said, "We were merry in an undertone at the very idea of making so large a cup of tea for the fishes."

To "make tea" in Boston harbor mocked the genteel tea ritual. Tea, as Mercy Otis Warren wrote, was "an article used by all ranks in America," but among the "better sort" the conduct of brewing, pouring, and serving tea was an elaborate, mannered class ritual managed by women. Among the well-to-do, it required the elegant silver teapots, creamers, and sugar bowls crafted by silversmiths like Revere, the tea caddies, serving trays, and tea tables made by skilled woodworkers, and the porcelain cups, saucers, and serving dishes imported from abroad. For the boarding parties—all but a minority of them men able to wield block and tackle and lift and break open 350-pound chests—to "make tea" in Boston harbor was a parody of class and gender. And for those among them who had broken into homes in 1765 destroying mirrors, glass windows, wine cellars, and fancy furniture, or who had gutted Hutchinson's house, this was another way to channel class resentments.[5]

The second element of the carnivalesque was the participants' Indian persona. An Indian war whoop at Old South signaled the exodus of one party for the wharf. They were "Mohawks." The minority with advance notice (the invited) donned Indian disguises; the majority (the semi-invited and the self-invited) did little more than blacken their faces with soot like Hewes, to improvise a disguise. But the minority set the Indian ambience.

"Playing Indian"—the historian Philip Deloria's apt phrase for a game that began earlier and has continued throughout American history—in this case performed several important functions. First, disguise protected the minority of recognizable participants from detection and possible arrest. Second, the Indian was intended to be a terrifying symbol. Anne Hulton, the sister of a customs commissioner, testified that she had been "frequently alarmed with the Sons of Liberty surrounding her house with the most hideous howling of the Indians, when they attack an enemy." Third, wearing a disguise gave the players a sense of license to do what they might otherwise have been too inhibited to do. It was a masquerade that released them from the usual norms. Fourth, for the leaders "behind the curtain," identifying the actors as Indians shifted responsibility for the action to unknown outsiders, the same ploy leaders had used to blame every politically embarrassing action since 1765 on "boys, Negroes, seamen or strangers," all outside the formal body politic. Of course, no one on either side really believed they were Indians. The British Admiral Montagu, watching the event on shore, called it the "Indian caper." It was a case of "implausible deniability."[6]

Bostonians played this wink and nod kind of joke for a few more months. A boarding party of sixty men disguised as Indians destroyed a cargo of tea on another arriving ship. The newspapers ran a mock exchange between the King of the Narragansetts and his followers; one of the guards at Griffin's Wharf was inspired to write a mock proclamation attributed to another chieftain. In 1774 Paul Revere used the Indian as an emblem in at least three engravings. For the cover of an almanac, for example, he copied a British caricature in which a British minister with a copy of the Boston Port Bill in his pocket forces tea down the throat of a half-naked Indian woman, while another minister peers lecherously up her skirts. For a moment, the Indian became the political personification of the country, and "playing Indian" may well have been one way in which colonial Anglo-American Bostonians assumed an American identity.[7]

Boston's tea action caught the popular imagination all over the colonies. Songs and verses glorifying it appeared in Boston, Philadelphia, northern New England, and elsewhere.[8] Comparable actions in other ports enabled others to grasp the event. More important, tea, as Timothy Breen has demonstrated, "was perhaps *the* major article in the development of an eighteenth-century consumer society, a beverage which appeared on the tables of the wealthiest merchants and the poorest laborers." In 1774 colonists spoke of tea as "a badge of slavery" and sought "to purge their communities of tea leaves." In many villages "the inhabitants publicly burned their tea," which gave them a sense of kinship with Boston.[9]

For Bostonians there were many reasons the tea action should be imprinted in *personal* memory. Men in almost every patriot family had taken part in the event, either attending the "body" meetings, watching the action on the wharf, or joining the boarding parties. Many were young and at an age when such emotional events would have been very meaningful. Women who had become politicized during the tea boycott and the massive funeral processions of 1770 egged their menfolk into action. Moreover, whether or not an individual was actually present, it was the kind of dramatic moment that was easy to grasp and remember. Boston was a port town in which everyone knew the business of ships; moreover, there were no two ways about what happened as there were, for example, with the Massacre. It was an electrifying event people remembered in later years by locating themselves in relation to it. Psychologists now call this "flashbulb" memory, and the reminiscences that surfaced forty and fifty years later would support this. Indeed, it was the kind of mythic event father and mother would pass on to son and daughter, grandparents to grandchildren, and artisan to fellow artisan during a drink break or in the neighborhood tavern.[10]

Yet there were factors working against *public* memory of the tea action. The "invited" in the boarding parties were sworn to secrecy; others knew that "mum's the word." Years later, John Adams said he did not know who was involved and never asked; he expected indictments. People feared prosecution, it seems, even after the American victory. The first printed reminiscences by participants surfaced only in the 1820s, and the first list of those involved only in 1835, when Thatcher published one in the appendix to his biography of Hewes. None of the leaders left an "inside" account of this or any other major event; ambivalent about their role as conspirators, they put little down in writing or, like Samuel Adams, were said to have burned their papers. The tea party songs did not last, probably because they had none of the irreverent mockery that made "Yankee Doodle" popular for generations.[11]

There were also political reasons for playing down the event. The patriot movement did not commemorate the tea action or turn December 16 into a sacred day to match March 5, and it never depicted the action in engravings (until the 1830s, the only pictures were British or European). Why not? One reason is that the tea action was devastating in its impact, in effect, precipitating the British retaliation that led to the Revolution. The action itself was rapidly overtaken by the crush of events that followed and within sixteen months led to war: the closing of the port of Boston, the British occupying army, the city an armed camp and then under siege, the mass exodus of patriots, amid widespread privation. Thus, in one sense, the patriot leaders never had a chance to celebrate the tea action; in another, they did not want to: it was to blame for a lot of suffering. Moreover, it simply did not fit the posture Massachusetts patriots assumed as the war began. According to their narrative, the British were the aggressors, and the colonists simply the defenders of their own liberties. This was the visual trope of the patriot cause in Revere's engraving of the massacre as in Amos Doolittle's engraving of the Battle of Lexington soon after 1775, where a British officer is ordering troops to mow down dispersing militia who are not returning fire. This was the literal image a New England militia man, James Pike, engraved on his powderhorn in 1776: "Regulars Attacking, Provincial Defending," a Liberty Tree in between, and he was not the only one to do so. There was no way to portray the tea action to fit this image.[12]

The tea action was carried out only after all other remedies had been exhausted, but it was unmistakably willful and provocative, a true act of revolution. Although disciplined and focused (one crew member even swept the deck after they were done), it was also an exhilarating reversal—aggressive, quasi-military, destructive, and carnivalesque. There is no puzzle about why it should stay in private memory. But is it any wonder that it presented a problem for the keepers of public memory?

[3]

Taming the Memory of the Revolution, 1783–1820

What does it take for a political event to pass into public memory? Public rituals, for one thing. From 1775 to 1783, as Boston's men marched off to war, and some nineteen hundred did, a father who wanted to instruct his children about the cause had already experienced an array of festive calendar days to remind him of the landmark events of the decade: the dinners on August 14 to mark opposition to the Stamp Act in 1765; the orations on March 5 to mark resistance to the Redcoats in 1770; November 5, the old Pope's Day of the apprentices and young men, a memento in the 1760s of effigies of British oppression; and December 16, memorable for the tea action, even without celebration.

By the end of the war, this festive calendar was no more. In 1783, the town decreed an annual oration on July 4 to replace the annual Massacre oration of March 5, "exchanging that Anniversary for Another." The Fourth of July swallowed up not only March 5, but August 14, November 5, and December 16. The action, intended to celebrate independence, thus helped to erase the popular, radical side of Boston's Revolution. Pope's Day, which

Charles Bulfinch's doric column commemorating the Revolution erected atop Beacon Hill in 1790 lasted only to the early 1820s when the hill was levelled, providing a vista for the new State House. *Chromolithograph courtesy Bostonian Society.*

was indispensable to members of the North End and South End companies in passing on the activities of the day, illustrates what happened when the ritual day disappeared. Coopted by Whig leaders, it exploded briefly in 1774, was banned in the army by General Washington and then by the Massachusetts government, and, with anti-Popery out of favor politically, it survived only as a vestige in sporadic turf wars between children from different neighborhoods.[1]

"Captain Joyce, Jun.," the apocryphal avenging figure created to control tarring and feathering, made a real-life appearance in 1777 as head of a price control crowd and a newspaper appearance in 1783 threatening British importers. In 1804 his name was invoked on a handbill menacing usurers. And then he too was no more. At the same time, as we will see, the forms of popular resistance—effigy burning, tarring and feathering, Liberty Trees, Liberty Poles, and Indian disguises—which could be passed down in personal memory through oral tradition, entered public memory in the repertoire of popular movements. They did not need print culture to be perpetuated.

For the half-century after the Revolution, the Stamp Act resistance, the Boston Massacre, and the tea action—the popular side of Boston's Revolution—were in eclipse. Their decline was measurable in almost every way Bostonians chose to commemorate the Revolution: the ceremonial public rituals that called them together, the monuments they erected, the heroes they chose to celebrate, and the sites they allowed to survive.

Public Rituals

From the 1780s into the 1820s, the Fourth of July, the chief day in the festive calendar, became a safe, conservative celebration. Boston "marshalled public fervor in a controlled respectable fashion," Len Travers writes, on a day in which "patriotic oratory and pageantry" were the central features. Politically, Boston was an overwhelmingly Federalist town until at least 1801 and even after. The town meeting instructed speakers for the celebration "to consider the feelings, manners and principles" that led to the event and its "important and happy effects," a mandate for optimism. The selectmen invariably chose conservative young orators, lawyers, or sons of respected artisans, for the most part Harvard graduates. The form of the ritual, orderly and hierarchical, put people in their place. The day's ceremony began with a procession of the governor, executive, and legislative officials to the meeting place, Faneuil Hall (and, after 1800, Old South meetinghouse). The chaplain to the legislature offered a prayer, a chorus sang odes, the orator orated, his speech capped by another ode, and the multitude adjourned, either to a repast at Faneuil Hall or to separate dinners of militia companies, the Cincinnati, or social groups. The militia paraded, and the Fourth in fact became a grand muster day for the militia, the principal vestige of the citizen participation of an earlier era. Sometimes there were fireworks.[2]

Oratory in "the Boston style," which President Theodore Dwight of Yale characterized as "a florid, pompous manner of writing" (also true, he said, of "most of the orations delivered on the fifth of March") was not suited to the narration and description of the mass events of the Revolution. Federalist orators usually had little to say about what happened in the Revolution and much to say about current issues, whether the Constitution, as in Harrison Gray Otis's speech in 1787, or the international crisis, as in Josiah Quincy's of 1798.[3]

Boston's official Fourth celebrated independence, not the Declaration of Independence much less the principles of the Declaration. In the 1790s, as the French Revolution entered its radical phase, and Democratic Republicans linked it to their efforts to rekindle "the spirit of '76," while conservative, monarchical England went to war with republican France, the Federalist Fourth was more accurately a celebration of antirevolution. Federalists— antidemocratic, Anglophile, and Francophobe—for the longest time would not even read the Declaration of Independence on the Fourth, fearful of the intense Anglophobia its list of grievances stirred and the democratic and equalitarian implications of its preamble, to say nothing of its justification of the right of revolution. The successful slave rebellions in Haiti in the 1790s made them even more guarded. And they were reluctant to broaden participation in the Fourth; as late as 1806 there were pleas to make the day a work holiday so that "the large and respectable class of Young Men and Apprentices" could be instructed by "this yearly festival."[4]

Although Democratic Republicans emerged as a party in Boston in the 1790s, they were unable to shape or rival the official Fourth, as they did to striking effect, for example, in New York City. Occasionally, they attempted to reenact popular rituals of the Revolution. In January 1793, to celebrate the victory of the French Revolutionary army at Valmy, Boston Republicans staged an egalitarian procession in which "citizens" marched pell-mell and attended a mammoth outdoor civic "feast of Liberty and Equality." The procession revisited the street theater of 1765, stopping at the stump of the Liberty Tree cut down in 1775, then at the site of the office of Andrew Oliver (the Stamp Tax commissioner designate), which was pulled down in 1765, and engaged in a ritual renaming of Oliver's Dock as "Liberty Square." But this was the only action of its kind.[5]

In the early 1800s, after some electoral victories—Boston elected its first Republican to Congress in 1801, after which Republicans were more often the minority—Republicans mounted an alternative celebration of the Fourth. They sought out sites of the Revolution, meeting in Faneuil Hall, on Bunker Hill, or in Lexington. In 1809 their procession featured a ship on wheels pulled by thirteen white horses, which wended its way from the Old State House to Old South through the North End. And wherever they met, they read the Declaration of Independence, to which the Republican paper devoted its front page every July 4.

But for all their differences with Federalists, Boston Republicans were heirs to the Samuel Adams tradition of dissociating themselves from embarrassing street actions in which they'd had a hand. Effigy burning, a heritage of the Revolution, stayed in popular memory without need for instruction from "betters." In 1795, it was said that John Jay, author of the conciliatory treaty with England, could travel down the Atlantic coast by the light of his effigies. Republicans in Boston covertly promoted burning Jay in effigy, organizing boys to parade around town with lighted lanterns carved out of watermelons. When the action got out of hand, Governor Samuel Adams issued a proclamation condemning "persons unknown," a joke to the Federalist press, and James Sullivan, the Republican Attorney General, read the crowd the riot act. A writer in the Republican *Independent Chronicle* then condemned mobs as "useless and inefficient," turning the history of Pope's Day on its head by claiming that in colonial days, "riots were encouraged in all the great towns in favor of the Hanoverian dynasty. Everybody canst remember our *Popes-days*—the effigies on those occasions, the Pope, the devil, and the pretender—all this was done with the connivance and gross encouragement of the Royal Governors." With such distortions, Republicans did their part to bury the plebeian heritage of the Revolution.[6]

Monuments

The monument to the Revolution conceived and executed by Charles Bulfinch, a Doric column erected on Beacon Hill in 1790 and pulled down just over twenty years later, in 1811, encapsulated the process of forgetting while commemorating. Bulfinch, Harvard class of 1781, and recently returned from a grand tour of Europe, was then at the beginning of a long career, as the city's first professional architect and president of the Board of Selectmen that would reshape Boston. Beacon Hill, the highest of three hills in the center of the peninsula, was so named for the sentry tower erected in the seventeenth century, whose torch could be set afire as a warning of invasion. In 1768, when British troops landed, the Sons of Liberty threatened to set it off to awaken the country militia. An anachronism after the war, it was blown down in a gale in 1789, and in its place Bulfinch proposed a monument to the Revolution. The selectmen gave the project their blessing but no public money. The monument went ahead with "voluntary contributions" from a handful of the well-to-do on land owned in part by the town and in part by John Hancock and other proprietors of the hill.[7]

The fifty-seven-foot monument, a single column of brick and stone encased in stucco cement and mounted on an obelisk pedestal, was topped by a Doric pediment and a gilded wooden eagle. Slate tablets set into the four sides of the obelisk featured commemorative inscriptions. The tablet on the south side stated the monument's purpose: "To commemorate that train of events which led to the American Revolution and finally secured Liberty and Independence to the United States." The tablet on the north side cataloged the events leading to independence in lifeless fashion: "Stamp Act Passed 1765. Repealed 1766. Board of Customs Established 1767. British troops fired on the Inhabitants of Boston, March 5, 1770. Tea Act Passed 1773. Tea Destroyed in Boston, Decem. 16. Port of Boston Shut and Guarded June 1, 1774. . . ." The tablet on the west side listed the major battles of the war and then, "Federal Constitution formed Sept 17, 1787 and ratified by the United States 1787–1790 . . . Washington Inaugurated President." It ended with "Public Debts funded Aug 4, 1790"—as Federalist-minded a synopsis as one could want. Newspapers reported the completion of the monument, but there was no public dedication.

The conception of the monument—a stark column with a catalog of words chiselled on slate—by its very nature disembodied the dramatic street events it memorialized. The passive voice used in the inscriptions—"Tea Destroyed in Boston" and so on—eliminated all sense of agency. Of the leaders, only John Hancock and James Bowdoin were mentioned, and then only as elected officials. The monument's lofty location in the fashionable West End symbolized its distance from both the scene of the revolutionary events in the center of town and the homes of most of the participants in the increasingly unfashionable North End. A short walk from the Common, and after 1795 a stone's throw from the new State House, it was accessible only by climbing up the steep hill, first up a long flight of wooden stairs and then on a gravel path in which footholds were worn. There was no way for a procession (let alone a crowd) to parade past it. It was, rather, a site for visiting tourists with a grand vista of the city.

Its fate was equally symbolic. "The hill was already doomed," as the memorial history of the city later put it, by one excavation after another, first by an "avaricious proprietor," then by the builders of the State House, then by the Mill Pond Corporation, which carted off landfill for the pond separating the North and South Ends, and finally by the heirs to Hancock's estate. Ironically, surviving depictions of the column show it amid the massive excavations of Beacon Hill that so fascinated Bostonians, first standing on half of the hill and then on a quarter of the hill. In 1811, the column was taken down before it caved in, and the eagle and slate tablets saved for the State House. In the early 1820s, the rest of the hill was leveled, obliterating what little memory remained. The monument had commemorated elitist hauteur, commercial avarice, and public indifference—in short, civic progress. This was erasing the *memory* of the memory of the Revolution with a vengeance. In 1823 the editor of the Republican *Independent Chronicle* was shocked to discover the tablets "once affixed to the violated monument of the now prostrate Beacon

Hill thrown as useless lumber behind the back door" of the State House. "Oh Boston! Though the cradle of Revolutionary patriots, thou art no temple for their memory."[8]

Heroes

The omission of Samuel Adams's name on Bulfinch's tablets epitomized the erasure of leaders identified with the radical "pulling down" phase of the Revolution, just as the recognition of Washington on the tablet signaled his emergence as the ultimate hero of its nation-building side. Adams had led the opposition to ratification of the Constitution. In the 1790s, Federalist voters refused to send him to Congress but tolerated him as lieutenant governor and governor. He and Hancock stood for what Ronald Formisano calls "the politics of the Revolutionary center" in Massachusetts, whose strength came from their record of service in the Revolution.[9]

When Hancock died in 1793, he received full public honors. When Adams died in 1803, a good number of Federalists were conveniently out of town for the funeral procession, and the legislature, as James Sullivan put it, "whittled down" a tribute to him. In 1809, John Adams singled out Samuel Adams and John Hancock as "almost buried in oblivion" in a wailing lament about "the extraordinary and unaccountable inattention in our countrymen to the History of their own country." The process went on. In 1817 John Adams wrote, "If the American Revolution was a blessing, and not a curse, the name and character of Samuel Adams ought to be preserved." Yet the result of the "inveterate malice of his enemies" was that "a systematic course has been pursued for thirty years to run him down." It was not until the mid-1830s that John Singleton Copley's portraits of Adams and Hancock (both of which belonged to the Hancock estate) were hung in Faneuil

Hall. There was no Adams biography published until 1865, no Adams statue commissioned until 1873.[10]

In 1823 the Republican *Independent Chronicle* paid tribute to Adams as "the great man [who] cleared the way for Washington," which said it all. Boston celebrated only one hero in the half-century after the Revolution: George Washington. In 1789, the whole town paraded for him, the mechanics in organized contingents on his republican royal entry as president, and did so again in 1800 on his death. Bostonians celebrated his birthday, his inauguration, his demise, and then his memory. Newspapers reprinted his proclamations and his farewell message. After his death they consumed his image, which was reproduced in countless ways. In 1806, to mark the reopening of the enlarged Faneuil Hall, the city commissioned Gilbert Stuart to paint a giant portrait of General Washington victorious at Dorchester Heights in 1776. They placed one bust in Old North Church and a heroic statue in the new State House. The Washington Monument Association even proposed tearing down the Old State House to clear a vista for an equestrian statue. Federalists, exploiting Washington for all he was worth, organized the Washington Benevolent Society, a fraternal order. And in 1810 the Society's procession of four hundred children and fifteen hundred members marching four abreast stretched a mile and half, "with twenty one youths carrying the society's 21 silken banners commemorating revolutionary victories, the events of Washington's life and a satin cushion with a relic of Washington."[11]

Historic Sites

In other Massachusetts towns, boys and girls grew up with revolutionary memories inspired by historic sites. As late as the 1830s, Thomas Wentworth Higginson, then a young boy in Cambridge, knew where the first Provincial Congress had met and in which church the militia had been quartered after Lexington: "a bullet mark in the porch still recalls that period. . . . We all knew the spot where Washington took command of the army. . . . We played the battle of Bunker Hill on the grass grown redoubts built during the siege of Boston. . . . Moreover there still were one or two wounded veterans whom we eyed with Reverence." In Boston, where the hills had been leveled, the waterfront filled in, and many crooked and narrow streets straightened, a boy would have had a harder time finding old landmarks.[12]

The fate of the Liberty Tree site was symbolic. The elm had been a place of popular resistance to the Stamp Act and the Tea Act—patriots brought the Stamp Act commissioner and then the tea consignees there to force resignations. They hoisted a flag on a pole high above to call people to meetings. They attached a plaque identifying the tree and bestowed the title "Captain General of the Liberty Tree" on the Pope's Day leader, Ebenezer McIntosh. The tree infuriated Tories. The Loyalist Governor Bernard said it "put him in mind of Jack Cade's Oak of Reformation," referring to the mid-fifteenth-century leader of a popular rebellion that stormed London. In 1775, when Loyalists and British soldiers chopped it down, a doggerel verse mocked it as the tree of Watt Tylers, Jack Cades, and Masaniellos, all leaders of popular rebellions. When patriots reoccupied the city in 1776 they erected a Liberty Pole on the site. The Liberty Tree stump, on the major incoming street, served as a point of direction for travelers. On occasion a Republican or Federalist procession stopped there. But the pole decayed and the site gradually faded in importance.[13]

Many of the buildings associated with the events or leaders of the Revolution were lost as well, the result not only of the decline of old neighborhoods but also of indifference. The two main meeting places of the Revolution, Old South meetinghouse and Faneuil Hall, still stood, as did the old State House, the principal site of the provincial and then the state government, but their functions changed. Fanueil Hall, the place of official town meetings, was enlarged to double its size by Bulfinch in 1806. But in 1822 conservatives finally abolished the town meeting, achieving a goal sought for generations, and replaced it with an elected mayor and aldermen. The hall then became a place of meetings that citizens had to petition to use. After the new State House on Beacon Hill replaced it, the old State House building was commercialized, "used by various tradesmen, insurance offices &c." until 1830 and then as the City Hall until 1841. Once a new City Hall was built it again became a commercial building smothered in shop signs. Old South meetinghouse reverted to its original function as a church. As the congregation grew wealthy, people seemed to forget that the building was the principal site of revolutionary protest. The huge granite plaque mounted before the Civil War—"Old South/Church Gathered 1669/First Built 1770/This House Erected 1729/Desecrated by British troops, 1775–76"—was striking in its omission of the years 1770–75.[14]

In the North End progress took its heaviest toll. The Green Dragon tavern, host to so many caucuses, was taken down to widen the street, and the site left unmarked. Congregations abandoned their old buildings as "young gentlemen who have married wives in other parts of the town have found it difficult to persuade them to become so ungenteel as to attend worship in the North End." In the South End, Griffin's Wharf, scene of the tea action, became Liverpool Wharf, its earlier role unmarked. As a result, in a short section on "Ancient Buildings" in *Picture of Boston*, a Baedeker to the city of the 1820s, Nathaniel Bowen could single out only a few buildings, the Old Feather store, the house of Franklin's birth, and several "old fashioned structures" he could not name when "the north end was the fashionable part of town." In the first history of the city published in 1825, Caleb Snow did not even refer to the sites of the historic events of the Revolution he described in detail. Any sense of the revolutionary meaning of those places had atrophied.[15]

There were no efforts either to mark the homes of the once famous, much less save them. Few cared. By the 1820s Samuel Adams's frame house on Winter Street, run down when he lived in it, was gone. John Hancock, for all his wealth, had so little hold on the historical imagination that in 1833, Nathaniel Bowen expressed surprise in his guidebook that Hancock's "mansion house" on Beacon Street was "yet standing." The new elite was not comfortable with a rich man who pledged his fortune to the cause of revolution; one president of the Massachusetts Historical Society could not refrain from a stream of profanities when he walked past the elegant stone mansion. Small wonder then that in 1859 the legislature refused to buy the house from his hardpressed heirs, and the city turned down an offer to take it over. In 1863 the building was pulled down. In short, for almost a century after the Revolution, there was a process of willful forgetting.[16]

Thus, thirty-five years after the Revolution, say, in 1810, an intrepid boy might still jump over the stump of the Liberty Tree, search for the graves of Samuel Adams and the Massacre victims in the Granary Burying Ground, rattle a stick along the fence in front of John Hancock's mansion, or even hunt for Griffin's Wharf. But who was there to tell him the stories about the people or the events associated with such sites?

[4]

Merchants, Mill Owners,
and Master Mechanics

What explains the erasure of the popular side of the Revolution in public memory? Why was it possible to tame the memory of Boston's Revolution? One explanation is that a large proportion of the people who retained personal memories of the great events of the Revolution—the mechanics and laborers who had participated in them—did not return to the city after the British occupation and the war. In the eighteenth century, out-migration of artisans from the city during hard times was common. After the war, the people who had remained or who returned were skewed toward those with a propertied stake in the city. Poor men like George Hewes had made their way to greener pastures. Meanwhile, there was a sizeable in-migration of businessmen on-the-make from the seaports of Essex county, who had not shared Boston's experience. These nouveaux riches were ultraconservative politically, their leaders later stigmatized as "the Essex Junto." In the 1770s, the population of Boston was about 15,000; by 1810, in a city of 34,000, only a small minority could claim living experience of the events of the 1770s; by 1820, in a

The association of Boston's master mechanics, headed by Paul Revere, celebrated the memory of George Washington as well as the tools and trades of master craftsmen in its certificate of membership, issued about 1800. *Courtesy American Antiquarian Society.*

city of 43,000, they amounted to only a handful; and by 1830, in a city of 61,000, they had dwindled still more.[1]

Second, passing on history to the young presented a problem. The institutions we take for granted to disseminate historical knowledge—school courses, textbooks, books, historical societies, museums—were in their infancy or nonexistent. History per se was not a subject in the school curriculum, even in Boston's much vaunted public schools. The first textbooks about American history did not appear until the 1820s. Frequently reprinted readers assembled by the Boston schoolmaster Caleb Bingham, like the *Columbia Orator* and *The American Preceptor*, and later, Noah Webster's readers, while patriotic, avoided prewar events. In general, the Revolution was not widely accessible in print, even in a city with as many bookstores and as high a rate of literacy as Boston. The libraries serving the town were, like the Boston Athenaeum, limited to gentlemen shareholders and those admitted to annual membership. There was no public library, and the circulating libraries charged a fee. The Mechanics Association did not establish a library for apprentices until 1822.[2]

The first American histories of the Revolution, the tomes by William Gordon (1788) and David Ramsay (1789), did not make much of a splash, and in 1805, Mercy Otis Warren's two volumes met with "deafening silence and weak sales." Novels and short stories set during the Revolution were similarly late blooming. Memoirs of veterans appeared slowly; by 1800 there were only a dozen for the country as a whole. Newspapers occasionally ran a personal recollection of a particular event, but the collections of primary sources were not under way until the 1820s, and scholars like George Bancroft, who would popularize American history, would not bring out their first volumes until the 1830s.[3]

Historical societies were more interested in collecting than in disseminating historical knowledge. The men who founded the Massachusetts Historical Society in the 1790s limited membership to thirty local and thirty corresponding members, preferring "learned gentlemen." After an initial effort to publish documents, the society was inactive until 1833, building a library and keeping a private "cabinet of curiosities," while a dozen members met occasionally in one another's homes. Commercial museums assembling odds and ends, pictures of historical worthies among them, came and went.[4]

Ordinary Bostonians were more likely to have their patriotic thirst quenched in the theater, but judging by a few well-known examples, theater managers staged the war, not the earlier history. John Daly Burk's wildly popular play *Bunker Hill* (1797) restaged the battle. Deborah Sampson Gannett's sold-out performances reenacted her exploits as a soldier (1802).[5]

Thus, given the state of the institutions that transmitted American history up to the 1820s, for knowledge of the events of the Revolution that was not based in their personal experiences or in oral tradition, ordinary Bostonians were heavily dependent on a public memory passed down in the sermons of ministers, on secular orations commemorating ceremonial occasions, and on the symbolism of annual festive events like the Fourth of July. But these were almost all carried out under the auspices of a conservative elite with a growing awareness of the uses of history.

Personal memory could not compete with the elite's political need for a safe public memory of the Revolution. The era of Bulfinch was the "formative era of the patriciate" of Boston, as Frederic Jaher, a historian of American urban establishments, argues: "By the 1820s the Brahmin enclave composed of some forty interlocking families was substantially established." In 1831, when the French aristocrats Alexis de Tocqueville and Gustave de Beaumont visited Boston, they thought the city's high society "resembles almost completely the upper classes in Europe. Luxury and refinement reign." Open to new wealth, Boston's elite rapidly developed a social cohesion that in time set them off as "proper Bostonians" and a snobbery about their city as "the cradle of liberty" and "the Athens of America." Although at what point they should be called "Boston Brahmins," a term Oliver Wendell Holmes is credited with using in print for the first time in 1860, is arguable, it is clear that by the 1830s the elite shared most of the traits Holmes described. He spoke of their "houses by Bulfinch, their monopoly of Beacon Street, their ancestral portraits and Chinese porcelains, humanitarianism, Unitarian faith in the march of the mind, Yankee shrewdness, and New England exclusiveness."[6]

This emergent elite was extraordinarily attentive to culture and history. As the most recent analysis contends, it "fostered the growth and flowering of an interlocking cluster of public and private cultural institutions," which included Harvard college, the American Academy of Arts and Sciences, the Massachusetts Historical Society, and the Boston Athenaeum. The elite, Harlow Sheidley argues convincingly, "recognizing that the American past might well be used to legitimize democratic and egalitarian cases rather than their own conservative ethos, exorcised its potential radical thrust so that it could reinforce deference, hierarchy and due subordination." It "established the interpretive framework of the American Revolution that predominated for decades and remains influential even today."[7]

Harrison Gray Otis (1765–1848) and Josiah Quincy (1772–1864) may be taken as the articulate history-minded spokesmen of this class. Both were immediately descended from leading revolutionary conservatives. Otis, Harvard class of 1783, congressman (1797–1801), senator (1817–22), and mayor (1829–31), was the nephew of James Otis, perhaps the most eminent firebrand among Boston's leaders, and of Mercy Otis Warren, poet, pamphleteer, and historian. His father was a patriot merchant. Josiah Quincy, Harvard class of 1790, congressman (1805–13), mayor (1823–27), and president of Harvard (1829–45) bore the same name as his father, who was famous as John Adams's co-counsel in defending British soldiers from "the rabble" in the Massacre trials, and for his oratory at the tea meetings and in the town meeting against the Boston Port Bill. In his son's interpretation, the "front ranks of opposition [in the Revolution] were filled not by a needy, promiscuous, unknown and irresponsible crowd," but by the colonists' natural leaders, "the calm and calculating merchant . . . the cautious capitalist . . . the sedate and pious divine . . . the far-looking, deep-read lawyer . . . the laborious and intelligent mechanic." The Quincy coat of arms was "a Liberty Cap surmounting a law book." For Otis, colonial leaders had instructed the populace to exercise their legally justifiable "rights of insurrection" and to practice "the restraint of discipline" so that they would "define and limit its objects." He would have been at one with the contemporary biographer of his uncle, who held that the "body meetings" that effected the tea action, however "orderly, had set a dangerous precedent" by inviting popular intervention in public affairs, a "habit" people were "reluctant to resign." Men like Otis and Quincy wanted to remember only the conservatism of their revolutionary ancestors.[8]

Charles Bulfinch, who reshaped Boston between 1790 and 1817, made the city over in the image of the elite clients he served, an image superseding that of the older city of the Revolution. The commercial, political, and cultural energies of Boston's elite found expression in his public buildings. Their neoclassical style befitted the pretensions of this new elite: the new State House with its glimmering dome was the most impressive public building in the United States until Bulfinch went on to Washington to work on the Capitol. Besides enlarging Faneuil Hall, he designed the court house that became the City Hall, public markets in the West End, and a host of charitable institutions capped by the Massachusetts General Hospital. He also designed a bevy of churches and the Boston Theater, and allocated space in Tontine Crescent for the Massachusetts Historical Society and the Boston Library Society.[9]

Bulfinch's brick, stone, and granite dwellings in the fashionable West End and South End contributed to the decay of the North End, with its wood-framed clapboard houses. For the wealthy who once lived there cheek by jowl with artisans, Bulfinch designed handsome residences, elegant and innovative "crescents," and "colonnades" of connected houses reminiscent of London and Bath that set them apart from the inferior classes. He built no less than three mansions for Harrison Gray Otis. His palaces of business were a registry of the changing patterns of investment among Boston's commercial gentry: the "spacious and extensive" India Wharf (1807) in a channel deep enough to dock the largest ocean-going ships of the Amorys, Higginsons, and Perkinses; five banks (of the thirty-five in the city by 1835) and four insurance offices (of the twenty-four in 1835), which together made Boston's "State Street" the financial capital of New England. Under his stewardship, Boston's businessmen prospered in foreign trade, made a killing in real estate as "developers" and speculators (as did Otis), and invested in the Mill Pond Corporation, which brought manufacturing mills to Boston. All this laid the basis for the capital of the "Boston Associates"—the Lowells, Lawrences, Cabots, Appletons, and Jacksons—whose textile mills created an industrial landscape in New England by the 1820s and were in full hum by the 1830s. This is what moved Boston's elite: they could not have cared less about Samuel Adams's house, the Green Dragon tavern, or Griffin's Wharf.[10]

This elite was able to have its way with the public memory of the Revolution, finally, because it entered into an alliance with the master mechanics, the only potential carriers of an alternative tradition. "Remember," wrote "A Mechanic" in addressing "The Mechanics of the Town of Boston" in 1804, "that by the constancy and spirit of the Mechanics of this town, the dreadful yoke of Britain was broken asunder. . . . the monied and mercantile interest were by no means forward to aid their country." But his was a lonely voice.[11]

From 1765 to 1775 Boston master artisans and journeymen acquired a high consciousness of themselves as citizens. After the war this consciousness bloomed as master artisans formed a trades union committee with delegates from each trade, the first of its kind in America, and campaigned politically for protection against British manufactures, appealing to mechanics in other cities "as a band of brothers whose interests are united."

The Federalists of 1787, bent on building a system "to last for the ages," as James Madison put it, demonstrated an extraordinary capacity to accommodate their mechanic allies in drafting the Constitution, defeating, for example, a propertied qualification for voting for congressmen that would have disenfranchised mechanics. In the nip-and-tuck ratification battle in Massachusetts, the "mechanic interest" was crucial. In 1788, in the midst of the ratifying convention, a caucus of 380 masters at the Green Dragon dispatched a delegation to Samuel Adams that stayed his anti-Federalism. A committee of mechanics then organized the victory parade, in effect the first labor-organized parade in American history, quite unlike the official hierarchical processions in other cities. In the dead of winter, some 90 percent of Boston's 1,250 masters marched, trade by trade, with tools or emblems of their craft, the merchants sandwiched in. Artisans plied their trades on floats carrying a mock shipyard and a print shop, while seamen manned a replica of a frigate that was hauled through the streets.

Federalist city fathers never allowed a repetition of so audacious an assertion of the mechanic presence. "I don't know but we are in danger of running to excess in regard to processions," wrote

Samuel Otis, a merchant Federalist. In 1789, on President Washington's triumphal entry into Boston, the town committee arranged the mechanic contingents in the proper hierarchy following officials, clergy, and merchants. Some forty-six trades marched in alphabetical order under banners of their own making with emblems of the English craft guilds, but subordinated. The same thing happened a decade later, in 1800, in the official mourning procession for Washington. Mechanics did not march again by trades until 1815 during the town's celebration of peace. After that, Boston's truckmen wearing white smocks and riding their horses, were the only trade regularly on display in community parades. The consequences were serious: on annual festive occasions, younger generations had no living reminder of the mechanic presence in the Revolution.[12]

Mechanics paid a price for accommodating the establishment. "A Mechanic" could claim in 1804 that Boston's mechanics "to their disgrace, too long submitted" to "that haughty tone of superiority" of wealth. As a result, they "have less influence in our State and National government than the mechanics of any commercial city or town in the United States of any considerable importance." The legislature denied a general association of masters, organized in 1795, a charter of incorporation until 1806, since merchants were fearful of their political and economic influence. After incorporation, the Massachussetts Charitable Mechanics Association never enrolled more than a small fraction of the masters in town. Their membership certificate honoring the mechanic arts paid obeisance to the memory of Washington, the State House, and merchants. They were courted with success by Federalists and then by Whigs. When Boston switched from a town meeting to a mayoral system, the first five elected mayors included on the one hand the aristocrats Josiah Quincy and Harrison Gray Otis, and on the other Charles Wells and Samuel Armstrong, past presidents of the Mechanics Association. But for all their conservatism, the mechanics as a whole had had their political wings clipped.[13]

The fate of Paul Revere catches some sense of the subtle erasure of the mechanics as a group in the glorification of one. A political leader of the town's artisans, in public memory Revere was reduced to a single role, that of courier, and to a single event, his "midnight ride" of 1775. A silversmith and jack-of-a-few-other trades, Revere was emblematic of the thriving skilled master tradesman. He was active in the patriot cause in many ways: as a leader in the North End, the center of the maritime trades; as a leader of the St. Andrew's Lodge of Masons drawn from the "middling" sort; as an engraver of propagandistic drawings, of which the Massacre print was only the most famous; as the impresario of public displays; and only after 1774 as a courier. He developed a keen sense of himself as an artisan. Around 1770 he allowed John Singleton Copley to paint him at his workbench, in his shirtsleeves, holding a tool and a product of his craft, one of the few portraits of a colonial artisan that breathes craft pride. In a song after the tea action, "bold Revere" was hailed as one of "our chiefs" among "the true North Enders."[14]

After the Revolution, Revere referred to himself as a "tradesman" and increasingly as a "mechanic." In the 1790s, when the new Massachusetts Historical Society asked him for an account of his ride to Lexington, already a source of fame, Revere began his recollection with the sentence, "In the fall of '74 and winter of '75, I was one of upwards of thirty who formed ourselves into a committee for the purpose of watching the movements of the British soldiers." He then went back and inserted a caret after "thirty" to add "chiefly mechanics." In the 1788 ratification battle, he was one of three spokesmen chosen by the caucus of "mechanics and tradesmen" to lobby for the Constitution, and in 1795 he was the indispensable first president of the mechanics association.[15]

Revere's own transformation in part accounts for the erasure of his mechanic past. He climbed up, out of his artisan beginnings, becoming the owner of a copper foundry and brass works, which supplied the copper sheathing for the dome of the new State House and for the frigate *The Constitution*, and bells for at least 150 New England churches. He moved from his old clapboard house in the North End to a brick mansion on Charter Street and enjoyed a country home near his factory, Canton Dale. In a second portrait commissioned by his son, Gilbert Stuart portrayed Revere as a successful white-haired patriarch. According to family lore, his descendants retired the Copley portrait of the craftsman at his bench to an attic. In spite of all this, on his death in 1818 he was spoken of as "a prosperous North End Mechanic" who was "a born leader of the people, and his influence was pervading, especially among the mechanics and workingmen of Boston, with whom his popularity was immense." As early as 1795, however, "Eb Stiles," a self-taught poet, was singling him out for his midnight ride, as was the historical society. Even in his own lifetime, according to Esther Forbes, Revere's modern biographer, the legend had already begun to swallow up the man, paving the way for Henry Wadsworth Longfellow's sentimental 1861 poem, "Paul Revere's Ride": "Listen, my children, and you shall hear / Of the midnight ride of Paul Revere."[16]

[5]

The Discovery of the Veterans, 1825

In the 1820s a new festive calendar had come into being in Boston, one that registered a massive shift in what was being commemorated. In 1824, Edward Everett, a young professor of classics, in a Phi Beta Kappa address at Harvard College, was convinced that "as long as the name of America shall last" there would be "a father, that will . . . take his children on his knee and recount to them the events of the twentieth of December, the nineteenth of April, the seventeenth of June, and the Fourth of July." He enumerated Forefather's Day, memorializing the Pilgrim founding fathers, previously celebrated only in the town of Plymouth, the Battles at Lexington and Concord, the Battle of Bunker Hill, and Independence Day.[1]

Long before the 1820s, as we have seen, Boston had simply stopped commemorating the once-famous political events of the Revolution. There was no observance of the fiftieth anniversary of the Stamp Act protests in 1815 or the Massacre in 1820. Even on the fiftieth anniversary of the tea action in 1823, there are no signs of a town-sponsored commemoration or of published sermons or orations. In the *Columbian Centinel,* the history-conscious Federalist newspaper, December 1823 passed without notice of the event. And on December 17, 1823, on the occasion of "the destruction of the tea . . . this memorable event," the Republican *Independent Chronicle* paid only a short, pious tribute to those who made the Revolution possible. "A few yet live. . . . But the rest sleep in silent dust. . . . Yet they are not forgotten." But they were.[2]

The "jubilees" of local military events, on the other hand, were observed in the mid-1820s on a scale without precedent, dwarfing the annual Independence Day celebration. Elites who had never been comfortable with prewar events—controversial, ambiguous, menacing—felt more at home commemorating the war, when ostensibly there was a consensus between people and leaders, soldiers were under hierarchical command, and battles were clear-cut, as they are only in retrospect. Such commemorations, moreover, had a much wider potential appeal. While tens of thousands in the cities had taken part in prewar political events, at least two hundred thousand served in the military during the war, and some fifty thousand of them were still alive in the 1820s and 1830s. And if the men in urban street actions might be put down as the "mob" or the "rabble," most veterans were country people—the oft-hailed sturdy American yeomanry who could not be so easily dismissed. "Conservatives orchestrated the ceremonial rituals," Harlow Sheidley writes, "but only by supporting a democratization of the festive ritual in a near revivalistic fashion, thus popularizing the Revolution to large masses of ordinary people."[3]

Several political developments set the stage for the new public memory of the Revolution. First, the victory over Britain in the War of 1812 (however ineptly the war was fought) led to an upsurge of patriotism. This "second" war for independence revived memories of the first; the sons wanted to be worthy of their fathers. Second, New England Federalists, who had openly opposed the war, had to accommodate in order to survive. It was the "era of good feelings," a phrase coined by Boston's Federalist *Columbian Centinel* on the occasion of President James Monroe's visit to Boston in 1817. "Old school" Hartford Convention Federalists (like Harrison Gray Otis) were in eclipse, at least for a while. "New school" Federalists who knew how to stoop to conquer (like Josiah Quincy) were in fashion, as were practitioners of a sentimentalized Federalism (like Daniel Webster), and all were aware that they had to compete with groups in Boston calling themselves "the middling interest" and with Jacksonian democratic politicians emerging in the 1820s.

Third, amid the wave of patriotism and guilt following the war of 1812, the country discovered—and celebrated—the veterans of the Revolutionary War, a sea change in American opinion, which had long held "regular armies" in contempt and soldiers of the Continental army in disrepute. On July 4, 1817, when forty thousand people turned out to greet him in Boston, President James Monroe consecrated the battlefield on Bunker Hill: "the blood spilt here roused the whole American people." Monroe, a battle-scarred veteran wearing a suit that made him look like a continental soldier, called attention to old soldiers "reduced to poverty" or "in real distress." In 1818, in response to a welling up of sympathy, Congress passed the first general pension act, limited, however, to veterans "in indigent circumstances."[4]

Courthouses all over Massachusetts witnessed the spectacle of "hoary headed" veterans filing their claims, many "poor, old, lame, blind, deaf, and forgetful [and] bandied about from pillar to post." In Boston 220 applicants appeared in the spring of 1818. In 1820, after a flurry of fraudulent claims, a penurious Congress amended the law to require "an oath of poverty," which was widely condemned as humiliating. In a few years, some thirty thousand men applied, the testimony of their applications a gloomy inventory of American poverty in a land of plenty. The angry voices of veterans eventually achieved a new pension act in 1832 eliminating the means test and requiring only "a full account of services," which, much to the surprise of politicians, led to another twenty thousand applications.[5]

Veterans were a clamorous presence. Like Hewes, they petitioned; when rejected, they pleaded again, often seeking the help of politicians. By telling their stories in public and in appearances at ceremonies, they laid claim to entitlement. Some twenty-two "memoirs," "reminiscences," "recollections," and "narratives" of veterans were published between 1801 and 1819; still more appeared in the decade that followed, among them dramatic accounts like Enoch Crosby's and Israel Potter's, which became grist for the novelists James Fenimore Cooper and Herman Melville. Some memoirs, like that of Joseph Plumb Martin, vented the long-pent-up rage felt by many veterans. A veteran of seven years of war and a farmer defeated in his struggles with the great proprietor Henry Knox for land in Maine, Martin wrote one of the most poetic and humorous, yet bitter narratives of privations, of unequal treatment of officers and enlisted men, and of an ungrateful government. Enlistees were promised a hundred acres of land, he claimed, but "when the country had drained the last drop of service it could screw out of the poor soldiers, they were turned adrift like worn out horses and nothing said about land to pasture them upon."[6]

Finally, among the other developments making for a shift in opinion, the history of the political Revolution was being recovered in print culture. The first textbook histories of the United States written for schoolchildren, works by Salma Hale, Charles

Goodrich, Emma Willard, and Noah Webster, appeared in the 1820s and 1830s. Before them, history had no place in the curriculum. "These books," a scholar of American historiography reminds us, "were very nearly the sole source of information on American history," and not only for children. They were conservative, condemning mobs and agrarian rebellions, and their very format constricted the events they described: a short, numbered paragraph describing each event was followed by an appendix of didactic questions keyed to each paragraph. Even so, these books called attention to lost pre-Revolution events. Noah Webster described the tea action (paragraph 446) and then asked, "When was the tea of the East India company destroyed and how was it done?" Salma Hale gave the most dramatic account of the tea action and then asked students to recite Josiah Quincy's speech at the tea meeting. Samuel G. Goodrich, writing as "Peter Parley," introduced a series of didactic, sugar-coated tales for children that would eventually sell in the millions.[7]

The history of Boston came into vogue. The first local history of the city appeared, and another one intended for children, along with the first history of Massachusetts and the final volume of Thomas Hutchinson's Loyalist history of the colony. All devoted chapters to the famous events in Boston. Biographies of James Otis and Josiah Quincy, the first about Boston's Whig leaders, were published. And Lydia Maria Child peopled the first historical novel set in revolutionary Boston, *The Rebels, or, Boston Before the Revolution* (1825), not only with Samuel Adams and James Otis, but with one heroine who defies the patriarchal authority of Thomas Hutchinson and another who "incarnates both the spirit of the Revolution and its plebeian origins" by defying British troops the night of March 5, 1770.[8]

In the Boston area, the mammoth fiftieth-anniversary celebrations of the 1820s—the "jubilees" so full of meaning to Bible readers—gathered up all these trends: the reception for the Marquis de Lafayette on his triumphal tour of the United States in August 1824; the observance of the anniversary of the battles of Lexington and Concord in April 1825; the laying of the cornerstone of the Bunker Hill monument, for which Lafayette returned, in June 1825, and finally, the observance of the anniversary of the Declaration in July 1826.

The commemorations of 1825 in Boston at which Lafayette was twice a central figure, showed elitist Federalist republicans bending to accommodate democratic sentiment. Lafayette, as Sarah Purcell writes, was the "greatest remaining republican military hero of the Revolutionary war and he was also a symbol of the liberal democratic political commitment for which he had suffered in the French Revolution." Yet he was still more. On his tour, the aristocrat was "a democratic gentlemen, clad in plain style." Everywhere he singled out soldiers, shaking their hands, conversing with them, sharing military memories, moving the men and himself to tears. Lafayette's tour validated the ordinary soldier as hero, lifting him to the level of the republican hero hitherto reserved for generals and other officers.[9]

The observance at the site of the Bunker Hill monument-to-be in June 1825 epitomized the "discovery" of the veterans. Bunker Hill was not only the first real battle of the war, it was one of two Bostonians could appropriate as their own. A small band of volunteer citizen soldiers defending an American redoubt (actually on Breeds Hill) again and again turned back waves of British regulars. The British eventually captured the hill, but not until they had lost seven hundred of their two thousand men. In 1794

Boston's Masonic lodges had erected a small obelisk monument to General Joseph Warren, the most famous of them to fall in the battle, but it never quite gave the site its due.

The Bunker Hill Monument Association, an effort by elites who sought support from "our wealthy and public-spirited men," was unable to control the drift of the commemoration. Whichever estimates one takes from contemporary accounts, the cornerstone ceremony drew the largest gathering ever held on the North American continent. People came from all over, along with dignitaries from private institutions and all branches of federal, state, and local government. Some five to seven thousand marched in the procession, watched by as many as a hundred thousand, the crowds drawn from "all classes of citizens," as the papers put it. The place of honor in the procession went to some hundred veterans of the battle followed by several hundred other veterans, and they alone, like Lafayette, rode in carriages. Everyone else walked, even the President of the United States. At the ceremony, some fifteen thousand to twenty thousand sat in a giant, improvised amphitheater, and another tier ringing the hill may have brought the total audience to fifty thousand. The ceremonial laying of the cornerstone was sacred: the program included prayers, hymns, music, and an oration by Daniel Webster in a ministerial gown. The emotion was palpable: a drummer who had been at the battle beat his drum to the tune of "Yankee Doodle," veterans, Lafayette sitting among them, were in tears at Webster's tribute. Afterwards, some four thousand or more selected guests sat down to a meal of sorts at twelve giant tables.[10]

Webster, already the "Demosthenes of America" and "the godlike Daniel" to his admirers, was at the beginning of a career in which he "consistently . . . remained the spokesman for the New England merchant-industrialist class." His oration was a conservative encomium to the "great wheel of political revolution" whose rotation in America was "guarded, regular and safe," unlike the European revolutions that had received "an irregular and violent impulse." He celebrated material progress since the Revolution: "Our proper business is improvement." Webster also paid a sentimental tribute to the veterans sitting before him as survivors: "Venerable men! You have come down to us from a former generation. . . . But alas! You are not all here! . . . Veterans, you are the remnant of many a well-fought field. . . . May the Father of all mercies smile upon your declining years and bless them!" To Nathan Appleton, Boston's merchant and mill owner magnate, the event was "splendid," and he and his friends retired to the most "brilliant and interesting private party" Boston had ever seen.[11]

The impact of this oversized event in revivifying the popular traditions of the Revolution is hard to measure. Lafayette's visit watered the Liberty Tree. The Liberty Pole, erected in 1776 on the site of the elm cut down by Loyalists, was gone by 1815. A Lafayette Hotel went up next to the site in 1823–24. It was Lafayette's first stop on his 1824 grand entry, where a dense crowd greeted him at a giant arch, "Lafayette and Washington." Lafayette accepted the welcome of Mayor Josiah Quincy and a goblet of wine proffered by a young girl draped in a red, white, and blue sash. "The world should never forget the site where once stood the Liberty Tree, so famous in your annals," said the Frenchman. A second Liberty Pole went up, a Liberty Tree Tavern opened at the site, and for the first time since the Revolution the Liberty Tree was depicted in engravings illustrating histories of Boston; in one, the tree was shown draped with bunting. The Liberty Tree was back in fashion, so much so that in 1850, when David Sears, a real estate developer of the Back Bay, a Whig, and

Vice President of the Massachusetts Historical Society (MHS) erected a four-story building on the site, he called it the Liberty Tree building. Its fashionable shops and elegant ballroom mocked the large wooden bas-relief of the Liberty Tree, carved by ship carpenters, mounted high on the outside. The motto "Law and Order" across its roots tamed the illegal acts with which the tree was associated from 1765 to 1775.[12]

The 1825 jubilees paved the way for the fiftieth anniversary of the Declaration of Independence in 1776. The trajectory of the Declaration resembled that of the loss and recovery of the memory of the tea action. In the 1770s and 1780s it "seems to have been forgotten," Pauline Maier writes. Then, in the 1790s, as I have noted, it was rejected by Federalists fearful of its revolutionary implications in proportion as it was claimed by Jeffersonian Republicans. In the 1820s, as old partisan lines were shuffled, the Declaration "began to assume a certain holy quality." In 1818, when John Trumbull brought to Faneuil Hall his monumental twelve-by-eighteen-foot painting of the drafting committee presenting the Declaration to the Continental Congress, he drew huge paying crowds for weeks. Bostonians could also choose one of two engraved and decorated copies of the document or an exact facsimile distributed by Congress, all suitable for framing. In 1826, the commemoration of the Declaration confirmed the entry of the document into the pantheon of conservative landmarks of the Revolution. By then, Boston's elitist *North American Review* could confess that when the French Revolution "made a recurrence to principles of the [American] Revolution . . . the instrument of party," there was not "intense interest in the history of our revolution." Now there was. The death of both Thomas Jefferson and John Adams on July 4, 1826, to contemporaries a sign of divine providence, was solemnly observed in Boston on

August 2: businesses closed, church bells tolled, and ships lowered their flags to half-mast. Their deaths confirmed the popular sense that the country was losing its last links with the revolutionary generation.[13]

A wave of sentimentality bathed the "hoary headed veteran." In 1831, Oliver Wendell Holmes, whose poem "Old Ironsides" had helped save the frigate *Constitution* from demolition, was inspired by Major Thomas Melville to write "The Last Leaf." Melville was the grandfather of the novelist and a veteran of the tea action who still walked the streets of Boston, "the last of the cocked hats" as he was sometimes called:

> I saw him once before,
> As he passed by the door,
>   And again
> The pavement stones resound,
> As he totters o'er the ground
>   With his cane.
> . . . .
> But now he walks the streets,
> And he looks at all he meets
>   Sad and wan,
> And he shakes his feeble head,
> That it seems as if he said,
>   "They are gone."

An immensely popular poem all over the country, it was memorized by, among others, Abraham Lincoln, a Whig legislator in Illinois. Lincoln gave voice to the widespread recognition that at one time "a living history" of the Revolution "was to be found in every family . . . a history that could be read and understood alike by all. . . . But *those* histories are gone. They can be read no more forever." Americans saw in each surviving veteran a "last leaf."[14]

Throughout the 1820s and 1830s politicians of all stripes exploited veterans at festive rituals. At the ceremony on July 4, 1835, in Worcester, "there were two or three pews stuffed full of survivors," four of them veterans of Bunker Hill, a cynical observer reported, and he supposed they "will be carted about the county as long as their bones hold together." Edward Everett, by now a prime oratorical star, went so far as to rehearse veterans as to when to stand up during his oration.[15]

All this—the veneration of the veteran as hero, the increased attention to the prewar Revolution in print, the political orchestrations of festive ritual, the recovery of the symbolism of the Liberty Tree and the Declaration of Independence—combined with a sense of the loss of the last links to the Revolution, set the stage for the "discovery" of George Robert Twelves Hewes and his triumphal reception in Boston in 1835. And yet there was something more, an unintended consequence of this giant leap forward in the democratization of the memory of the Revolution.

[6]

Claiming the Revolution:
The Radical Challenge, 1835

In 1834, the year before Hewes returned to the city, there were no less than six celebrations of the Fourth of July in Boston, a sign of the fragmenting of the old political culture as new, radical movements emerged to claim the Revolution. The reporter who joyfully made the rounds for the *Boston Daily Advocate* (most likely the editor, Benjamin Franklin Hallett, before long a Jacksonian Democrat) filled no less than four columns with his vivid descriptions of the "pomp, parade, procession and feasting." The city was "a moving mass of people from morning till night," he wrote, "the whole population and multitudes from the neighboring towns seeming to be in the streets." The Common was covered with "numerous tents arranged in a line . . . busy in dispensing their edibles and beverages."[1]

At eight-thirty in the morning, William Emmons, a well-known Jacksonian and "the butt of the day" (wrote Hallett), spoke on horseback, haranguing some fifteen hundred persons on the Common about the evils of the Whigs, corporations, the Bank of the United States, and the new trades unions. At nine, the assembled children of the Baptist Sabbath School Union heard a "Peter Parley-style" talk relating "the prominent causes and events of the Revolution." About ten, the New England Anti-Slavery Society, meeting in Boylston Hall, listened as an orator from Maine "dissected the Declaration of Independence and the Constitution which legalizes Slavery" in a keen lawyer-like way, and then heard hymns from "a choir of fifty colored children." The official celebration sponsored by the city government in Old South "was dull and formal as usual." "All the world were on the Common or attending another celebration." The Whigs, who had formally come into being as a party in the spring, sponsored a handsomely decorated pavilion on the Common where a "tall mast surmounted by a liberty cap" flew the flag. The pavilion was jammed all day with "a genteel and well dressed crowd." At one, a procession Hallett counted at 1,916 persons, along with bands and military units, marched to the Whig pavilion and sat down to tables covered with white cloths. "Distinguished citizens" of city, state, and federal governments were honored guests, and Whig orations were followed by endless Whig toasts and expressions of regret from Whig politicians like Daniel Webster, who could not attend.

To Hallet, "the most complete and imposing" celebration was offered by the unions, whose parade included "the grand spectacle of the day," "the Frigate Mechanic," and whose orator, Frederick Robinson, was "the most eloquent." Organized only that March, the Trades Union of Boston and Vicinity, comprising delegates from fourteen trades, was the first central association of journeymen mechanics in the town. Hallett, an enthusiastic quantifier, counted a total of 1,074 "operatives" (a count others put closer to 2,000) marching in a dozen contingents with nine banners. The main banner was "a large and rich ensign with appropriate devices"; 88 masons carried as their slogan "Labor Is the Property of Those Who Produce It," while 54 Coopers bore a flag marking the birth of the association with the slogan, "All Men Are Born Free and Equal." The procession, which took two hours to move from the State House to Fort Hill, "attracted the gaze of the whole city." Headed by the Mechanic Riflemen, a militia company, it included two floats echoing those of the ratification parade of 1788: one of printers working a press and the other a miniature ship constructed for the occasion, rigged and manned by sailors in white uniforms and pulled by twenty-four horses, one for each state.

The outdoor ceremony was held in the park at Fort Hill, a site where Stamp Act collector Andrew Oliver's effigy had been burned and where one group had assembled for the action against the tea ships. The band played the "Marseilles hymn," Dr. Charles Douglas of the Trades Union read the Declaration of Independence and someone else the Declaration of the Rights of the Trades Unions of Boston, after which Robinson offered the oration. Some eight hundred paraders then adjourned to a dinner at Faneuil Hall. "Our mechanics, and our most useful men," Robinson said, "have been so long shut out from public festivals, or admitted only to be set down at the tail of the feast." They were now setting their own table. It was the first time Boston's mechanics, masters, or journeymen, held their own public observance of the Fourth.[2]

The ceremony was a coming-of-age for the journeymen unionists. Beginning in the mid-1820s, journeyman had taken action in Boston, as they had all over the east coast. Throughout the era of the Revolution and well into the nineteenth century, class lines between masters and journeymen were blurred, perhaps longer in Boston than elsewhere. Today's journeymen, tomorrow's master, or so the aphorism went, and often vice versa. On those infrequent occasions in Boston when the trades marched in a community procession (1789, 1800, 1815), journeymen in most trades very likely fell in with masters. But by the mid-1820s, as Christopher Tomlins points out, "the skin of craft homogeneity had grown brittle and was at the point of cracking." In April 1825, six hundred out of Boston's six hundred and fifty journeymen carpenters went on strike for the ten-hour day, "one of the most notable strikes in American labor history." The strike failed when master mechanics—the employers of journeymen—gave in to the pressure of their employers.[3]

"When conflict revived in the 1830's," Tomlins observes, "things were clearly different." Self-organization, which was rife, was expressed in strikes; "almost every year between 1830 and 1836 saw significant numbers of journeymen involved in strikes, mostly focused on the ten-hour day, in independent working-men's political activity, and in city-wide trade organizations." Labor papers in eastern cities—the *New England Artisan*, (later the *Daily Reformer*), *The Man*, *The Working Man's Advocate*, and *National Trades Union*—and itinerant agitators like Seth Luther spread the message from one city to another. In Massachussetts in the early 1830s, a Workingman's Party ran candidates for governor and Congress before Jacksonian Democrats succeeded in "embracing them to death," as Ronald Formisano puts it.[4]

This new labor movement staked its claim to the American Revolution. In New York City, George Henry Evans drafted a "Working Men's Declaration of Independence" (1829), the first of many in the nineteenth century that would mimic the language of 1776. On July 4, 1826, Robert Owen delivered a declaration of "mental independence." Between 1834 and 1836, the general trades unions, Bruce Laurie writes, "breathed new life into the Glorious Fourth and infused it with fresh meaning." This rhetorical claiming of the Revolution had several distinctive components: a recognition that mechanics had played an important part in the political events of the Revolution and in the war; that the revolution of '76 was incomplete, the promise of the Declaration unfulfilled, and working men now confronted a new "tyranny"; and a conviction that it was necessary for workers to act collectively, as had the patriots, forming "combinations" to confront employers and politicians.[5]

The Fourth of July, to conservatives never more than the anniversary of independence, to others had become a symbol of liberation. The New York act emancipating the state's slaves went into effect on July 4, 1827, the law of the radical Democrat Frederick Robinson abolishing imprisonment for debt and thus presumably liberating prisoners went into effect July 4, 1834, and Henry David Thoreau would make a personal Declaration of Independence when he went to live at Walden Pond on July 4, 1846. African Americans on the other hand, in Boston, as elsewhere, had "a hate-love" relationship with the Fourth. Since 1808, they had marked the anniversary of the ending of the slave trade by a parade on July 14, close enough to July 4 to taunt white Americans with their hypocrisy.[6]

Seth Luther, "the leading figure of the New England labor movement" and prominent in Boston during these years, exemplified the rhetoric of claiming the Revolution. Born in Rhode Island, the son of a veteran who had received his pension, Luther was a carpenter who had worked in New England textile mills and traveled widely in the west and south. In 1832, after masters broke the ten-hour-day strike of the Boston shipwrights and caulkers, Judge Peter Oxenbridge Thacher of the municipal court fumed to a grand jury about the danger of "combinations."

From 1832 to 1835, Luther delivered a scorching address in Boston and nine other towns. He invoked Bunker Hill as Webster had never intended: "When we look towards that *Holy Hill* where Warren fell and where blood flowed like water from the hearts of Freemen," the alarm had to be sounded. "Our rights are not only endangered, but some of them already wrestled from us by the powerful inhumanized grasp of monopolized wealth." The unfinished monument (not completed until 1842) was "a most excellent emblem of our unfinished independence. There let it *stand* unfinished, until the time passes away when aristocrats talk about mercy to mechanics and laborers. There let it stand unfinished, until our rights are acknowledged."[7]

Luther rebutted Judge Thacher head on: "The Declaration of Independence was the work of a combination and was as hateful to the Traitors and Tories of those days as combinations of workingmen are now to the avaricious monopolist and purse-proud aristocrat." Boston's iconic events were vivid in his mind. "Was there no combination," Luther asked, "when the leather aprons of the farmer and mechanic were seen mingling with the shining uniform of the British Regulars?"—an image that could be taken to refer to either the Boston Massacre or the Battle of Bunker Hill. "Was there no combination when Bostonians in the disguise of Mohawk Indians made a dish of TEA at the expense of *King George the Third* using Boston harbor for a teapot?," words that echoed the cries of the "body" meeting of 1773.

Frederick Robinson, the orator of 1834, portrayed a society riven by class conflict. "For the interests of the thousands," he proclaimed, "are always contrary to the interests of the millions." It was the "industrious classes," "the producing classes" against "the aristocracy." The working man required "trades unions," declared Robinson, laying into Judge Thacher. "The very judge who had on the bench condemned the open Trades Union of the people was himself a member of the secret society of the Suffolk bar." Well might "the capitalists, monopolists, judges, lawyers, doctors and priests" complain of combinations of workers, especially "the combination of lawyers." Hallett reported that the speech rallyed support for Jackson in the war against "the great monster," the Bank. But in his printed text, Robinson contended that the two major political parties were both enemies. The aristocracy continually contrived to change their party name: "it was first Tory, then Federalist, then no party, then amalgamation, then National Republican, now Whig and the next name they may assume perhaps will be republican or democrat."[8]

In 1835, Boston workers acted in the spirit of these appropriations of the Revolution. In May, when the journeymen house carpenters, masons, and stonecutters went on a "turn-out," an early term for a strike, they adopted a "ten hour circular" drafted by a committee on which Luther served. The shorter work day was a "Natural Right" and one of "the Rights of Man." "We claim by the blood of our fathers shed on our battlefields in the War of the Revolution," they wrote, "the rights of American Freemen, and no earthly power shall resist our righteous claims with impunity." In July, the carpenters, Seth Luther among them, carrying their rules, the emblem of their trade, paraded through the wards of the rich to the tune of the "Marseillaise." In 1835 this would have been a reminder not only of 1789 but also of the 1830 revolution, when working men had manned the barricades in Paris.[9]

The strikers heard a speech from Theophilus Fisk justifying an eight-hour day: "eight hours for work, eight hours for sleep, and eight hours for amusement and instruction." A former Universalist minister and the editor of the Boston *Reformer,* he spoke in Julien Hall, after some twenty churches refused him a platform.

It is not clear which they feared more, the passionate anticlerical-
ism of the editor of *Priestcraft Unmasked* or his labor radicalism.
"The great fear of those who grow rich upon your industry," Fisk
held, "is that if you get time to improve your minds, you will get
your eyes open to the monstrous frauds that have been perpetrated upon you by the heathen idolaters—the worshippers of
Mammon," among which were the political parties. "Throw
away all party names—all parties are and ever have been opposed
to your interests."[10]

Nationally, 1835 was "the height of the ten hour movement"
and "the turning point in the history of American labor's effort
to reduce its working day." In Boston, as a speaker to the masters
put it, a "portion of our journeymen" displayed "a restless and turbulent spirit." And not only skilled artisans were restless. It required little prescience for Luther to charge that the "capitalists"
of Boston were afraid that "the contagion" of the journeymen's
demands for shorter hours "will reach their SLAVE MILLS."
In February 1834, eight hundred women in a Lowell textile mill
turned out against a reduction of wages, marching in a procession
to an outdoor rally at which "one of the leaders mounted a pump
and made a flaming Wollstonecraft [sic] speech on the rights of
women" and the inequities of "the *monied* aristocracy," in all "an
Amazonian display" to a reporter for a Boston paper. A petition
circulated among "all who imbibe the spirit of our patriotic ancestors."[11]

Class resentments surfaced against still other targets. On August 11, 1834, a crowd "composed largely of poor Protestant laborers" of Boston and Charlestown bearing banners of "No Popery"
and "Down with the Cross," burned down the Catholic Ursuline
convent in Charlestown, which was used principally as a school
for the daughters of wealthy Boston Unitarians. Contemporaries

identified the rioters as "brickmakers, sailors, firemen, apprentices, youthful hooligans, etc." "No Popery" appropriated another
part of Boston's Puritan revolutionary heritage, save that it owed
more to the competition of native-born workers with the Irish
immigrants now entering the city than to the highly politicized
Pope's Day of colonial and revolutionary Boston. The wealthy
imputed antirich motives to the rioters.[12]

Violence in the nation as a whole reached new heights in the
mid-1830s. From 1828 to 1833 there were twenty riots, in 1834 sixteen, and in 1835 thirty-seven, producing what David Grimsted
has called "a climate of national near-hysteria." "The spirit of
mob-law is becoming too common," President Andrew Jackson
wrote in August 1835, "and must be checked, or, ere long, it will
become as great an evil as servile war." Boston's elite grew tense in
response to this range of threats. A day after the convent riot, the
committee formed at an "indignation meeting" at Faneuil Hall
read like a Who's Who of Boston's wealthy. In the debate in the
Massachusetts legislature, Robert Winthrop, a leading Whig,
spoke of the convent "besieged by a mob, sacked pillaged and
burned"; nothing was safe if this "spirit of violence is to have free
vent." "The heart of upper class reaction to the convent riot,"
writes Theodore Hammett, "was anxiety, concern in stability,
law and order."[13]

Judge Thacher took up the gauntlet thrown down by these declarations of class war. In a charge to a grand jury in December
1834, Thacher lumped riots and combinations into one monstrous
evil. The riot at the convent was a "a scene of popular madness"
invoking the Reign of Terror in the French Revolution. The riot
and the unions were signs of "that leveling spirit" that would
"array one portion of our free and happy society against the
other." "When one class of citizens is taught to consider another

as enemies, it will inevitably tend to disturb the peace of society. It has late been fashionable even in this commonwealth, to excite the employed against their employers, and borrowers against lenders, and thus to lead the poor to wage a civil war against the rich." At Harvard, Theophilus Parsons exhorted listeners to his Phi Beta Kappa address to reach out to the masses with "the clear simple truth on which the rights of property rest." In 1835, a panicky legislature rewrote the law (last revised in 1786, the year of "Shays's Rebellion") permitting the mayor or an alderman to read the riot act to disperse would-be rioters and eliminating the waiting period of one hour before they could take action.[14]

Boston's establishment seemed in even more of a frenzy over the threat of radical abolitionism. As a center for antislavery agitation, the city was second only to New York. In 1829 David Walker, a free black who had migrated from North Carolina and become an organizer for the General Colored Association of Massachusetts, issued *Walker's Appeal*, a fiery pamphlet calling for slave rebellion. In 1831, William Lloyd Garrison launched *The Liberator*, 1,700 of whose 2,300 subscribers were free blacks, 150 of them living in Boston. In 1833 the popular Boston writer Lydia Maria Child published *An Appeal in Favor of That Class of Americans Called Africans*, which converted such future leaders of the antislavery cause as Wendell Phillips and Thomas Wentworth Higginson.[15]

In the wake of Nat Turner's rebellion in Virginia in 1831, for which both *Walker's Appeal* and *The Liberator* were scapegoats, outraged southern slaveholders demanded that Boston suppress Garrison's paper (Walker had since died). Boston's elite responded, fearful of abolition's radical threats to property rights, the Constitution, and the union, and, implicitly, their southern trade. Harrison Gray Otis, as mayor, placated southern officials.

Then in August 1835, at a mass meeting in Faneuil Hall attended by invited southerners and "the best people" of Boston, Otis, nephew of James Otis, the revolutionary, railed against the antislavery society as "a *revolutionary society*." George Thompson, an English abolitionist touring the country, was a prime target: a handbill promised a purse of one hundred dollars to the first person who could bring "that foreign scoundrel [to] the tar kettle."

On August 1, a mob invaded a meeting of the Boston Female Anti-Slavery Society, but Thompson escaped with the aid of Lydia Maria Child and others. In this atmosphere, threatened by a hangman's gallows outside his house, Garrison left town. In October, after he had returned, a "broadcloth mob" again stormed a meeting of the women's society in search of Thompson, found Garrison next door, tied a rope around his body, and dragged him through the streets. He escaped lynching only because he was spirited off to jail. It was a mob, as a Boston newspaper put it, of "gentlemen of property and standing." The establishment that had condemned the convent riot the year before condoned the anti-abolitionist riot. The abolitionists were "a threat to social order, their attackers were depicted as defenders of the peace."[16]

Boston's antislavery advocates, like the labor radicals, expressed an extraordinary affinity with the radicalism of the Revolution. David Walker ended his tocsin to insurrection, "See your Declaration, Americans!!! Do you understand your own language?" Garrison had chosen to launch his crusade in Boston, as he put it, to be *"within sight of Bunker Hill and in the birthplace of liberty."* He excoriated Harrison Gray Otis as a traitor to his ancestors. In his account of the "mobocracy" that almost lynched him, Garrison stressed that "the outrage was perpetrated in Boston—the Cradle of Liberty—the city of Hancock and Adams." He was dragged through State Street, he wrote, "over the ground that was stained with the blood of the first martyrs . . . by the memorable massacre of 1770."[17]

Understandably, in view of these multiple claims to the radical traditions of the Revolution—including advocates of tarring and feathering and anti-Popery—the dominant, history-conscious elite felt a need to recover what Boston's prominent Whig legal scholar called *The True Uses of American Revolutionary History*, marked by "moderation and compromise." The very adoption of the name "Whig" for their party in 1834 staked their claim on their revolutionary forebears.[18]

Thus the extraordinary tensions of 1834–35 laid bare rival claims to Boston's revolutionary heritage. As Tomlins aptly puts it, the stage was set for "spasmodic guerrilla warfare between trade unionism and its judicial critics." In the summer and fall of 1835, Mayor Theodore Lyman thought the populace in "a very heated, irritable state." Movements subversive of conservative values had emerged at different points on the political spectrum —journeymen trades unionists, nativist laborers, free blacks, antislavery advocates of the middling sort, women and men. Seth Luther and Theophilus Fisk, William Lloyd Garrison and Wendell Phillips, David Walker and Lydia Maria Child were, in different ways, laying claim to the radical heritage of the Revolution long submerged by the city's dominant conservative culture. Who would claim the tea party? Who would claim George Hewes? What political function might the tea party and Hewes perform?[19]

[7]

The Recovery of the Tea Party

When George Hewes arrived in Boston a few days before July 4, 1835, a reporter for the *Boston Traveller* who "had an interview with the venerable man" called the event the "Tea Party," in quotation marks. Hewes did not. "On first setting foot in Boston," the reporter wrote, "Mr HEWES exclaimed, 'O, that I could see one of the band who assisted, with me, in destroying the British tea—then would my joy be complete.'" A few minutes later Colonel Henry Purkitt, another survivor of 1773, was introduced to Hewes, "and it was a meeting of intense interest." They "minutely recapitulated" details of the event and "the statements of both were alike in nearly every particular." The apposite terms used by Hewes and the reporter to describe the event suggest a clash of generations: Hewes, a man out of the past clinging to the older usage, in effect "the destruction of the tea," the reporter adopting a term then coming into popular usage. The old term was serious and reverential, the new term faintly comic and irreverent. By putting "tea party" in quotation marks, the reporter was straddling the two, distancing himself from what some of his genteel readers might have considered vulgar usage.[1]

Thus, the answer to the teasing question I started with, "When did they begin calling it the Boston Tea Party?," turns out to be something like this: ordinary people in their everyday speech, that is, the vernacular, may possibly have called the event the "tea party" or some variant of making tea in Boston harbor during and after it and may have continued to pass on this usage in oral tradition. But their betters referred to it as "the destruction of the tea," the serious, proper term. In print culture this is what it remained: one paper in 1835 referred to Hewes as "among the spirited destroyers of the tea." In fact, as I have mentioned, the term "tea party" does not seem to have appeared in print until the early 1830s. Surprising as it may seem, the two biographies of Hewes, in 1834 and 1835, marked the first time any author used "tea party" in the title of a book, and possibly the first time it appeared in any book. I don't find it in any of the Massachusetts-oriented histories, national or local, or in the biographies, memoirs, or children's books prior to 1835 that I have examined. I therefore suspect that for the longest time the genteel considered it a vulgar expression, and authors who were trying to reach respectable audiences avoided it. It was not something proper Bostonians joked about.[2]

If this pattern of evidence holds up, what can we make of it? For purposes of analysis, we can differentiate three overlapping subjects: first, the recovery of the tea action, under whatever name, as an important historic event; second, the use of the term "tea party" to describe it; and third, the "discovery" of George Hewes, who until 1834 was unknown as a historical figure in either print or oral culture, save, of course, to his family and the circles around him. How do these three fit together in the contest for the memory of the Revolution very much in the air the year Hewes appeared on the scene?

The action against the tea seems to have washed back into historical consciousness in the wake of the commemorations of 1825.

Beginning in the 1830s, we can detect an assumption in public discourse that when someone referred to the action against the tea, it was a familiar event. Three examples suggest that this taken-for-granted quality held across the political spectrum. The peripatetic Seth Luther, in a speech given to audiences of workers in the 1830s, could ask, as we have noted, "Was there no combination when Bostonians in the disguise of Mohawk Indians made a dish of TEA at the expense of *King George the Third* using Boston harbor for a teapot?" So too, did Benjamin Franklin Hallett, the newspaper editor, in response to the "Mashpee Revolt." In 1833, the Mashpee Indians of Cape Cod petitioned the legislature demanding "that we as a tribe will rule ourselves and have the rights to do so as all men are born free"—an appropriation of the Declaration that shows how it had rippled throughout the country. They wanted, among other things, to deny permission to "any white man to come into our Plantation to cut . . . wood." On July 4, 1833, when William Apess, himself a Pequot and a Methodist minister, and several others dumped the cart of a white man collecting wood, Apess was arrested, tried, and imprisoned. This was the onset of the "Mashpee Revolt" that would rile the state for several years. The governor threatened to call out troops, but Hallett thought "the persons concerned in the riot, as it was called, and imprisoned for it . . . were as justifiable in what they did, as our fathers were who threw the teas overboard."[3]

A third example is telling for what it reveals about the contest for the memory of the event. In 1837, at a meeting in Faneuil Hall to debate a resolution of indignation over the murder of the abolitionist editor Owen Lovejoy by a crowd in Alton, Illinois, the tea action became an unintended focus of debate. James T. Austin, the Whig attorney general of Massachusetts and an ardent racist defender of slavery, likened the crowd in Alton to the "orderly mob" that threw the tea overboard. Young Wendell Phillips was moved to an extemporaneous speech—his first in Faneuil Hall. "Mob, mob, forsooth!," exclaimed Phillips. "The 'orderly mob' which assembled in Old South to destroy the tea were met to resist not the laws but illegal exactions." Pointing to the portraits of Revolutionary worthies recently hung in the Hall, Phillips said, "When I hear the gentleman lay down principles which place the murders of Alton side by side with [James] Otis and [John] Hancock, with [Josiah] Quincy and [Samuel] Adams, I thought these pictured lips . . . would have broken into voice to rebuke the recreant American."[4]

As to the second issue, when the "destruction of the tea" became the "tea party," we have to resort to guesswork. We are on uncertain ground on the question of when any phrase is in everyday speech, because evidence usually comes to the attention of scholars only when it appears in print, which may not be until many years, if not several generations later. I have searched in three genres that typically registered popular usage, children's textbooks, songs, and pictures, choosing them in part because they were accessible and well indexed.[5] The children's textbooks I have touched on already were unanimously proper in the 1820s and 1830s, and none referred to the Tea Party. I also found no evidence of the phrase in songs. Those composed soon after the event did not use it; songsters, which presumably reprinted the most popular songs of the Revolutionary era, reprinted none about the event.[6]

In the 1830s, one new song showed that genteel Bostonians were able to treat the event humorously, even without calling it the Tea Party. "The Tea Tax: A Yankee Comic Song," was touted as "sung with unbounded applause by Mr Andrews at the respectable Federal Street Theatre." The words were by "a gentleman of

Boston," and the sheet music for the pianoforte, an instrument still reserved to the well-to-do, but the tune was so popular it was the subject of a parody at the Whig Fourth of July celebration in 1834. The singer took on the country bumpkin persona that had made "Yankee Doodle" a long-lasting hit, beginning with "I sum I am a Yankee lad and I guess I'll sing a ditty." But unlike "Yankee Doodle," which had the satiric bite of a comic reversal, "The Tea Tax" was a nonsense song that played on the changes in Boston over the sixty years gone by since the tea action:

> And t'other day we yankee folks, were mad about the taxes,
> And so we went, like Indians dress'd to split Tea chests with axes
> I mean, t'was done in seventy five, an we were real gritty
> The Mayor he would have led the gang but Boston warn't a City.

The verse ended with the inversion theme of making tea in the harbor on a grand scale:

> And then we went aboard the ships, our vengeance to administer,
> And didn't care a tarnal curse, for any King or minister;
> We made a plaguey mess o'Tea, in one of the biggest dishes,
> I mean, we steeped it in the Sea and treated all the fishes.[7]

Evidence from pictures reproduced for popular consumption also suggests that the tea action was making its way into popular culture, although not under the name "tea party." In the 1830s, for the first time, children could see the tea action pictured in engravings. This is important because it would be hard for children (or adults, for that matter) to imagine grown men disguised as Indians throwing chests of tea overboard: "Why, father? How did they do it?" The first American depictions were all engravings in books aimed at children and published in New England between 1833 and 1835.[8]

None of these representations—the songs, the textbooks, the

pictures—called the event the "tea party"; nor did most political writers or orators. But the newspaper reporters in Providence and Boston who interviewed Hewes in 1835 did, as did a volunteer who toasted Hewes on July 4 and a number of Boston newspapers. The *Morning Post* captioned an article "The Tea Party" and spoke of "the memorable Tea Party" (how rapidly an event so long ignored became "memorable"). Indeed Hewes's appearance created a hubbub in town as "some dozen or more persons have presented their claims to the 'last survivorship.'" The paper was dismissive: they were "no doubt spectators," that is, people on the wharf, as opposed to those who boarded the ships, but whatever the basis of their claim, at least a score of claimants were still alive in 1835, a good many of them in the Boston area. By mid-year, the phrase, as well as the event, was in the air, and people wanted to get into the act. Otherwise, why would James Hawkes in New York have entitled his 1834 biography of Hewes *A Retrospect of the Boston Tea-Party*, or Benjamin Bussey Thatcher in Boston in 1835 entitled his *Traits of the Tea Party*? Both were trying to sell a book about a nobody in a competitive book market; "Tea party" may have given the title the appeal of slang. They hoped to cash in on the sudden emergence of the now "memorable" event as to validate an otherwise unknown artisan. Each wrote a work devoted primarily to prewar political events in Boston, virtually the only account of a military veteran to do so. Yet they were obviously under no temptation to call their books *Retrospect of the Boston Massacre* or *Traits of Tarring and Feathering*, events on the dark side of the Revolution.[9]

Sixty years after it took place, the Tea Party may have been on its way to becoming an iconic event in the making of the Revolution, at least in the North. And from the point of view of Boston's elite in a state of near hysteria about radicalism and mob violence, compared to other events (the ambiguous Stamp Act riots, the mobbish Massacre, the grim tarring and featherings), it was by far the safest. After all, both Austin and Phillips could refer to the participants as "an orderly mob."

What did it mean, then, in the second quarter of the nineteenth century, to speak of the event as the "tea party" and not as the "destruction of the tea"? Very likely the new term served both conservative and radical claimants to the Revolution. "Tea party" could have had several meanings. First, it was a comic, frivolous way of referring to a serious event. It thus put the user on familiar terms with a somewhat frightening, somewhat puzzling distant event. It restored some of the mood of the original participants in 1773, who had engaged in this ridiculous reversal, but it had none of that derisive, mocking quality, and it softened the terrifying carnivalesque theme of the Indians—indeed eliminated it altogether. Second, as in the previous century, in this context the phrase implied a parody of the tea ritual associated with the genteel. Thus, when the Providence reporter wrote of Hewes that "his etiquette may be tea party etiquette, but it was not acquired at tea parties in Beacon Street or Broadway," he was using a shorthand he did not have to explain. His readers knew that Beacon Street in Boston and Broadway in New York City were fashionable enclaves of the rich. Third, the term carried a parody on the level of gender: among the well-to-do and middling sort, women presided over the elaborate ritual of making, pouring, and serving tea. The term "tea party" applied to strong, muscular men throwing heavy chests of tea overboard reversed gender as well as class: the image of working-class men "making tea" in the harbor mimicked the actions of their betters and women.

Indeed, the tea ritual became even more pervasive in early nineteenth-century Boston. The daughters of Mayor Josiah

Quincy described in delicious detail the joys of an elaborate tea party. Others wrote about "lap teas," "a party . . . in the real old fashioned style," or "delightful and cosy tea parties." Henry Sergent called his oil painting of a social gathering in a luxurious Beacon Street home *The Tea Party*. In 1827 Robert Roberts, an African American who was a Boston house servant, published a guidebook laying out the elaborate procedures for serving tea, a sure sign that upstarts aspiring to gentility were in need of instruction.[10]

Two striking examples suggest the use of "tea party" as a mocking parody of class. The first American minstrel song, popularly known as "Backside Albany," burlesqued the patriotic song "The Battle of Plattsburgh," which celebrated the American victory at the end of the War of 1812. It originated in Albany, where it was first performed by Micah Hawkins, in time a leading minstrel performer. It was printed on a broadside in Boston in 1815 side by side with the patriotic song. In the song, the British general, Sir George Prevost, is satirized by a black sailor in a black dialect burlesque as "Gubbener Probose an he British soger / Come to Plattebug a tea party courtin." McComb, the American general, sends Prevost into fast retreat. "Probose scare so, he lef all behine / Powder, ball, cannon, tea-pot an kittle. / Uncle Sam berry sorry / To be sure for he pain," but the British general is unlikely to try again "When he notion for a nudder tea party." The white working-class audience in eastern cities, among whom minstrel shows became immensely popular, could have connected "tea party" to Boston, but more likely they thought of the tea parties of the upper classes.[11]

In the Baltimore riot of August 1835, the targets of crowd wrath were "swindlers" of the failed Bank of Maryland, which left a trail of "Ruined Widows and Orphans," and the Mayor and officials trying to maintain law and order. In what the historian David Grimsted calls a saturnalia, the crowds sacking the homes of the elite "emptied their victims' wine cellars," drinking wine they called "American Blood," burnt a law library, and destroyed chinaware from Mayor Jesse Hunt's house. A crowd leader broke the mayor's china in the street, crying, "Gentlemen, who wants to go to a tea party? But stop, I'll go get the plates." A carpenter assuming the role of mayor completed the parody, saying, "Damned if he wasn't mayor of the city."[12]

Still another level of parody is implicit. Genteel adults generally would not have called the social functions at which they served tea a "tea party." They formally invited guests to "take tea" or "come to tea" or "drink tea." Women gossiped about "tea parties." But then as now, it was children who held tea parties in imitation of grownups, especially the children of the well-to-do. Peggy Livingston, growing up in an aristocratic family, at the age of five invited "by card . . . 20 young misses" to her own "Tea Party & Ball." The use of imported toy "Chinaware" tea sets, advertised in Boston as early as the 1770s and available in the early nineteenth century, is evidence that this symbol of the consumer revolution was spreading downward. We can risk saying that in the nineteenth century, pretend tea parties became so much a part of children's play that the Mad Hatter's tea party Alice attended in Lewis Carroll's *Alice's Adventures in Wonderland* (1865), "an American success from the start," was instantly recognizable in the literate Anglo-American world. Calling the historic event the "tea party" enabled the genteel to reduce it to child's play.[13]

In these reductions of class, gender, and age, "tea party" can be read in two contradictory ways: as mocking a genteel custom or as a playful way of making the most revolutionary event of the era "safe." For conservatives, using "tea party" may have helped to tame the inherent radicalism of the event for popular consumption. We are on the way to its codification in the *Oxford English Dictionary* as "a humorous name for the revolutionary proceeding in 1773" and to its inclusion in dictionaries of slang. Of course, over time, as "tea party" passed into common usage, high and low, verbal and written, the term was taken for granted so that it either had no meaning or assumed whatever political inflection the user attached to it. The term had a protean quality; it could serve a plebeian purpose by parodying the rich or it could serve a conservative purpose by reducing a revolutionary action to child's play.[14]

Perhaps, but not quite. There were accommodating conservatives and fearful conservatives. Later in the century, such ardent keepers of the conservative flame as the members of the Massachusetts Historical Society, would remain extraordinarily sensitive to the political implications of names given to the events of the Revolution, especially after they were claimed by the hoi polloi. Robert C. Winthrop and others would continue to refer to "the destruction of the tea," and put the tea party in quotation marks (suggesting the "so-called" tea party), just as they referred to the "so-called" Boston Massacre, establishing their distance not only from the vulgar but also from the events themselves.[15]

What did it mean, finally, in the second quarter of the century to bring back the tea party in which Americans "played Indian"? The Indian disguise was not emphasized. Noah Webster, for example, did not ask children in the catechism to his textbook, "Why did the patriots disguise themselves as Indians?" But this aspect was increasingly represented in visual depictions after Currier and Ives's vivid lithograph of the event appeared in the mid-1840s. We are left to speculate. The tea party was not revived while Indians threatened Americans—not in the 1790s in the midst of Indian wars in the Northwest, not in the War of 1812 when the country was battling Tecumseh. In the 1830s the country carried out Andrew Jackson's removal of the Cherokees from Georgia. And U.S. Supreme Court Justice Joseph Story of Massachusetts could say of Indians that "by a law of nature they seemed destined to a slow but steady extinction." In Boston playgoers watched the dying Indian chieftain Metamora on the stage. Only when the stereotype of "the vanishing Indian" was in place was it safe to "play Indian."[16]

[8]

The Appropriation of a Shoemaker

And what of poor George Robert Twelves Hewes, who, in the course of this exploration of the discovery and etymology of the tea party, we have left stranded in his stagecoach on the way from Providence to Boston, poised to enter the "cradle of liberty" in July of 1835? If now, in the context of competing conservative and radical claims to the Revolution, we revisit the ways in which Hewes was presented to the public in 1835 by politicians at Fourth of July observances, by the painter Joseph Cole in a portrait ready for public display in July, and by Benjamin Bussey Thatcher in his biography appearing later in the year, I would argue that Hewes was put to conservative uses.

If Hewes was aware of the competing claims for the Revolution swirling up from below in Boston, he gave no sign of it. He was, in a sense, a real-life Rip Van Winkle who had lived for some thirty years after the war in sleepy rural Wrentham and for the twenty years since 1815 in Richfield Springs, a hamlet sixty miles west of Albany. The reporter for the *Traveller* added several touches relevant to his memory I did not catch earlier: "His memory, in reference to any event that occurred in 'the times that tried men's souls' [i.e., the Revolution] is singularly retentive, and he

In his oil portrait painted in 1835, which he called "The Centenarian," Joseph Cole celebrated Hewes for his age, hale, happy, and respectably dressed, with no hint of either the famous event in which he took part or his life as a mechanic. *Courtesy Bostonian Society.*

recounts his various exploits with great perspicuity and distinctness." This we knew. "But later and passing events are soon forgotten," he wrote, drawing a distinction between long-term and short-term memory that psychologists now recognize as a commonplace in the elderly. "His hearing," the reporter added, "is considerably impaired, and one has to elevate his voice to a pretty high key to be understood." He was not much of a reader, and we also know it was hard to talk to him. The implication of all this is that Hewes had little opportunity to absorb the new currents running through the country from 1815 to 1835 and no incentive to encode them in his memory if he did. He had encoded his memory of events of the Revolution as he had experienced them and that's the way they stayed with him. In the construction of his memories, I don't think he was much affected by the historical events of the 1820s and 1830s.[1]

Nothing in his own experience would have prepared him, say, for a parade of a union of Boston journeymen shoemakers. As an apprentice in the 1760s, he became a master with a little shop of his own without having been a journeyman. And in rural Wrentham and frontier Otsego, it is not likely that he learned about the rash of turn-outs by journeymen cordwainers in six cities in the early 1800s, for which they were hauled before the court on charges of conspiracy. He arrived in a city full of dazzling wonders: a hotel with 180 rooms, water flowing through cast iron pipes, and gaslights in the City Hall. On July 4 two railroads and a steamboat line in the harbor offered holiday excursions out of the city.

"The fourth," several papers wrote in 1835, "was celebrated this year with more than usual interest" and an absence of partisanship. There was no assembly of the antislavery society as in 1834, possibly because the orgy of denunciation of abolitionists was intimidating to blacks. But the journeymen trades unions, which were in the midst of a strike, paraded again; craft contingents again carried banners and a float displayed a miniature ship, the whole affair, however, perhaps not quite as big and brassy as the one the year before. They ended up in the First Universalist Church, where they heard an oration that was "spirited and to the point" by Theophilus Fisk, champion of their strike. The ceremony Hewes attended in South Boston was the principal celebration for the city as a whole. South Boston, "the newest and most unsettled part of the city," was connected to Boston by two bridges; it had been annexed in 1804. It included Boston's other hill of Revolutionary fame, Dorchester Heights, which Washington had fortified by surprise in 1776, forcing the British to evacuate the city—the first American victory of the war.[2]

The South Boston celebration at a Baptist church was bipartisan and conservative. A procession included "the officers of the general, state and city governments" among them the lieutenant governor, officers and soldiers of the Revolution, several units of artillery, the militia, and citizens all shepherded by some fifty marshals. Hewes quite literally was supported by leaders of the Whig master mechanics: he walked into the church on the arm of Lieutenant Governor Samuel Armstrong, past president of the Mechanics Association and a wealthy printer who campaigned as "a mechanic and workingman." When he rose to accept the applause of the assemblage, he was supported on one side by Colonel Henry Purkitt, a cooper who as an apprentice was at the tea party, and on the other by Benjamin Russell, another past president of the Mechanics Association and a Federalist office holder, who for forty-four years was editor of the staunchly Federalist and Whig *Columbian Centinel*.[3]

Conservative Democrats had a hand in the affair. The orator of the day, Dr. Samuel Van Crowninshield Smith, the quarantine physician and a prolific medical writer, had written a campaign biography of Andrew Jackson in 1828. Hewes's nephew and host, Richard Brooke Hewes, was an inspector in the United States Customs House from 1829 to 1839, which patronage was dispensed by the conservative Democrat, David Hinshaw (thus showing him to be a Democrat), and, according to the family genealogist, "never an admirer of the mob that made the tea party" (thus making him a conservative Democrat like his fellow Customs House employee, Nathaniel Hawthorne). Dr. Smith's oration was conservative Jacksonianism. He praised a political system in which "the obscurest occupant of a hut may aspire to the highest places of distinction" and there were no limits to a native-born citizen, "however humble," in his "onward and upwards march." But he eschewed all talk of a "monied aristocracy" as the "bugbear of a politically disturbed imagination." In America "the rich and the poor are mutually dependent on each other."[4]

There was nothing about the speech or the festivities that "the Honorable Abbott Lawrence," the recently elected Whig congressman from Boston, could fault. At the dinner Lawrence, whose father had fought at Bunker Hill, toasted the memory of patriots of the Revolution. A leading merchant, a leading mover of the Boston Associates (whose portrait depicted a bucolic industrial mill town in the background), Lawrence was a major domo in the Whig party, its "guiding genius" in the 1840s, under whose tutelage Boston Whigs were learning to masquerade as commoners. They elected as governor John Davis, a cosmopolitan lawyer who campaigned as "the furrow turner" and "Huge Paws." The year before, Lawrence had squired Davy Crockett through his mill in Lowell, Tennessee's frontier congressman, self-created as "a half horse half alligator sort of man," and a Whig apostate from Jacksonian democracy. The Whigs were well on the way to the log cabin and hard cider presidential campaign of 1840, which in Boston would be decked out with all the imagery of Bunker Hill.[5]

As Hewes walked into the packed church, the Whig *Daily Atlas* reported, "high and low did him homage and heads were almost involuntarily uncovered as he approached." Hewes "was seated on a platform in front of the pulpit" and "when the orator had occasion to speak of the destruction of the tea in Boston harbor"—using the old, dignified term proper to the occasion—"he alluded to the venerable patriot who arose and received the united and enthusiastic congratulations of the audience." Afterwards, there was a procession to Mt. Washington on Dorchester Heights, where some six hundred were served dinner in a pavilion "within the old entrenchments." At the dinner, Hewes "requested permission of the President of the day" to offer a remark and then made his emotional toast.[6]

In defining Hewes, age had replaced class and citizenship. Smith's comments about Hewes were a replay of Daniel Webster's words to the veterans at Bunker Hill. A newspaper had reported that Hewes was born September 5, 1735, so that on July 4 he "will want only 63 days of being one hundred." In speaking of him as a man "on the verge of eternity," Smith celebrated Hewes not for his actions in the Revolution but for his age. "How wonderful!—nearly one hundred years of age—yet in the full possession of his faculties," he intoned, ignoring the newspaper account of Hewes's deafness. "Venerable old man! May heaven's blessings rest upon your frosted head," said Smith. "Though you come to the land of childhood leaning upon a staff and feeling your dependence on the charities of a selfish world, you are surrounded by friends. . . . May your last days be peaceful and happy."[7]

Joseph Cole's portrait of Hewes portrayed him in a similar vein. Cole was an up-and-coming young portrait painter: one of his next commissions was John Davis, president of the Massachusetts Historical Society and U.S. Attorney. He commanded a fee, which was paid by a member of the Hewes family. Begun July 4, by mid-July the oil painting was on display at the gallery of the Boston Athenaeum, "a place of fashionable resort" where Cole had recently exhibited his work, not exactly a site journeymen mechanics were likely visit. It would hang for a while amid portraits of Washington and Webster and landscapes by European masters. The portrait then went to relatives in Massachusetts. Painter, family sponsors, prospective audience (as well as the sitter, who had a stake in his own persona) all combined to present a most respectable Hewes.[8]

The portrait was called *The Centenarian*, not *The Patriot* or *The Citizen*. It gave no hint that Hewes had been a shoemaker all his life. He was not shown with either a tool or an emblem of his trade as a good many workers had themselves painted and soon photographed in the nineteenth century, much less as a craftsman at his bench, as Copley had portrayed Paul Revere (although his portrait of the lawyer John Davis a year later would portray his sitter holding a law book). Nor was there a clue, as a reporter bluntly put it, that "the venerable patriot is in very destitute circumstances." And Cole obviously did not make use of a scene through an open window, a common trope in portraits of the era, to suggest the iconic event with which Hewes was associated. Cole did not even portray the deep wound on Hewes's forehead made in 1774 by John Malcolm's cane, which left an "indentation" Thatcher in 1835 found as "plainly perceptible as it was sixty years ago."[9]

The painting, while immensely flattering to Hewes, was also reassuring to the viewer. There was nothing in it to offend the sensibilities of the ladies and gentlemen who visited the Athenaeum gallery. Hewes's face was not nearly as wrinkled as it was in an engraving made for James Hawkes's biography the previous year, and his head not nearly as shriveled as in a painting completed a few years later. He was shown as a happy old man with a twinkle in his eye, leaning on a cane, a signifier of both age and gentility. Although the portrait clearly conveyed Hewes's triumph in his survival, it comforted the viewer to see that he looked so hale and that his clothes were not threadbare. The painting congratulated the viewer: America took care of its veterans.

The biography by Benjamin Bussey Thatcher (writing under the pseudonym "A Citizen of Boston"), the third medium to present Hewes to the city, reflected a far more conservative response to the radical challenges of the day than I recognized when I first wrote about Hewes. Thatcher brought to Hewes "the same compassion for the lowly and a sense of the uses of history" that he brought to his biographies of Indian chieftains and the African American poet Phillis Wheatley, but the scholarship of this very present-minded historian served respectable causes. Thatcher (1809–1840) grew up in Maine, where his father, Samuel, the son-in-law of no less a personage than General Henry Knox and Federalist sheriff of Lincoln county, had put down the rebellions of angry settlers against the great land proprietor. Sheriff Thatcher "awoke one morning," Alan Taylor writes, "to find that overnight the insurgents had thoughtfully left an open coffin on his doorstep." Bowdoin College, which young Thatcher attended, was founded as an outpost of "civilization" among such barbarians. There he absorbed attitudes toward New England's revolutionary heritage akin to those that would be demonstrated by his fellow students of the Class of 1825, Nathaniel Hawthorne and Henry Wadsworth Longfellow. In Boston in his early twenties, as a lawyer who defined himself as a writer, he was a would-be member of the genteel literary circle connected with the Federalist/Whig *North American Review*. "He numbered most of the prominent authors of America among his friends," a biographer reports.[10]

Thatcher was antislavery but no abolitionist, a term I originally used too loosely. He was a leader of the young men's branch of the American Colonization Society, whose goal was the voluntary removal of free blacks to Africa—a plan that drew enthusiastic support from leading southern slaveholders—and editor of their journal in 1833–34. In Boston, abolitionists like William Lloyd Garrison and colonizationists were at loggerheads. For Thatcher the chief aim of the Society was to make Liberia "a desirable home for the free colored man," and he offered his volume of the poems of Phillis Wheatley as proof of the "African intellect" that might arise in "a region now overspread with an intellectual and moral midnight." His compassion for the lowly oozed condescension. He wrote a "Prayer for the Blind" that was printed on a piece of satin and sold to raise funds for the Institution for the Blind. In no fewer than three books on Indians, he portrayed their customs sympathetically but regarded them "as an extraordinary but unfortunate people" in the process of "disappearance"—the stereotype of the "vanishing Indian." He saved his praise for those who became Christian and "civilized."[11]

Thatcher, I think it is safe to say, was a Whig. He composed a hymn for the Whig dinner on July 4, 1834. His views—colonizing free blacks, sympathy to assimilating Indians, condescension to "the humble classes"—were Whig doctrine. Thatcher did not see or hear Hewes on July 4; he was off giving an oration in Brattleboro, Vermont. He began Hewes's biography on his return, and a Whig paper reported it ready for the press in late August. Given Whig elite hysteria about the mob at the time between the nativist riot of 1834 and the anti-abolitionist riot of 1835, putting down the mob of the Revolutionary era would have been on Thatcher's mind much more than I allowed.

This was the political context that required Thatcher to play down the mobs of the revolutionary era and minimize Hewes's involvement. But there was also a personal context. Hewes had become a celebrity in a surprisingly modern way. The newspapers reported his every move: Hewes went to church; Hewes was having his portrait painted; Hewes left for Maine to visit relatives; Hewes was the guest at a tea party in Augusta; Hewes sang songs in the stagecoach; Hewes returned. The portrait went on exhibit. A biography was under way; indeed, the family was supporting yet another biography. And then, a touch of tarnish on the persona he had been given: a paper reported that according to town records, Hewes was born August 25, 1742, which would make him nearly 93, not 100. The family then revealed that before he left, Hewes had recalled that he was christened in Old South. A grandson checked their records and found that the date was September 6, 1742. The family apologized. Neither they nor Hewes had any intention of deceiving the public. They were convinced "the old gentleman had forgotten his age."

Thatcher's challenge was to make an acceptable hero of the actor without condoning the actions. If he was to reach his fear-ridden readers, he had to distance himself from the mob and find a way to romanticize this lowly artisan. If he needed conservative literary exemplars, he had two in Hawthorne and Longfellow, his classmates at Bowdoin.[12]

Hawthorne offered a vision of the revolutionary era mob as nightmare. In his suspenseful short story "My Kinsman Major Molineux" (1831), Hawthorne amalgamated the most terrifying features of a decade of Boston street actions, which he saw through the eyes of Thomas Hutchinson's history, a book he had read. Robin, a young country boy on a visit to Boston, encounters a well-to-do kinsman as the victim of a horrifying mob, which has tarred and feathered and then carted him through the streets. Hawthorne combined elements of the generic Boston mob ("a mighty stream of people," "a band of fearful wind instruments,"

"shrill voices of mirth and terror"), the apocryphal avenging figure of "Joyce, Jun." leading ("a single horsemen clad in military
dress" with "a fierce and variegated countenance"), the tea party
("In his train were wild figures in the Indian dress and many fan-
tastic shapes without a model"), and the tarring and feathering of
John Malcolm. Hawthorne presented a "perception of tremen-
dous ridicule" of Major Molineux ("On they went like fiends that
throng in mockery around some dead potentate").[13]

Longfellow, by contrast, "a skillful purveyor of gentle, lovable
ideals," blended "the romantic, the sentimental and the moralis-
tic." In his poems, whether "The Building of the Ship," "The
Ropewalk," or ultimately, "Paul Revere's Ride," he sentimentalized craftsmen. He became a master of the romantic glow, as in
"The Village Blacksmith":

> Under a spreading chestnut tree
> The village smithy stands
> . . . .
> His brow is wet with honest sweat
> He earns what'er he can
> And looks the whole world in his face
> For he owes not any man.[14]

Thatcher took a leaf from both Hawthorne and Longfellow.
Although his picture of the mob was not nearly as dark as Hawthorne's, his language was often similar. At the Stamp Act, "the
flame" burst with "a fury"—"it came in the shape of a mob" and
"the ill humors . . . went on growing worse and worse till the
whole people became the *mob*." The destruction of Hutchinson's
house was "unjustifiable." But, it must be said, Thatcher did not
demonize townspeople, either at the Massacre or at the tarring
and feathering of Malcolm. He was at pains to separate the Tea
Party from the mob. It was "a *lawless* enterprise" but it was "the
only course for preventing more revolutionary and bloody re-

sults," which was also John Adams's stance. It was "an expression of the principles of a whole people;—facts alone sufficient to distinguish it from all *mobs*."[15]

Thatcher's sentimentalism, like Longfellow's, presented a sunny Hewes: the child as a lovable bad boy. By emphasizing his short size and long name, which made him the butt of ridicule, Thatcher created a comic figure. By dwelling on his advanced age, he obscured the youthful militant and allowed readers to admire the benign old man. In patronizing him as "one of the humble classes," Thatcher ignored the implications of Hewes's consistently bold, defiant actions, which were anything but deferential.

Thatcher's condescension toward Hewes stands in sharp contrast to James Hawkes's respect. Hawkes, as I have only recently discovered, was most likely James Hawkes of Richfield Springs, Otsego county, the town where Hewes lived. He was a country school teacher, then sheriff, then assemblyman, and in 1820–21 a congressman elected as a Republican. In the context of the political culture of the 1830s, his biography of 1834 has a distinctly democratic flavor. He thought Hewes as a boy had the same spirit of independence shown by the boy Andrew Jackson. He compared Hewes to other heroic soldiers, the three Westchester farmers who captured the treasonous Major André, and to Deborah Sampson Gannett, "the celebrated heroine." He saw Hewes as "obscure and illiterate," reflecting that "in the distribution of public favors the idle and powerful are generally preferred to the useful and obscure." Hawkes, moreover, allowed Hewes to speak at times in his own voice.[16]

Taken together, these Boston representations of Hewes—the venerable survivor of the Fourth of July, the centenarian of Cole's portrait, and the unmobbish patriot of Thatcher's memoir—served conservative ends. How might we test such a claim? By what historians call a counterfactual hypothesis. What if Hewes had been taken in hand by labor radicals when he appeared in Boston? And suppose he had arrived not in 1835 but, say, in time for July 4, 1834, when the trades unions celebration stole the day. What might have happened? The sixty-four journeymen bootmakers in the procession might have invited him to ride in a carriage with their contingent. From the platform in Fort Hill park, where the mechanics gathered, Hewes might have spoken of the memorable events that had taken place at the site: the burning of Pope's Day effigies, the bonfire the night of the Stamp Act protest, the rendezvous of a boarding party that sallied down to nearby Griffin's Wharf. Frederick Robinson, the orator, himself a former shoemaker, might have paid tribute to Hewes as an illustrious member of the "gentle craft." And, as the author of the law abolishing imprisonment for debt, Robinson might have pointed to Hewes as a man who could no longer be imprisoned for a paltry debt, as he once was. He most certainly would have noted the injustice of granting a veteran a pension of sixty dollars per year in a city of "monied aristocracy." And at the dinner at Faneuil Hall, Seth Luther would surely have toasted him as one of the "combination" of mechanics that threw the tea overboard and made the Revolution possible.

What if the painter intended the portrait of Hewes not for an audience at the Athenaeum but for Faneuil Hall, frequented by every Tom, Dick, and Harry, where it might hang on a wall next to Copley's Samuel Adams and John Hancock. Or suppose he thought of it as hanging in the tavern on the site of the old Liberty Tree? What if Hewes had been painted for such venues, and not by young Joseph Cole but by, for example, John Neagle of Philadelphia, who in 1827 had portrayed Pat Lyon, the Jeffersonian blacksmith/locksmith at his forge in his leather apron (a painting that hung in the Athenaeum Gallery). Through the window Neagle showed the courthouse, the scene of Lyon's triumph over an unjust, politically inspired Federalist prosecution. Hewes would not have wanted himself portrayed at his cobbler's bench, but he would have pointed with pride to a background scene of himself and his "associates" drowning the tea in Boston harbor.

And what if his biography had been written not by Benjamin Bussey Thatcher but by the young George Bancroft, the intellectual who was then in a full flush of sympathy with the radical labor movement? In 1834, Bancroft filled his notebooks with such aphorisms as "The farmers achieved the Revolution aided by the mechanics" and "The furtherance of our liberty rests on the mechanics." (Bancroft, we know, acquired the Hawkes *Memoir* of Hewes, but when is unknown.) Had Bancroft come in from Northampton to Boston and met Hewes, he might have portrayed him for what he had been: a shoemaker, an active member of the mechanic class, and a would-be citizen of a democracy in the making.

Set against this counterfactual portrayal, the actual appropriations of Hewes came at a price. They erased Hewes's membership in a class, minimized his agency in making history, and dismissed his aspirations for equality. As it was, Hewes gained the kind of recognition no other ordinary Bostonian of the Revolutionary era had received (or has received since): hero of the day on the Fourth of July, a portrait eventually displayed in a public place, and not one but two biographies. Moreover the recovery of this survivor and his testimony in the as-told-to memoirs played a part in the recovery of the tea action in public memory and the transformation of "the destruction of the tea" into "the tea party." What they made of him in Boston in 1835 is not necessarily what others made of him then or later. Nor need it be what we make of him today.

[9]

Into History: The Ongoing
Contest for the Revolution

In 1873, at the centennial celebrations of the Tea Party in Boston, it was clear that the event was secure in public memory as an icon of the Revolution, that it *was* the "tea party" (to all but a handful of "saints," as they called themselves, in the Massachusetts Historical Society), and that the contest between left and right for the meaning of the event would continue.[1]

Nothing better illustrates the tea action's hold on the popular imagination than the way Chicago seized on David Kennison as "the last survivor." In 1848, Chicagoans were so desperate for a link to the Revolution and so credulous that they embraced Kennison, who migrated to the burgeoning city advertising himself as 112 years old, a participant at the Tea Party, and a veteran of every battle from Lexington to Yorktown. In reality, Kennison was only nine or so in 1773 (which put him in his eighties in the later 1840s), he may have served in the army late in the war, and he seems to have been a veteran of the War of 1812. A laboring man down on his luck and injured, he opened a museum in downtown Chicago and charged admission. He was the chief exhibit,

Boston's Young Women's Christian Association celebrated the 1873 Tea Party Centennial with a tea party at which men dressed as Mohawks and women in colonial garb sold miniature chests of tea. From *Frank Leslie's Illustrated Weekly*. *Courtesy Newberry Library*.

along with a vial of tea he attested was from the Tea Party—a bittersweet story. In 1852, thousands turned out for the funeral of this man they presumed to be 115 years old to give him full military honors.[2]

In crowd actions in the decades before the Civil War the Tea Party joined effigy burning and tarring and feathering in the repertoire of popular rituals from the Revolution that ordinary people could call upon. In the cities, as David Grimsted concluded after an exhaustive study of rioting, "sometimes the tea party was invoked and often general precedents" of the Revolution justifying violence but not often Indian disguises. In Philadelphia in the mid-1830s, for example, an anti-abolitionist mob lugged antislavery pamphlets out to the Delaware River, tore them up, and threw them into the water. In Cincinnati a town meeting encour-

Bostonians streaming into a mass meeting at Old South Meeting House in 1876 at the eleventh hour to protest the threatened demolition of the building, here bedecked with banners and slogans. *Courtesy Old South Meeting House/Old South Association.*

aging anti-abolitionist action praised "the noble and fearless example set for us" by Boston patriots.[3]

The "downrent" movement that toppled the anachronistic landlord system of the Hudson Valley in the 1840s was unusual in appropriating both the Tea Party and the Indian persona. In agrarian protests the Indian disguise predated the tea party and continued after the Revolution, drawing on deeper Anglo-American traditions of "rough music," commonly known in America as "skimmingtons" and "riding a man on a rail." Indian "posturing and costuming," Alan Taylor tell us, "was typical of Vermont's Green Mountain boys and Pennsylvania Whiskey Rebels and Wild Yankees," as well as of the Liberty Men in Maine who assumed a full "white Indian counterculture" in their land struggles with "great men" proprietors like Henry Knox.[4]

In a movement that at its height embraced fifty thousand farmers in eleven Hudson Valley counties, as many as ten thousand men disguised as Indians organized in small bands to conduct guerrilla warfare against evictions, attempted auctions, and arrests. They wore elaborate Indian regalia and masks, and bonded through secret rituals. The movement turned to the Tea Party as justification for extralegal action. As Dr. Smith Boughton, their leader, explained, "Our all was at stake. The law was on their [the landlords] side and we were at their mercy. We resolved to adopt the same kind of protection resorted to by the people of Boston [when the tea] was thrown into the harbor."[5]

Meanwhile, the Tea Party was making its way into the culture of respectable mainstream America, betokened by the lithograph of the event produced by Currier and Ives, the country's chief publishers of cheap, popular pictures, and the books of George Bancroft, America's most popular historian. The Tea Party was the only prewar event of the Revolution Currier and Ives chose to

Currier and Ives's 1846 lithograph gives the viewer his favorable opinion of the destruction of the tea by looking at the "Indians" aboard the ships from the perspective of the respectable cheering crowd on the wharf. *Courtesy Chicago Historical Society.*

illustrate. Nathaniel Currier's lithograph, first issued in 1846, was sold for decades at the firm's store in New York City and by peddlers throughout the country (6 cents wholesale, 15 to 25 cents retail, fully tinted at slightly additional cost). Currier, an apprentice to a Boston lithographer, grew up in the midst of the city's revived awareness of the tea action. He clung to the traditional, more dignified title, "The Destruction of the Tea at Boston Harbor" (Currier and Ives did not joke about American history) but made it into a safe, romanticized scene suitable for the parlors of middle-class Americans.[6]

Unlike the first American engravings of the 1830s, which emphasized either a tea ship or the crowd on the dock, Currier's lithograph combined the two: The large and enthusiastic crowd, all men in gentlemen's clothing, wave tricornered hats, cheering on the handful of "Indians" aboard the ships. But the scene is overrun with historical inaccuracies: there were three ships, not two; those gathered on the docks stood in awed silence; only a minority on the ships were disguised as Indians (and few would have risked such nakedness in Boston's December weather); they did not drop sealed chests into the water but broke them open with axes and threw them overboard with the tea; and, to top it all, the actual boarding occurred at night, the darkness broken only by lanterns and the light of the moon. In exercising artistic license, Currier recast what might otherwise have appeared threatening. Because viewers witness the action through the eyes of the crowd whose size and appearance suggest majority approval and respectability, they are unlikely to regard it as radical or bizarre. Yet for all this sanitizing, it was still the "tea party": bold, wild, extralegal. People could make of it what they would.

By the time George Bancroft (1800–1891) reached the Tea Party in the 1850s, in volume six of his ten-volume history of the United States, he was already America's Herodotus, unrivaled among historians in scholarly reputation or sales. Not surprisingly, given the trajectory of his politics, Bancroft provided a synthesis of radical and conservative readings of the Revolution. The radical intellectual with a doctorate from the University of Göttingen who in the 1830s had fled stultifying Boston for Northampton was in the 1850s a Jacksonian Democrat mellowed by years of political power as chieftain of the Democratic Party of Massachussets, Secretary of the Navy in James K. Polk's cabinet, and then minister to England. Bancroft's history, it was said then and has been said since, "voted for Andrew Jackson." He admired "the people"—when they followed their leaders. He erased the mechanics politically from the Revolution as had the Jacksonian Democrats, who swallowed the working man's movement whole.

He removed the patriots "playing Indian," as one might expect from a devotee of Jackson, architect of Indian removal, nor were African Americans an active presence in his narrative.[7]

But for all this, Bancroft legitimated the tea action in the American historical narrative. He devoted an entire chapter to "The Boston Tea Party," exalting December 16, 1773, as "a day by far the most momentous in [Boston's] annals." In his dramatic account Bancroft reserved a place of honor for the bold leaders guiding "the spirit of the people." He devoted most of the chapter to the meetings in Old South and no more than a paragraph to the action at Griffin's Wharf, yet it was a rendering that would have delighted Samuel Adams, John Adams, and possibly George Hewes.[8]

In Boston the contest for the memory of the Revolution emerged starkly during the centennial celebrations of 1873, which showed uncanny parallels with the lineup of the 1830s. There were three major public celebrations as well as a private gathering by the historical society. At each public event the sponsors served tea, blissfully unaware of the irony of consuming the very beverage whose destruction they were celebrating.[9]

On December 15 at Faneuil Hall, the Woman's Suffrage Association introduced the theme by draping an evergreen banner reading "Taxation Without Representation Is Tyranny" across the stage. The galleries were jammed, a paper reported: "there were old ladies, young ladies, middle-aged ladies, colored ladies . . . in fifteen minutes every seat had its occupant." The speakers were the old warhorses of abolition and reform, Thomas Wentworth Higginson, who presided, Wendell Phillips, William Lloyd Garrison, and Frederick Douglass, and two stalwarts of women's rights, Lucy Stone and Mary Livermore. "If Sam Adams could speak today," said Phillips, reprising the metaphor from his maiden speech in 1837, he would "stand exactly where he did in his age—at the very head of the van of the reformers of his age," in favor of woman suffrage and with those who were trying "to prevent money from accumulating in the aristocratic class."

The next day, December 16, at the city-sponsored celebration that also packed Faneuil Hall, "the oldest [Boston] families were fully represented." Mayor Josiah Quincy, grandson of the Revolutionary patriot, presided. In the principal address, Robert C. Winthrop, the long-term Whig/Republican congressman and long-term president of the Massachusetts Historical Society, a foe of mobs for forty years, all but disavowed what he still called "the destruction of the tea." Winthrop raced though the action of December 16, 1773, in a few sentences. "We are not here today I think to glory over a mere act of violence, or a merely successful destruction of property." Children should not be taught that "anything but evil and mischief and wrong is to be accomplished by a resort to lawless violence." In an act of historical revisionism, Winthrop claimed that "we know not exactly . . . whether any of the patriot leaders of the day had a hand in the act. It seemed to have been performed by a spontaneous rising of the young blood of the town from the workshops and the printing offices of men like Benjamin Edes and Paul Revere."[10]

The third major public celebration, sponsored by the Young Women's Christian Association (YWCA) in Tremont Temple, was, in effect, a parody of the Tea Party. The atmosphere was festive, the participants well-dressed. Young women in "ye olde costumes" served tea and men as "young Mohawks in the dress of the native tribe" distributed miniature souvenir chests of tea. With the United States Army out west, pacifying the plains Indians, in Boston it was safe to "play Indian." The orator of the day, however, was sensible of the mission of the recently founded

YWCA, whose Boston branch provided a shelter and an employment bureau for working women. General Nathaniel Banks, former governor, congressman, and Union officer, made an appeal to extend "a helping hand" to "the working women of the city," chastising well-to-do women for displaying "criminal extravagance" in the midst of unemployment, hunger, and suffering. During all this, the audience faced a stage decorated with a banner saying "Boston Tea Party, December 16, 1773," and to one side, the 1835 oil portrait of George Hewes labeled "The Last Survivor of the Tea Party."

On the evening of the official celebration, the historical society conducted a genteel anticelebration in the home of a granddaughter of Josiah Quincy of Revolutionary fame. President Winthrop presided. Relics of the Tea Party were displayed: a bottle with tea from December 16, 1773, John Adams's diary opened to his conservative defense of the action, Quincy's speech on the Port Bill, and a silver bowl bearing the Quincy coat of arms. Winthrop said he was more proud to be associated with Quincy's "eloquent and noble plea for moderation . . . than with the act itself on Griffin's Wharf," which in any case he thought was the work of "a volunteer band of Liberty-Boys," without the sanction of their leaders. The historian Richard Frothingham was a shade more sympathetic because the action did not have "a single feature of a riot." Oliver Wendell Holmes, by then Boston's poet laureate, added the only jarring democratic note of the evening by reading his "Ballad of the Tea Party." It was a tribute to "our old Northenders" who gathered "from stall and workshop" to do the job: "the cooper' boys" and "ship yard lads," the "lusty young Fort Hillers," the "prentice crew" from the ropewalk. What would Holmes's genteel listeners make of his gentle play on the rituals of upper-class tea parties?

An evening party,—only that,
No formal invitation,
No gold-laced coat, no stiff cravat,
No feast in contemplation,
No silk-robed dames, no fiddling band,
No flowers no songs no dancing—
A tribe of red men, axe in hand
Behold the guests advancing.[11]

In the *Proceedings* of the historical society, the event remained "the tea party"—in quotation marks.

At the centennial of Independence in 1876, the radical-conservative divide over the meaning of the Revolution and how its memory should be perpetuated was once again epitomized by Robert Winthrop and Wendell Phillips. The celebration took place in the third year of a great depression, and Boston's conservative elite seemed as haunted by the threat of social upheaval as they had been in 1765–75 and 1834–35. It was also the moment when two of the three public buildings of the Revolution, Old South and the Old State House, were threatened with demolition. In June 1876, Old South, abandoned by its wealthy congregation for a site in the Back Bay, had been auctioned off and was on the verge of being dismantled for salvage. The Committee on Streets of the Board of Alderman voted to remove the Old State House to improve traffic. The city of Chicago, ever searching for a link to the Revolution, offered to buy it.

Winthrop, the official town orator, devoted most of his Faneuil Hall address—which droned on for hours and took up ten columns of newsprint—to a state-by-state tribute to the great men of the Continental Congress for the achievement of Independence. He omitted Boston's great public events, however, save by negation. The Revolution "was no wild breaking away from all authority. . . . It was no mad revolt against every thing like government." Winthrop granted that "doubtless our Boston mobs did not always move 'to the Dorian mood of flutes and soft recorder.' But in all our deliberative assemblies . . . there was respect for the great principles of Law and Order." He called for a renewal of "the spirit of subordination and obedience to law."[12]

Winthrop seemed reconciled to the demise of the threatened buildings. "If these sacred edifices . . . are indeed destined to disappear, let us see to it that some corner of their sites, at least, be consecrated to monuments which shall tell their story, in legible lettering, to our children." Winthrop's ideal was Bulfinch's chaste doric column of 1790, which he had petitioned the state to reproduce in a replica. He now proposed a joint statue of John Adams and Thomas Jefferson, "side by side and hand in hand."

By contrast, Wendell Phillips, in an oration at Old South in June at the eleventh hour—to some the most eloquent of his long career—pleaded passionately to save the meetinghouse as a living monument. "You spend forty thousand dollars here, and twenty thousand dollars there to put up a statue of some old hero. . . . But what is a statue of Cicero compared to standing where your voice echoes from pillar to wall that actually heard his philippics?" It was not only that Old South echoed with the eloquence of Otis, Adams, Warren, and Quincy but that it was associated with the great popular events of the era. It stood near State Street, "just below where [Crispus] Attucks fell (our first martyr), and just above where zealous patriots made a teapot of the harbor." Phillips's liberalism was at an opposite pole from Winthrop's conservatism. "What does *Boston* mean?" he asked. "Since 1630 the living fibre running through history which owns the name means jealousy of power, unfettered speech, keen sense of justice, readiness to champion any good cause. That is the Boston

[Archbishop] Laud suspected, [Lord] North hated and the negro loved."[13]

Phillips peroration stood the conventional picture of leaders and followers in the Revolution on its head. "It was the mechanics of Boston that threw the tea into the dock; it was the mechanics of Boston that held up the hands of Sam Adams; it was the mechanics of Boston, Paul Revere one of them, that made the Green Dragon immortal. . . . the men that carried us through the revolution were the mechanics of Boston. . . . It was the message of the mechanics of Boston that Sam Adams carried to the governor and to Congress. They sent him to Salem and Philadelphia; they lifted and held him up." Phillips proposed that Old South be preserved as a "Mechanics Exchange" for "the common run of the people—the bone and muscle" of the city.

Old South was saved, thanks especially to the fund-raising activities of women, and became a museum. The aldermen spared the Old State House and the building, restored to its 1830 condition, housed a museum established by the newly formed Bostonian Society. The long neglected popular side of the Revolution, it seemed, was receiving its due. A statue to Samuel Adams was put up—"A Patriot / He Organized the Revolution"—while a plaque called him "The Father of the Revolution." At the site of the Massacre, a circle of paving stones was embedded in the road. Under the auspices of the new patriotic societies, plaques went up all over town honoring John Hancock, the Cromwell's Head, the Green Dragon, and the Salutation (taverns where various caucuses had met). The site of Griffin's Wharf, now inland, was marked, as was a house in which one group of men disguised themselves for the Tea Party.[14]

A monument to the martyrs of the Boston Massacre, erected in 1888, registered the state of the public memory of the Revolution much as Bulfinch's Beacon Hill monument had in 1790. Since the 1850s, Boston's African American community, with the support of abolitionists like Phillips, had campaigned unsuccessfully for a monument to Crispus Attucks. In 1887, in response to their renewed petitions, which now had the support of leading citizens and Boston's Irish mayor, the state legislature authorized the sum of ten thousand dollars for a monument on the Common and headstones in the Granary Burying Ground to honor all five martyrs. The "saints" of the MHS were beside themselves. To the society's president, Charles Francis Adams, "the so called massacre" was the result of a riotous mob, to be distinguished from the "peaceful, earnest, patriotic protest and resistance by our wise and resolute popular leaders." One member claimed that "the so-called victims were the aggressors," another thought "a monument to perpetuate the fame of rioters was preposterous," and still another held that "the martyrs crown" was being placed "on the brow of the vulgar ruffian." The society's belated protest to the governor, however, was to no avail and the monument went up. A female figure of "Free America" held aloft a broken chain of oppression, above her the names of the five martyrs and at eye level a bronze bas-relief depicting the massacre adapted from Paul Revere's engraving. It was popularly known as the Crispus Attucks monument.[15]

Where was George Hewes in this contest? His portrait, as we have noted, was displayed on the stage at the YWCA celebration, amid Mohawk Indians and philanthropic ladies. He was identified as "the last survivor of the tea party," his ticket to immortality. In 1885, the Bostonian Society bought the Cole portrait of Hewes from a grandson and hung it in their new museum in the Old State House. The Hewes family genealogist gave the shoemaker an enthusiastic write-up in a thick compendium of the many generations of the Heweses. And in the last quarter of the century Hewes was treated with deference in the sometimes garbled accounts of standard histories of the Revolution, the Tea Party, and Boston.[16]

Perhaps because of such recognition, Hewes, like the other "vulgar ruffians," rankled the MHS. In a long diatribe about "recollections as a source of history" in their *Proceedings*, Edward Pierce singled out Hewes's memoirs as a prime example of "the untrustworthiness of old men's memories." A conservative lawyer known for his treatises on railroad law, Pierce invoked standards of the courtroom that would rule out most historical evidence. The list of participants published in Thatcher's appendix was "worthless," he wrote, because "no person was identified upon any evidence on which a plaintiff or prosecutor could expect a verdict." Hewes's testimony was "impeached" by his insistence that Adams and Hancock were on board ship. The reason participants never talked about their action, he said, was because of "the instinctive shrinking of civilized people to confess a share in any deed of violence." At bottom, Pierce was hostile to the "the Boston Tea Party" itself, which he was careful to put in quotation marks.[17]

He was wrong, of course, on every count. Memories of the aged can be reliable even if they do not meet the criteria of the courtroom. In weighing evidence, a historian has to serve as defense attorney, prosecuting attorney, judge, and jury. What to the lawyer is flawed testimony to the historian often reveals the meaning of the event. Many "civilized people" like Hewes had talked about their participation in the Tea Party; the elites had not listened. Other participants did not talk about it because they believed no one considered the event important. It took more than half a century for public memory to catch up with private memories. The Tea Party, lost, buried, and willfully forgotten in public memory, was recovered in the context of popular movements claiming the Revolution. Hewes was appropriated at the time to serve a conservative version of history, but other Americans were free to make of him what they would, as they still are. The Tea Party became an iconic event in public memory because men like Hewes came forward with their private memories. We are doubly in their debt—for what they did in history and for the history they have helped to recover.

Afterword

The place of the Tea Party in American history is assured. It is an American icon, a sacred moment if ever there was one. But what of George Robert Twelves Hewes, Mr. Man-in-the-Street, whose life is as full a record of an ordinary person in the American Revolution as we are likely to find? Hewes, was "discovered" in the 1830s, lost again, and then "recovered" in the 1980s to the extent that a historical publication can recover anyone. Now that we have found him once again, what do we do with him? Now that we know that the public memory of the Revolution was contested, how can it help us to understand and present history today?

These questions are part of a growing challenge to those who think of themselves as "keepers of the past" and accept responsibility for a more inclusive American history. As historians bring to light groups long excluded, or condescendingly treated only as victims, they are recovering the life stories of more and more "unknowns" and coming up with more and more unsung heroes and heroines. But when historians recover the lives of ordinary people who have played a part in great events we need to ask ourselves, How should we as a society recognize them in public memory?

The contest for the symbolism of the tea party goes on. In April 1998, two Republican congressmen prepare to dump a copy of the federal tax code from the tea party ship as two protesters shout, "Your tax will sink the working family." *Reprinted by permission of* Boston Globe.

As I jumped from the centennials of the 1870s to the bicentennials of the 1970s, I was struck by how, in the last quarter of the twentieth century, Americans, and Bostonians in particular, have continued to appropriate Boston's iconic events and to contest the public memory of the Revolution. Indeed, the best sign that the Tea Party has become a national icon is that it is claimed by people at so many points on the American political spectrum.

Take the confrontations in Boston in 1973 at the two-hundredth anniversary of the Tea Party. "Bicentennial in Tradition of Revolutionary America in More Ways Than One" ran the headline in the *Boston Globe*. The official celebration arranged for *Beaver II*, a replica of a tea ship built on the structure of a 1906

Danish brig, to be sailed to Boston for the occasion and docked near to what would have been Griffin's Wharf. There was a polite tea party at the Museum of Fine Arts and a dutiful ecumenical meeting in Old South conducted by religious leaders and attended by representatives of the Daughters of the American Revolution and the Girl Scouts, at which the principal speaker said he did not know "if the actual dumping of the tea was a good or bad idea." The National Organization for Women picketed for the Equal Rights Amendment and carried a banner proclaiming "Taxation without Equal Rights is Tyranny." Shades of 1873.[1]

At a jammed Faneuil Hall meeting, the crowd cheered speeches (one by Thomas Boylston Adams, a descendant of the revolutionary family) calling for the impeachment of President Richard Nixon and for action against oil companies profiteering in the energy crisis. As in 1773, before the last speaker had finished the audience joined a march to the harbor, this one organized by the People's Bicentennial Commission, along with environmentalists, the Disabled American Veterans, and the Boston Indian Council, the latter protesting negative stereotypes. At the tea ship there was an officially sponsored reenactment of the Tea Party. Then, six protestors in colonial garb boarded the *Beaver II*, hanged a tarred and feathered effigy of President Nixon, and finally dumped it and three empty oil drums into the harbor. The crowd, estimated by the police at close to forty thousand, cheered and dispersed.

The Tea Party continues to be claimed by left and right. In 1970, as the historian Howard Zinn remembers the event, "feelings about the war [in Vietnam] had become unbearably intense. In Boston about a hundred of us decided to sit down at the Boston Army Base and block the road used by buses carrying draftees off to military duty" as a "symbolic act." They were arrested for obstructing traffic, and when Zinn and seven others came to trial, they represented themselves. "We talked about how the American political system seemed incapable of stopping a war which was both unconstitutional and immoral. And therefore how acts of civil disobedience, in the great tradition of the Boston Tea Party and the anti-slavery actions were necessary." A year later, at a rally of fifty thousand on the Boston Common, Zinn spoke on the same theme, as he did at trials of others for acts of civil disobedience to the war.[2]

Almost thirty years later, in April 1998, the ultraconservative Republican House Majority leader from Texas and a fellow Congressman from Louisiana, crusading for tax reform, came to Boston, boarded *Beaver II*, the tea ship replica, put a copy of the federal tax code in a chest marked "tea," and dumped it in the harbor. But two protesters paddling by in a rubber raft marked "Working Family Liferaft" stole the show, shouting "Your tax will sink the working family" before they tipped over into the water. And so it goes and not only in Boston.[3]

Appropriations of the Boston Massacre, like the event itself, are grim. In 1970, after the National Guard fired into a peaceful demonstration at Kent State University in Ohio, killing several students, an antiwar poster took the stark photograph of a horror-stricken young woman leaning over a fallen student and superimposed it on Revere's iconic engraving of Bostonians shot down by troops in 1770.

In 1975, at the reenactment of the Massacre in Boston, Irish working-class opposition to court-ordered busing of African American children to the schools of South Boston and Charlestown and of their own children away from neighborhood schools, led to a bitter confrontation, described vividly by J. Anthony Lukas in a Pulitzer Prize–winning book. "Not surprisingly," writes

Lukas, "the violent anti-bussing demonstrations, the sight of police on horseback clattering through the narrow streets, the placards, banners and effigies, had stirred recollections of an earlier battle over men's rights." Charlestown's Irish were divided. Fourscore were members of a militia company who claimed the heritage of the Battle of Bunker Hill and were scheduled to perform at the Massacre reenactment. On the day of the event, "some 400 anti-bussing demonstrators loomed in the street. Led by two drummers beating a funeral dirge, eight black-clad pall bearers carried a pine coffin marked 'R.I.P. Liberty Born 1770–Died 1974.' Behind them came rank and upon rank of marchers, keening to the high pitched wail long used to mourn the Irish dead."[4]

At the site of the Massacre, in response to a plea from an Irish-American legislator, "the demonstrators grew still. The Massacre proceeded with Medford's 64th Regiment of Foot portraying the squadron of seven British soldiers who fired into the crowd of colonials, killing five of them. But as the shots echoed off the glass-and-steel skyscrapers, all 400 demonstrators dropped to the pavement, lying there for a moment as still as Liberty in her coffin, as if to say We too are victims."

On a recent visit to Boston, I was struck by the ways in which the Liberty Tree, from 1765 to 1775 the single most important symbol of the Revolution in Boston, has inspired quiet appropriation. The site of the Liberty Tree is not on the Freedom Trail even though it is only a few blocks from the major downtown sites. Located in "the Combat Zone," an area of porn shops, it is as much an embarrassment to the historical establishment as to its neighbors in Chinatown. A plaque on the ground across the street commemorates the tree, but the Liberty Tree building put up on the site in 1850 is still there, and if you look up above the second story, you see the old bas-relief carving of the Liberty Tree (touched up, it would seem, with a coat of fresh paint), proclaiming "Liberty 1766, Independence of Their Country, 1776," with "Law and Order" across its roots. On the adjoining building the bright yellow sign of the Royal Hotel (accompanied by Chinese script) spans the front, and on the ground floor another sign identifies the "Liberty Tree II Adult Entertainment Complex," a porn store. Over the entrance the owner has mounted a small replica of the Liberty Tree bas-relief, an act that appropriates the symbol on behalf of freedom of expression.[5]

As these few examples attest, it is not hard to see what keeps the public memory of the Revolution so alive and so contentious. Just as in the "jubilee" anniversaries of the 1820s and the centennials of the 1870s, official commemorations revive the memory of famous events and new movements embrace them, claiming the heritage of the Revolution. But in contrast to the first half-century after the Revolution, today a different mix of holidays, statues and monuments, and historic sites keeps public memory alive.

Bostonians celebrate their own holidays of the American Revolution: March 17 is Evacuation Day, marking the departure of British troops in 1776 (which conveniently coincides with St. Patrick's Day); the third Monday in April is Patriot's Day, for the encounters at Lexington and Concord (a field day for reenactors in the uniforms of local militias); June 17 is Bunker Hill Day, in commemoration of that battle. December 16, while not a holiday, is the occasion for an annual reenactment of the Tea Party.

Boston's public statues overwhelmingly convey a sense of history and serve as another reminder of the layers of commemorations by successive generations. Boston has to be the most bestatued city in the country, and the sway of past conservative public memory is strong. Even Bulfinch's Federalist column of 1790, pulled down when Beacon Hill was excavated in the 1820s, is resurrected behind the State House in a half-size replica erected in 1898 and including the tablets from the 1790 monument. But memorials now recognize Samuel Adams and the once-scorned martyrs of the Boston Massacre, as do prominent gravestones in the Granary Burying Ground, fittingly side by side. Statues honor not only Daniel Webster and Josiah Quincy, the establishment heroes of the nineteenth century, but the radical agitators Wendell Phillips and William Lloyd Garrison. And statues, too, are reclaimed by new movements. The monument erected in 1897 to pay homage to Robert Gould Shaw, the white commander of the Massachussetts Fifty-Fourth Regiment in the Civil War, is now the first stop on the Black Heritage Trail, honoring the black enlisted men who fought. And while John Winthrop, the Puritan colony's first governor, is exiled to the Back Bay (and Harvard Yard), Anne Hutchinson, the religious dissenter he banished to Rhode Island, and Mary Dyer, the Quaker the colony later hanged, occupy prominent places on the State House lawn and are included on the Boston Women's Heritage Trail.[6]

The major public buildings on Boston's Freedom Trail are the political sites where the Revolution was made. Old South Meeting House and the Old State House, almost demolished a century ago, have been rehabilitated and faithfully restored over the past decade, together with Faneuil Hall, thanks to tens of millions of dollars of federal money. And they are interpreted as sites of contention, Faneuil Hall for its historic debates, Old South as a venue for free speech, the Old State House as a place of legislative resistance to the British and as the site of the Massacre. Every December, a debate in Old South launches the march to the replica of the Tea Party ship, and during the year Old South plays host to ten thousand elementary and high school students who take part in a program called "Resisting for Justice." They debate the pros and cons of civil disobedience, first over destroying the tea in Old South, and then over disobeying the Fugitive Slave Law of 1850 in the African Meeting House.[7]

The now venerable Freedom Trail is not without its anachronisms and ironies. A thick red line running along sidewalks and streets, it links some sixteen sites, from the Common through downtown Boston and into the old North End, and out as far as Bunker Hill in Charlestown. Each time I have walked the Trail as it has changed over the past thirty years it is with a sense of wonder. As the city all around booms with one redevelopment after another, the Trail retains its historical integrity, resisting thus far the pressures of tourism to sanitize history. It is not Disneyland. It is not Colonial Williamsburg.[8] Yet it is true, as a recent report put it, that "when the Trail was first set up, the nation of 1950 emerging from World War II sought consensus and saw the American Revolution through its heroes and great events." The permanent exhibit in the Old State House, for example, which is organized around five "Leading Persons"—Thomas Hutchinson, John Hancock, James Otis, John Adams, and Samuel Adams—is a throwback to an older interpretation. It is as if in the transition "From Colony to Commonwealth," the exhibit theme, there were no rebels against patriot "leading persons," no Abigail Adams imploring her husband, John, to "remember the ladies" in making new laws and then enlisting Mercy Otis Warren (James Otis's sister) to "foment a rebellion" by women; no Mum Bett bringing a court suit for freedom from slavery and then adopting the name Elizabeth Freeman; no Isaac Backus urging Baptists to civil disobedience to win religious liberty from the established Congregational church; and no Daniel Shays demanding justice for debt-ridden western Massachusetts farmers.[9]

In the old North End, Longfellow's legendary Paul Revere, the midnight rider, casts a long shadow. People come to see the Old North Church, where the lanterns were hung, and are reassured by the heroic statue of Revere astride his horse. Paul Revere's house, restored a century ago by the Brahmin-led preservation movement to its seventeenth-century state, is now vigorously interpreted by the Paul Revere Memorial Association as the dwelling of an artisan and leader of artisans in the Revolution. With its next-door neighbor one of the two surviving colonial dwellings in the city, the house still cannot carry the burden of representing the North End's community of shipwrights and seamen, shoemakers and seamstresses of that era. No other houses, no workplaces, no taverns survive from the eighteenth century.[10]

Successful restorations, perhaps inevitably, tug against history. Boston's restored public buildings inspire reverence; the Revolution was irreverent. The sites are quiet; the Revolution was noisy. Indoors there are no passionate orators, no buzz of people vying for the floor. The Revolution also took to the streets, but outdoors no Indian war whoops or shrill whistles summon crowds to action. (On a recent visit, I viewed a temporary exhibit on the Boston Massacre in the Old State House that gave me a sense of the noise and chaos of the event the pavement marker outside cannot.) But how, amid the skyscraper caverns of a bustling downtown, could you convey the picketing boys, the massive funeral processions of men and women, the hanging of effigies, the tarring and feathering—the stuff of the popular revolution?

There is no plebeian presence on the Freedom Trail; for that matter, neither is there a patrician presence, terms familiar to a class-conscious eighteenth-century city. No homes of the aristocracy of the Revolutionary era survive. You would have to stare at the array of John Singleton Copley portraits in the Boston Museum of Fine Arts to sense the arrogance of the would-be ruling class of colonial Boston.[11] What a difference if the city had saved and preserved John Hancock's mansion in 1863. Then visitors might ask what kind of revolution it was that brought together, often literally, the richest man in Boston, a middling artisan like Revere, and a poor shoemaker like Hewes. And perhaps they might go on to ask what the words "all men are created equal" in the Declaration of Independence that Hancock signed so boldly meant to Hewes and the other unequals of colonial America.

Can George Robert Twelves Hewes stand for this missing plebeian presence? Perhaps. But how do you focus attention on an ordinary person unknown to visitors who come with no expectations? Revere survives because he is the stuff of legend, because his house, the silverware he crafted, and a portrait by Copley exist today. Phillis Wheatley survives as the first African American poet and one of America's first women poets because generations of crusaders for equal rights have won a place for her as a symbol of black achievement. Hewes's claim to fame in the nineteenth century was his reappearance as "the last survivor of the tea party" (which wasn't even true).

Once again, Hewes has arrived on the scene, so to speak, although with hardly the splash he made in 1835. His portrait, long hanging in the Old State House and then put in storage, is now back on display and a reproduction hangs in the tea ship museum. For several summers I have talked to Boston elementary school teachers about Hewes and shown the video *Tea Party Etiquette*, which dramatizes his life. The National Park Service's new guidebook to Boston in the Revolution, a model of the new history, features Hewes and other unknowns, and Park Service rangers know about him. An exhibit in Old South, "Voices of

Protest," will mount silhouettes of Hewes and Phillis Wheatley.[12]

And this brings us to consider how Hewes should be portrayed—in a museum exhibit, a classroom play, a dramatization for television, a movie? What moments should one choose from the life of this very unheroic-looking five-foot, one-inch man for a series of tableaus or living sculptures? He would have to be shown with other people (he never claimed to act alone), and surely not as "The Centenarian," the safe, ninety-year-old codger of 1835, or as a poor young cobbler in an artisan's leather apron at his bench as the sheriff serves him a writ for nonpayment of his debts and carts him off to jail. It would not be his choice. At the Liberty Tree, an effigy hanging from a branch, Hewes side by side with his fellow shoemaker Ebenezer McIntosh, "Captain General of the Liberty Tree"? Perhaps. On the street the night of the Massacre, angry but unarmed, at the moment shots ring out: Hewes aghast at the carnage, catching a wounded James Caldwell in his arms? In Old South at six o'clock on December 16, 1773, on his feet cheering Samuel Adams's closing remarks, perhaps giving the whistle for the boarding parties to assemble?

How about at the railing of a tea ship, his face smeared with soot, side by side with a gentleman whose ruffles peek out from his Indian disguise (someone who could be taken for John Hancock), the two of them axing open a chest of tea and about to heave it into the harbor? If there is only one choice, I suspect that this would be his, a moment of equality between plebeian and patrician. Perhaps at the tarring and feathering of John Malcolm, his head bandaged from the blow Malcolm dealt him, rushing after the crowd with a blanket to cover the victim. Or during the war, on a dock after he has agreed to serve on the *Hancock*, telling a ship's officer he would not take his hat off for any man. Isn't it remarkable at how many important points Hewes appears and how little he fits the stereotypes of "motley rabble" or "vulgar ruffian"? Why not an entire exhibit devoted to Hewes: "The Man in the Street in the American Revolution"?

An exhibit about Hewes would say that ordinary people were there playing a part in important events. But does this say enough? How did their presence change the story or affect the outcome? "Revolutions always begin with the populace," Wendell Phillips said in 1851, in pleading for a monument to Crispus Attucks, "never with the leaders. They argue, they resolve, they organize; it is the populace that, like the edge of the cloud, shows the lightning first."[13] His sweeping claims about revolutions aside, Phillips got to the nub of the matter. In a time of upheaval, ordinary people make events possible, and they have done so time and time again in American history.

But to do justice to men like Hewes and their impact you would have to depict political events in which such men and women were "a presence" even though they were not "present." I am not posing a riddle. The American Revolution was not a plebeian revolution, but there was a powerful plebeian current within it. Patricians all over "had to learn to yield to the torrent if they hoped to direct its course," as one of them so aptly put it.[14] Massachusetts's patriot leaders mastered this strategy, each in different ways, John Hancock by a patronizing noblesse oblige, Samuel Adams by democratic politicking, John Adams by framing constitutions intended to balance "aristocratic" and "democratic" interests. If these constitutions were to last, James Madison wrote, the makers of the federal Constitution had to "consult the genius of the people." Mechanics like Hewes were a presence in framing a political system so that politicians would have to take into account the aspirations of people who refused to take their hats off for anyone. This long struggle to achieve equal rights and to expand the meaning of liberty in the "Liberty Tree" is one of the grand themes of American history. We do well to keep it in public memory.

Notes

Introduction

1. The essay "George Robert Twelves Hewes (1742–1840): A Boston Shoe-maker and the Memory of the American Revolution" originally appeared in *William and Mary Quarterly*, 3rd ser., 38 (October, 1981): 561–623. It received the award of the Daughters of Colonial Wars for the best article of the year and the Douglass Adair Award for the best *Quarterly* article in six years. In 1993 it was voted one of the eleven "most influential" articles in the previous fifty years of the *Quarterly* and was reprinted in *In Search of Early America: The William and Mary Quarterly, 1943–1993* (Williamsburg, 1993). It has been translated into Spanish and reprinted in its original or in condensed form in numerous anthologies.

2. Peter Novick, *That Noble Dream: The "Objectivity Question" and the American Historical Profession* (New York, 1988), chaps. 10, 11; John Higham, *History: The Development of Historical Studies in the United States* (Englewood Cliffs, N.J., 1965), chap. 6.

3. Jesse Lemisch, "The American Revolution Seen from the Bottom Up," in *Towards a New Past: Dissenting Essays in American History*, ed. Barton Bernstein (New York, 1968), 3–43; Lemisch, "The American Revolution Bicentennial and the Papers of Great White Men," *AHA Newsletter* 9 (1971): 7–21; E. P. Thompson, *Making of the English Working Class* (New York, 1963), 12. I discuss the postwar scholarship on the Revolution in Young, "American Historians Confront 'The Transforming Hand of Revolution,'" in *The Transforming Hand of Revolution: Reconsidering the American Revolution as a Social Movement*, ed. Ronald Hoffman and Peter Albert (Charlottesville, 1995), 387–454.

4. David J. Garrow, *Bearing the Cross: Martin Luther King and the South-*

ern Christian Leadership Conference (New York, 1986), chap. 1; Howard Zinn, *SNCC: The New Abolitionists* (Boston, 1964).

5. Jacques Barzun and Henry Graf, *The Modern Researcher* (New York, 1957), chap. 7 at 135.

6. Daniel L. Schachter, *Searching for Memory: The Brain, the Mind and the Past* (New York, 1996), 4.

7. Schachter, *Searching for Memory*, chaps. 1, 2, 3.

8. David Thelen, Introduction to a special issue, "Memory and American History," *Journal of American History* 75 (1989): 1117–29. For recent efforts to analyze memories of the Revolution, see Robert C. Cray, Jr., "Major John André and the Three Captors: Class Dynamics and Revolutionary Memory Wars in the Early Republic, 1780–1831," *Journal of the Early Republic* 17 (1997): 371–97; Robert E. McGlone, "Deciphering Memory: John Adams and the Authorship of the Declaration of Independence," *Journal of American History* 85 (1998): 411–38; and my essay, "*Common Sense* and *The Rights of Man* in America: The Celebration and Damnation of Thomas Paine," in *Science, Mind and Art*, 3 vols., ed. Kostas Gavroglu, et al. (Dordecht, Neth., 1995), 3, 411–39.

9. Michael Kammen, Introduction to *Mystic Chords of Memory: The Transformation of Tradition in American Culture* (New York, 1991), citations at pp. 9–10; Kammen, *A Season of Youth: The American Revolution and the Historical Imagination* (New York, 1978), is the indispensable starting point for mapping the subject.

10. "Civil War, Alternate Names of," in *Encyclopedia of Southern History*, ed. David C. Roller and Robert W. Twyman (Baton Rouge, 1979), 228.

11. Mark Mayo Boatner III, *Encyclopedia of the American Revolution* (New York, 1974). Ronald Formisano, "Teaching Shays/The Regulation: Historiographical Problems as Tools for Learning," *Uncommon Sense* [A Newsletter of the Omohundro Institute for Early American History] 106 (1998): 24–35, argues that the term "Shays rebellion not only distorts a complex populist movement but also obscures its central meaning."

Part One: George Robert Twelves Hewes (1742–1840)

This essay is reprinted with only minor clarifications. In the notes, where I update citations or add information, I indicate these emendations with square brackets.

1. A Bostonian [Benjamin Bussey Thatcher], *Traits of the Tea Party; Being a Memoir of George R. T. Hewes, One of the Last of Its Survivors; With a History of That Transaction; Reminiscences of the Massacre, and the Siege, and Other Stories of Old Times* (New York: Harper & Brothers, 1835), 52–55, hereafter cited as Thatcher, *Memoir of Hewes*.

2. Ibid., 226–27.

3. A Citizen of New York [James Hawkes], *A Retrospect of the Boston Tea-Party, with a Memoir of George R. T. Hewes, a Survivor of the Little Band of Patriots Who Drowned the Tea in Boston Harbour in 1773* (New York: S. Bliss, printer, 1834), hereafter cited as Hawkes, *Retrospect.*

4. *Evening Mercantile Journal* (Boston), July 6, 1835.

1. A Man in His Nineties

1. C. Vann Woodward, "History from Slave Sources," *American Historical Review* 79 (1974): 470–81. For the related problems in slave memoirs see John W. Blassingame, *The Slave Community: Plantation Life in the Antebellum South*, rev. ed. (New York, 1979), 369–78.

2. Michael Kammen, *A Season of Youth: The American Revolution and the Historical Imagination* (New York, 1978), 26; Richard M. Dorson, ed., *America Rebels: Narratives of the Patriots*, 2d ed. rev. (New York, 1966), 17. Dorson, defining "narrative" somewhat loosely, counted over 200 entries in the Library of Congress catalog; in his appendix he lists 37, 11 of which appeared between 1822 and 1833.

3. J. Todd White and Charles H. Lesser, eds., *Fighters for Independence: A Guide to Sources of Biographical Information on Soldiers and Sailors of the American Revolution* (Chicago, 1977), lists under "Diaries, Journals and Autobiographies" 538 entries, both published and in manuscript. Walter Wallace, "'Oh, Liberty! Oh, Virtue! Oh, My Country!' An Exploration of the Minds of New England Soldiers During the American Revolution" (M.A. thesis, Northern Illinois University, 1974), is based on 164 published diaries. Also relevant is Jesse Lemisch, "The American Revolution Bicentennial and the Papers of Great White Men," American Historical Association, *Newsletter* 9 (Nov., 1971): 7–21, as well as "The Papers of Great White Men," *Maryland Historian* 6 (1975): 43–50, and "The Papers of a Few Great Black Men and a Few Great White Women," ibid., 60–66.

4. John C. Dann, ed., *The Revolution Remembered: Eyewitness Accounts of the War for Independence* (Chicago, 1980), introduction. For other scholars who have made use of the pension applications see the works cited in Chapter 6 below. John Shy and Dann are directing a project, "Data Bank for American Revolutionary Generation," William L. Clements Library, University of Michigan, Ann Arbor, Mich., based on samples from the 1818 and 1832 pension applications. [The project was not funded.]

5. Catalogers attribute the book to James Hawkes on the basis of the copyright entry on the overleaf of the title page. I am indebted to Walter

Wallace for searching for Hawkes in the New York Public Library, unfortunately without success. See Part Two, chap. 8, n. 16.

6. The body of Hawkes's book with the memoir runs 115 pages, about 27,000 words; a lengthy preface and an appendix bring it to 206 pages.

7. *Dictionary of American Biography*, s.v. "Thatcher, Benjamin Bussey." See also Nehemiah Cleaveland, *History of Bowdoin College. With Biographical Sketches of its Graduates . . .* , ed. Alpheus Spring Packard (Boston, 1882), 356–58. See Part Two, chap. 8.

8. Thatcher's book has 242 pages, about 49,000 words, plus a short appendix.

9. Hawkes, *Retrospect*, 13–16, 85–93.

10. Thatcher, *Memoir of Hewes*, iv, 250–53.

11. Ibid., 250, and examples at 52, 89, 95, 112.

12. For example, Hewes gave Hawkes, who had no way of prompting or correcting him, the more or less correct names and occupations of the five victims of the Boston Massacre, five leading Loyalist officials, and half-a-dozen relatives he visited in 1821. A typical error was "Leonard Pitt" for Lendell Pitts as his "Captain" at the Tea Party.

13. Hawkes, *Retrospect*, 28.

14. See Ian M. L. Hunter, *Memory* (London, 1957), esp. chap. 6.

15. According to John R. Sellers, "many [veterans who applied for pensions under the 1818 act] did not know how old they were" ("The Origins and Careers of New England soldiers, Non-Commissioned Officers, and Privates in the Massachusetts Continental Line" [unpubl. paper, American Historical Association, 1972], 4–5, cited with the author's permission). Sellers was able to compute the ages of 396 men in a sample of 546.

16. Dann, ed., *Revolution Remembered*, xx. For examples in which narratives faulty in some respects still checked out as essentially credible, see ibid., 204–11, 240–50, 268–74.

17. Paul Thompson, *The Voice of the Past: Oral History* (Oxford, 1978), 113 and chap. 4. For a remarkable example of this in a black sharecropper interviewed in his eighty-fifth year, see Theodore Rosengarten, *All God's Dangers: The Life of Nate Shaw* (New York, 1974). See also John Neuenschwander, "Remembrance of Things Past: Oral Historians and Long-Term Memory," *Oral History Review* 6 (1978): 45–53.

18. Hawkes, *Retrospect*, 93; Thatcher, *Memoir of Hewes*, 251.

19. See David Hackett Fischer, *Growing Old in America*, expanded ed. (New York, 1978), esp. chap. 2.

2. A Boston Childhood

1. Based on a computer printout of all wills at probate entered at Suffolk County Court, kindly loaned to me by Gary B. Nash. For analysis of

the context see his "Urban Wealth and Poverty in Pre-Revolutionary America," *Journal of Interdisciplinary History* 6 (1976): 545–84, and *The Urban Crucible: Social Change, Political Consciousness, and the Origins of the American Revolution* (Cambridge, Mass., and London, 1979), chap. 7. Before 1735, eight shoemakers on the probate list ended up in the top 10 percent of wealthholders (albeit most at the bottom of that bracket), but from 1736 to 1775 only one did.

2. Allan Kulikoff, "The Progress of Inequality in Revolutionary Boston," *William and Mary Quarterly*, 3rd ser., 28 (1971): 375–412; James A. Henretta, "Economic Development and Social Structure in Colonial Boston," ibid., 22 (1965): 75–92. The 1771 tax assessment does not list occupations; the 1780 assessment, which does, is incomplete; the 1790 list is the first point at which occupations can be measured for wealth.

3. In Nash's list of 61 shoemakers, 1685–1775, 7 names are repeated, appearing twice; after 1752, no name is repeated (see above, n. 1). For examples of trades passed down within families, see Esther Forbes, *Paul Revere & the World He Lived In* (Boston, 1942). For a family engaged in shipbuilding over six generations, see Bernard Farber, *Guardians of Virtue: Salem Families in 1800* (New York, 1972), 104–8.

4. Lawrence W. Towner, "The Indentures of Boston's Poor Apprentices: 1734–1805," Colonial Society of Massachusetts, *Transactions* 43 (1966): 417–68. The maritime, shipbuilding, and leather trades each accounted for about 8 percent of the boys; about 40 percent went into husbandry. From 1751 to 1776, 26 boys were put out to cordwainers, 6 in Boston, 20 in country towns.

5. Eric Hobsbawm and Joan Scott, "Political Shoemakers," *Past and Present*, No. 89 (1980): 86–114, which the authors kindly allowed me to see in MS. See also Peter Burke, *Popular Culture in Early Modern Europe* (London, 1978), 38–39.

6. *The Most Delightful History of the King and the Cobler* ... ([Boston, 1774]), reprinted from an English chapbook; and also printed in *Crispin Anecdotes; Comprising Interesting Notices of Shoemakers* ... (Sheffield, Eng., 1827).

7. John Adams, June 17, 1760, in L. H. Butterfield et al., eds., *Diary and Autobiography of John Adams*, vol. 1 (Cambridge, Mass., 1961), 135.

8. Hawkes, *Retrospect*, 17–18.

9. Thatcher, *Memoir of Hewes*, 11.

10. For a very full genealogy and family history of the several branches of the Hewes family see Eben Putnam, comp., *Lieutenant Joshua Hewes: A New England Pioneer and Some of his Descendants* ... (New York, 1913).

11. William B. Trask, "The Seaver Family," *New-England Historical and Genealogical Register* 26 (1872): 303–23.

12. Will of Shubael Seaver, Suffolk Co. Probate Court 52, 20–21, a copy of which was provided by Gary Nash.
13. Trask, "Seaver Family," *NEHGR* 26 (1872): 306; Putnam, comp., *Joshua Hewes*, 318.
14. Hawkes, *Retrospect*, 18, 86.
15. Thatcher, *Memoir of Hewes*, 26–33. Hewes did not volunteer these anecdotes to Hawkes.
16. Ibid., 129, 132. Warren was his grandmother's sister's son.
17. Petitions by Nathaniel Cunningham and George and Robert Hewes, 1740–1743, MS, Massachusetts Archives, Manufactures, 59, 316–19, 321–24, 334–337, 342–45, State House, Boston. I am indebted to Ruth Kennedy for running down Hewes and his family in a variety of legal and other sources in Boston, and to Gary Nash for his help in interpreting the sources. [David Ingram of Foxborough, Mass., points out in a letter to me of Oct. 15, 1996, that the family economic woes were even more severe. Robert Hewes was jailed, as was Solomon Hewes, the grandfather who also lost his farm in the Land Bank fiasco of the 1740s. As late as 1775, Dr. Joseph Hews of Providence wrote a diatribe, *A Collection of Occurrences and Facts*, about the troubles visited on his brothers, which meant the issues rankled in the family for decades.]
18. Thatcher, *Memoir of Hewes*, 38.
19. Letter of Administration, Estate of George Hewes, Suffolk Co. Probate Court, 1766, Docket No. 13906.
20. Alexander Keyssar, "Widowhood in Eighteenth-Century Massachusetts: A Problem in the History of the Family," *Perspectives in American History* 8 (1974): 98, 116–19. A census of 1742 showed 1,200 widows, "one thousand whereof are in low circumstances," in a population of 16,382 (Nash, *Urban Crucible*, 172).
21. Petition of Robert Hewes, Nov. 1752, MS, Mass. Archs., Manufactures, 59, 372–74. He is not to be confused with Robert Hewes (1751–1830) of Boston, a highly successful glassmaker (*DAB*, s.v. "Hewes, Robert"), or the father of this man, also Robert, who migrated from England c. 1751. See petitions of Robert Hewes to the General Court, May 25 and June 8, 1757 (in a different hand from that of Uncle Robert), Mass. Archs., Manufactures, LIX, 434–35.
22. Benjamin Franklin, *The Autobiography of Benjamin Franklin*, ed. Leonard W. Labaree et al. (New Haven, Conn., 1964), 57.
23. George P. Anderson, "Ebenezer McIntosh: Stamp Act Rioter and Patriot," Col. Soc. Mass., *Transactions* 26 (1927): 15–64 (hereafter cited as Anderson, "Ebenezer McIntosh"), and "A Note on Ebenezer McIntosh," ibid., 348–61.
24. The Overseers of the Poor first put out Thomas Banks, age eight, to a

farmer, William Williams. In 1770 Williams informed the Overseer that Thomas "is now seventeen years . . . old and about as big as an ordinary Country boy of thirteen . . . and scarcely able to perform the service of one of our boys of that age," and so he placed him with a cordwainer. Williams to Royal Tyler, Jan. 23, 1770, in Towner, "Boston's Poor Apprentices," Col. Soc. Mass., *Transactions* 63 (1966): 430–31.

25. James Biddle to David Conner, Aug. 9, 1813, Fourth Auditor Accounts Numerical Series, #1141, Record Group 217, National Archives, kindly brought to my attention by Christopher McKee.

26. Hobsbawm and Scott write that "there is a good deal of evidence that small, weak or physically handicapped boys were habitually put to this trade" ("Political Shoemakers," *Past and Present*, No. 89 [1980], 96–97).

3. The Apprentice

1. Hawkes, *Retrospect*, 23–24; Franklin, *Autobiography*, ed. Labaree et al., 57. For a boy whose threats forced his parents to allow him to go to sea, see Lemisch, "Life of Andrew Sherburne," sec. III.

2. Thatcher, *Memoir of Hewes*, 17–18. For a boy in the laboring classes who fell into a cistern of rainwater and was rescued from drowning, see Isaiah Thomas, *Three Autobiographical Fragments* . . . (Worcester, Mass., 1962), 7.

3. Thatcher, *Memoir of Hewes*, 18–26.

4. Ibid., 25.

5. Hawkes, *Retrospect*, 21–22.

6. Thatcher, *Memoir of Hewes*, 29–47. Thatcher presented this story as occurring shortly after Hewes became twenty-one, which might make it 1764, the year of a massive smallpox inoculation campaign in Boston.

7. Hawkes, *Retrospect*, 23–25. See also *By His Excellency William Shirley, Esq.* . . . (Boston, Apr. 17, 1755), with the eligibility requirement, and *By His Excellency Thomas Pownall* . . . (Boston, Apr. 10, 1758, and Mar. 14, 1760), broadsides, Lib. Cong.

8. Thatcher, *Memoir of Hewes*, 47–49. For the anti-impressment riots of 1747 see Jesse Lemisch, "Jack Tar in the Streets: Merchant Seamen in the Politics of Revolutionary America," *William and Mary Quarterly* 3rd ser., 25 (1968): 371–407, and John Lax and William Pencak, "The Knowles Riot and the Crisis of the 1740's in Massachusetts," *Perspectives Am. Hist.* 10 (1976): 163–214.

9. This may have been the Great Fire of 1760. I find no record of a Downing in the claims filed by 365 sufferers in "Records Relating to the Early History of Boston," *Report of the Record Commissioners of the City of Bos-*

ton (Boston, 1876–1909), vol. 29, hereafter cited as *Record Commissioners' Reports*, but the published records are incomplete.

10. Thatcher spelled his name Rhoades (*Memoir of Hewes*, 49–50). Henry Roads is listed as a cordwainer assigned an apprentice Oct. 30, 1752, in Towner, "Boston's Poor Apprentices," Col. Soc. Mass., *Transactions* 43 (1966), Table, [441]. If the apprenticeship ran the customary seven years, Rhoades (or Roads) would have needed another one in 1760, which would fit Hewes's story.

11. Alfred Young, "Pope's Day, Tar and Feathers, and Cornet Joyce, Jun: From Ritual to Rebellion in Boston" (unpubl. MS, Anglo-American Labor Historians' Conference, 1973). See also Thomas, *Three Autobiographical Fragments*, 22–25, for one apprentice's near-fatal participation.

12. Thatcher, *Memoir of Hewes*, 50–52. For another anecdote about a gift of food during the siege of Boston see ibid., 204.

4. The Shoemaker

1. Hawkes, *Retrospect*, 26–27.
2. Thatcher, *Memoir of Hewes*, 58–64.
3. My estimate. There were 78 shoemakers in Boston in 1790, when there were 2,995 people on the assessment rolls in a population of 18,000 (Kulikoff, "Progress of Inequality," *William and Mary Quarterly*, 3rd ser., 28 [1971], 412). I count 26 shoemakers in 1780, when there were 2,225 on the assessment rolls in a population of less than 15,000 and at a time when poorer men were apt to be at war (Boston Assessing Dept., *Assessors' "Talking Books" of the Town of Boston 1780* [Boston, 1912]). If the population of Boston was 20 percent smaller in 1774 than in 1790, with a proportional loss of shoemakers, it would have included 63 shoemakers. For comparisons of occupational breakdowns see Jacob Price, "Economic Function and the Growth of American Port Towns in the Eighteenth Century," *Perspectives Am. Hist.* 8 (1974): 176, 181.
4. See Thatcher, *Memoir of Hewes*, 39–40, 85, for evidence that he made and repaired shoes. Griffin's Wharf was in the area of the tenth and eleventh wards where in 1771 the mean tax assessment was £193 and £254, twice as high as the mean in the crowded North End wards but considerably below the mean of £695 in the center of town (see Kulikoff, "Progress of Inequality," *William and Mary Quarterly*, 3rd ser., 28 [1971], 395, map).
5. Putnam, comp., *Joshua Hewes*, 335.
6. "Boston Town Records," in *Record Commissioners' Reports*, vol. 3, 65; "Boston Marriages, 1752–1809," ibid., vol. 30, 65; and Samuel Stillman,

"Record of Marriages from the Year 1761" indicate marriage by Still-man. The records of the First Baptist Church, including the Minutes, List of Adult Baptisms, and Pew Proprietors Record Book, do not show the names of either the Sumners or the Heweses as members or of Sumner (or anyone else) as sexton (MS, Andover Newton Theological Seminary, Andover, Mass.). Researched by Elaine Weber Pascu.

7. The First Baptist Church had "not 70 members" before 1769 and about 80 more during the next three years (Isaac Backus, *History of New England, with Particular Reference to the . . . Baptists*, III [Boston, 1796], 125–26). See also Nathan Eusebius Wood, *The History of the First Baptist Church of Boston (1665–1899)* (Philadelphia, 1899), 266–67. After the Great Fire of 1760 the church gave £143 to charity compared, for example, to £1862 from Old South and £418 from Old North. See Franklin Bowditch Dexter, ed., *Extracts from the Itineraries and Other Miscellanies of Ezra Stiles . . .* (New Haven, Conn., 1916), 120.

8. Writ of Attachment on George Robert Twelves Hewes, including Hewes's note of indebtedness to Courtney, Sept. 3, 1770, Suffolk Co. Court, Case #89862. Ruth Kennedy discovered this document. For Courtney see E. Alfred Jones, *The Loyalists of Massachusetts: Their Memorials, Petitions and Claims* (London, 1930), 103.

9. Bettye Hobbs Pruitt, ed., *The Massachusetts Tax Valuation List of 1771* (Boston, 1978), 14–15. Hewes is listed only for one "Polls Rateable." Christopher Ranks is listed as the owner. Stephanie G. Wolf brought this publication to my attention. Ranks is listed in the Thwing File, Massachusetts Historical Society, as a shopkeeper in 1750, a clockmaker in 1751, and a watchmaker in 1788.

10. Thatcher, *Memoir of Hewes*, 84, 204.

11. *Massachusetts Gazette and Boston Weekly News-Letter*, Jan. 27, 1774, discussed below, Chapter 6.

12. See *At a meeting of the Freeholders . . . the 28th of October, 1767* (Boston, 1767), broadside, Mass. Hist. Soc.

13. Blanche Evans Hazard, *The Organizations of the Boot and Shoe Industry in Massachusetts before 1875* (Cambridge, Mass., 1921), 128, chap. 6, and appendices on 256–264. Lynn shoes were being sold in Boston at public auctions by the hundred pair, dozen pair, or single pair. Moreover, there were several hundred petty retailers, predominantly women, who would have been driven to the wall by the boycott and eager to sell such items. See Thatcher, *Memoir of Hewes*, 139–40, for a reprint of a newspaper notice, Feb. 14, 1770, from Isaac Vibert implying a putting-out system.

14. *Peter Oliver's Origin & Progress of the American Rebellion: A Tory View*, ed. Douglass Adair and John A. Schutz (San Marino, Calif., 1961), 54–

55. Similarly in 1771, one in six Philadelphia shoemakers was on poor relief (see Billy G. Smith, "Material Lives of Laboring Philadelphians, 1750 to 1800," *William and Mary Quarterly*, 3rd ser., 38 [1981]: 163–202).

15. Hawkes, *Retrospect*, 20, 89, 92; Thatcher, *Memoir of Hewes*, 251–252; Richard Saunders, *Poor Richard Improved: Being an Almanac and Ephemeris . . . for the Year of Our Lord 1758 . . .* (Philadelphia, 1758), also appearing as *Father Abraham's Speech . . .* (Boston, n.d. [1758, 1760]), a compilation of aphorisms from the previous 26 almanacs. See Leonard W. Labaree et al., eds., *The Papers of Benjamin Franklin*, vol. 7 (New Haven, Conn., 1963), 326–355.

16. J. E. Crowley, *This Sheba, Self: The Conceptualization of Economic Life in Eighteenth-Century America*, The Johns Hopkins University Studies in Historical and Political Science, vol. 92 (Baltimore, 1974), 84. See especially James A. Henretta, "The Study of Social Mobility: Ideological Assumptions and Conceptual Bias," *Labor History* 18 (1977): 165–78.

17. Hewes is listed in the baptismal records of Old South as having been christened on Sept. 26, 1742 (O.S.). See Thatcher, *Memoir of Hewes*, 255. There is no other trace of Hewes in Old South records, searched by Elaine W. Pascu. I am indebted to Charles W. Akers for help in identifying and locating Boston church records.

18. Chilton Williamson, *American Suffrage: From Property to Democracy, 1760–1860* (Princeton, N.J., 1960), 13, 16. See *Notification to Voters, William Cooper, Town Clerk, May 1, 1769*, publicizing the property requirement, and *Notification, Mar. 17, 1768*, warning that "a strict scrutiny will be made as to the qualification of voters" (broadsides, Lib. Cong.). The average total vote in annual elections at official town meetings from 1763 to 1774 was 555; the high was 1,089 in 1763 (see Alan and Catherine Day, "Another Look at the Boston Caucus," *Journal of American Studies* 5 [1971]: 27–28).

19. For the father see Putnam, comp., *Joshua Hewes*, 321, and for McIntosh see Anderson, "Ebenezer McIntosh," 26–28. I find no record of Hewes in "Records Relating to the Early History of Boston," in *Record Commissioners' Reports*, vols. 14–20. For the wealth of leaders of the town meeting see Edward M. Cook, Jr., *The Fathers of the Towns: Leadership and Community Structure in Eighteenth-Century New England*, The Johns Hopkins University Studies in Historical and Political Science, vol. 94 (Baltimore, 1976), chaps. 2, 3.

20. For Shubael see Putnam, comp., *Joshua Hewes*, 332, and for McIntosh see Anderson, "Ebenezer McIntosh," 25.

21. For the low level of associations see Richard D. Brown, "Emergence of Voluntary Associations in Massachusetts, 1760–1830," *Journal of Voluntary Action Research* 2 (1973): 64–73.

22. Mary Roys Baker, "Anglo-Massachusetts Trade Union Roots, 1130–1790," *Labor History* 14 (1973): 335, 362, 365–67, 371, 381–83, 388, 394.

5. The Massacre

1. Thatcher, *Memoir of Hewes*, 68, 72. For crowd events in Boston the most reliable guide is Dirk Hoerder, *Crowd Action in Revolutionary Massachusetts, 1765–1780* (New York, 1977). Hoerder has generously shared with me his detailed knowledge.
2. Thatcher, *Memoir of Hewes*, 84–87. Bostonians were "shocked by the frequency and severity of corporal punishment in the army" (John Shy, *Toward Lexington: The Role of the British Army in the Coming of the American Revolution* [Princeton, N.J., 1965], 308).
3. Hawkes, *Retrospect*, 31–32. My statement on the composition of the crowd is based on my analysis of participants, witnesses, and victims identified in the trial record, depositions, etc., and is supported by Hoerder, *Crowd Action*, 223–34, and James Barton Hunt, "The Crowd and the American Revolution: A Study of Urban Political Violence in Boston and Philadelphia, 1763–1776" (Ph.D. diss., University of Washington, 1973), 471–479.
4. Hawkes, *Retrospect*, 43; Thatcher, *Memoir of Hewes*, 88–95. Hewes told about the event after he recounted the Massacre. He correctly remembered Seider, reported as "Snider" by Thomas Hutchinson and other contemporaries. His recollection is borne out in essentials by Hoerder, *Crowd Action*, 216–23. See Hutchinson to Thomas Hood, Feb. 23, 1770; to Gen. Gage, Feb. 25, 1770; and to Lord Hillsborough, Feb. 28, 1770, Hutchinson Transcripts, Houghton Library, Harvard University, Cambridge, Mass.
5. Hawkes, *Retrospect*, 31–32; Thatcher, *Memoir of Hewes*, 96–99. For verification by another contemporary, see "Recollections of a Bostonian," from the *Boston Centinel*, 1821–1822, reprinted in Hezekiah Niles, *Principles and Acts of the Revolution in America* . . . (Baltimore, 1822), 430–31. For the fray at the ropewalk, accepted as a precipitating cause by contemporaries on both sides, see Richard B. Morris, *Government and Labor in Early America* (New York, 1946), 190–92.
6. Hawkes, *Retrospect*, 30–31; Thatcher, *Memoir of Hewes*, 118–19. For the trial see L. Kinvin Wroth and Hiller B. Zobel, eds., *Legal Papers of John Adams* (Cambridge, Mass. 1965), 50, 52, 56, 93–94, 108.
7. Hawkes, *Retrospect*, 29. For the event itself see Hiller B. Zobel, *The Boston Massacre* (New York, 1970), in conjunction with Jesse Lemisch, "Radical Plot in Boston (1770): A Study in the Use of Evidence," *Harvard Law Review* 84 (1970): 485–504, and Pauline Maier, "Revolution-

ary Violence and the Relevance of History," *Journal of Interdisciplinary History* 2 (1971): 119–35.

8. Hawkes, *Retrospect*, 29–32; Thatcher, *Memoir of Hewes*, 110–12.

9. Hawkes, *Retrospect*, 30.

10. Zobel, *Boston Massacre*, 206–9; Hoerder, *Crowd Action*, 232.

11. Deposition No. 75, in *A Short Narrative of the Horrid Massacre in Boston ... To Which is Added an Appendix ...* (Boston, 1770), 61. Thatcher reprinted this in *Memoir of Hewes*, 116–18. Hewes's deposition testified to the soldiers' threats to kill more civilians and to someone entering the Custom House at the time of the Massacre, both themes emphasized by Whig leaders.

12. Thatcher, *Memoir of Hewes*, 95. Thatcher did not give the words. I suspect that what Hewes remembered was the verdict brought in by the jury after a dramatic trial repeatedly interrupted by what Peter Oliver called "a vast concourse of rabble." The verdict was "Guilty of Murder," at which "the Court Room resounded with Expressions of Pleasure" (*Oliver's Origin & Progress*, ed. Adair and Schutz, 86). The judges delayed the sentence until the Crown granted a pardon. The case aroused a furor. See Wroth and Zobel, eds., *Legal Papers of Adams*, vol. 2, 396–430, and Zobel, *Boston Massacre*, chap. 15, and 423–426. For the way in which the killing of Seider and the killings of the Boston Massacre were linked politically, see *A Monumental Inscription in the Fifth of March Together with a few lines on the Enlargement of Ebenezer Richardson Convicted of Murder* [1772], broadside, Mass. Hist. Soc.

13. Hawkes, *Retrospect*, 32. Thatcher does not even mention this claim of Hewes, possibly because he was skeptical.

14. Wroth and Zobel, eds. *Legal Papers of Adams*, vol. 3, has no record of Hewes at the trial, but see L. H. Butterfield's "Descriptive List of Sources and Documents": "This operation has been a good deal like that of an archeological team reconstructing a temple from a tumbled mass of architectural members, some missing, many mutilated, and most of them strewn over a wide area" (ibid., 34). For Shubael Hewes see ibid., 176–77, 224–75, and for Robert Hewes ibid., vol. 2, 405, 418.

6. The Tea Party

1. Hutchinson to Lord Dartmouth, Dec. 3, 1773, Hutchinson Transcripts. For Daniel Hewes see Francis S. Drake, *Tea Leaves: Being a Collection of Letters and Documents Relating to the Shipment of Tea ...* (Boston, 1884), xlvi.

2. Hawkes, *Retrospect*, 36–37. Hewes's account is verified in its essentials by Hoerder, *Crowd Action*, 257–64, and is not inconsistent with the less

detailed account in Benjamin Woods Labaree, *The Boston Tea Party* (New York, 1964), chap. 7. For analysis of the participants see Hoerder, *Crowd Action*, 263–64, and Hunt, "The Crowd and the American Revolution," 481, 485.

3. Joshua Wyeth, "Revolutionary Reminiscence," *North American* 1 (1827): 195, brought to my attention by Richard Twomey.

4. Hawkes, *Retrospect*, 38–39.

5. Thatcher, *Memoir of Hewes*, 180–181, 261. Maxwell's reminiscence is in *New England Historic Genealogical Register* 22 (1868); 58.

6. Hawkes, *Retrospect*, 40–41; Thatcher, *Memoir of Hewes*, 182–83.

7. Tar and Feathers

1. *Mass. Gaz. and Boston Wkly News-Letter*, Jan. 27, Feb. 3, 1774. Hewes told this story to Hawkes essentially as reported in this paper but with only some of the dialogue. He may have kept the clipping. Thatcher added dialogue based on the account in the paper but also extracted additional details from Hewes not in either the *Gazette* or Hawkes.

2. Frank W. C. Hersey, "Tar and Feathers: The Adventures of Captain John Malcolm," Col. Soc. Mass., *Transactions* 34 (1941): 429–73, which also reprints the documents. The full letter, Hutchinson to Lord Dartmouth, Jan. 28, 1774, is in K. G. Davis, ed., *Documents of the American Revolution*, 1770–1783, vol. 8 (Shannon, Ireland, 1972), 25–27.

3. *Mass. Gaz. and Boston Wkly News-Letter*, Jan. 27, 1774.

4. Thatcher, *Memoir of Hewes*, 132; Hawkes, *Retrospect*, 33–35.

5. *Mass. Gaz. and Boston Wkly News-Letter*, Jan. 27, 1774. For other comments from the crowd, see *Boston-Gazette, and Country Journal*, Jan. 31, 1774.

6. Hawkes, *Retrospect*, 44; Zobel, *Boston Massacre*, 102.

7. *Mass. Gaz. and Boston Wkly News-Letter*, Jan. 27, 1774.

8. See Albert Matthews, "Joyce, Jun," Col. Soc. Mass., *Publications* 8 (1903): 89–104, and Young, "Pope's Day, Tar and Feathers," sec. VI.

9. For the newspaper accounts and prints see R. T. H. Halsey, *The Boston Port Bill as Pictured by a Contemporary London Cartoonist* (New York, 1904), 82–94, 121n, 132–33; Mary Dorothy George, comp., *Catalogue of Political and Personal Satires . . . in the British Museum*, vol. 5 (London, 1935), no. 5232, 168–69; and Donald Creswell, comp., *The American Revolution in Drawings and Prints; A Checklist of 1765–1790 Graphics in the Library of Congress* (Washington, D.C., 1975), nos. 668–670. For the impact on the king and his ministers see Peter Orlando Hutchinson, comp., *The Diary and Letters of His Excellency Thomas Hutchinson . . .*, vol. 1 (London, 1883), 164.

10. Thatcher, *Memoir of Hewes*, 132.
11. Ibid., 133.

8. The Patriot

1. Thatcher, *Memoir of Hewes*, 181, 263; *Oliver's Origin & Progress*, ed. Adair and Schutz, 74–75.
2. Hutchinson to Lord Dartmouth, Jan. 28, 1774, in Davis, ed., *Documents of the Revolution*, 25–27.
3. Hawkes, *Retrospect*, 42–44.
4. Ibid., 18–19.
5. Ibid., 87. Hewes made an allusion to having brought with him what could only have been *Copy of Letters Sent to Great Britain, by His Excellency Thomas Hutchinson, the Hon. Andrew Oliver, and Several Other Persons* ... (Boston, 1773). See Bernard Bailyn, *The Ordeal of Thomas Hutchinson* (Cambridge, Mass., 1974), 222–24. For Dorr see Bailyn, "The Index and Commentaries of Harbottle Dorr," Mass. Hist. Soc., *Proceedings* 85 (1973): 21–35, and Barbara Wilhelm, *The American Revolution as a Leadership Crisis: The View of a Hardware Store Owner*, West Georgia College Studies in the Social Sciences, vol. 15 (Carrollton, Ga., 1976), 43–54.
6. Robert Hewes attended the 1769 dinner commemorating the Stamp Act action of 1765 (see "An Alphabetical List of the Sons of Liberty who Dined at Liberty Tree, Dorchester, August 14, 1769," MS, Mass. Hist. Soc.). "Parson Thatcher" called Robert "a great Liberty Man" in 1775 (see Thatcher, *Memoir of Hewes*, 217). Daniel Hewes was a guard at the tea ships, Nov. 30, 1773 (see Drake, *Tea Leaves*, xlvi). For Shubael Hewes, who testified for the defense at the Massacre trial, see Putnam, comp., *Joshua Hewes*, 331.
7. See Alfred Young, "The Rapid Rise and Decline of Ebenezer McIntosh" (MS, Shelby Cullum Davis Center, Princeton Univ., Jan. 1976). Masaniello was a fisherman who led the seventeenth-century plebeian rebellion in Naples.
8. "Jack Cobler," *Massachusetts Gazette* (Boston), Feb. 20, 1776; "Crispin," *Massachusetts Spy* (Boston), Jan. 16, 1772. Lord Bute was the Earl of Bute, an advisor to King George III.
9. For derogatory references in New York, Baltimore, and Savannah, see Philip S. Foner, *Labor and the American Revolution* (Westport, Conn., 1976), 120, 197, 151, and for Charleston see Richard Walsh, *Charleston's Sons of Liberty: A Study of the Artisans, 1763–1789* (Columbia, S.C., 1959), 70.
10. Edmund S. Morgan, "The Puritan Ethic and the American Revolu-

tion," *William and Mary Quarterly*, 3rd ser., 24 (1967): 3–43, esp. sec. II; "Declaration of the Massachusetts Provincial Congress, Dec. 8, 1774," in Merrill Jensen, ed., *English Historical Documents: American Colonial Documents to 1776* (New York, 1955), 823–25. Thatcher dwelled on the patriot promotion of American manufactures without, however, attributing such ideas to Hewes (*Memoir of Hewes*, 58–60).

11. Hawkes, *Retrospect*, 62, 64.
12. Charles W. Akers, "John Hancock: Notes for a Reassessment" (unpubl. paper, Univ. of Michigan–Flint Conference, Oct. 1976), which the author kindly allowed me to read.
13. Thatcher, *Memoir of Hewes*, 192–93.
14. Ibid., 261–62.
15. L. F. S. Upton, "Proceedings of Ye Body Respecting the Tea," *William and Mary Quarterly*, 3rd ser., 22 (1965): 298. The standard sources are dubious. See Edward L. Pierce, "Recollections as a Source of History," Mass. Hist. Soc., *Proceedings*, 2d ser., 10 (1896): 473–90, and Labaree, *Boston Tea Party*, 144, and chap. 7.

9. Soldier and Sailor

1. Hawkes, *Retrospect*, 59–62; Thatcher, *Memoir of Hewes*, 198–220. For verification of the context see Richard Frothingham, *History of the Siege of Boston* . . . (Boston, 1849), and Justin Winsor, ed., *The Memorial History of Boston, Including Suffolk County Massachusetts* . . . , vol. 3 (Boston, 1881), chap. 2. The Hewes family was not listed among the five thousand or more Boston families who received charity from the Friends, although over a score of shoemakers were (see Henry J. Cadbury, "Quaker Relief during the Siege of Boston," Col. Soc. Mass., *Transactions* 34 [1943]: 39–179).

2. Hewes claimed five separate stints, two as a privateersman and three in the militia, in his Pension Application and Statement of Service, Military Service Records, MS, No. 14748, Nat'l Archs., hereafter cited as Pension Application. The two privateering expeditions can be verified from corroborative evidence (see Chapter 9, nn. 15, 16). Of his three claims for militia service, two are verified in Massachusetts Secretary of the Commonwealth, *Massachusetts Soldiers and Sailors in the Revolutionary War* (Boston, 1896–1908), vol. 7, 792–93, s.v. "Hewes, George" and "Hewes, George R. T.," hereafter cited as *Mass. Soldiers*. This compilation attests to one of the three months he claimed for 1777 (Sept. 25–Oct. 30) and more than the three months he claimed for 1781 (July 23–Nov. 8). Using unnamed "official records" that could only have been the

as-yet-unpublished MS records in the Mass. Archs., Putnam found evidence for four separate enlistments, one more than Hewes claimed, two of which (1777 and 1781) are printed in *Mass. Soldiers*, VII, and two of which (Aug. 17–Sept. 9, 1778, and July 28–Oct. 21, 1780) are not (see Putnam, comp., *Joshua Hewes*, 335–36). Putnam's 1778 finding verifies Hewes's pension claim for three months in 1778 for dates he did not specify (but which places him at the Battle of Newport Island at the right period). Hewes did not claim the 1780 stint Putnam found. There is corroboration for his pension claims in the Attleborough records (see below, n. 3). There is thus good evidence for his two privateering claims, direct verification for two of his militia claims, and evidence for two more he did not claim.

3. George Hewes's name is not on the militia musters for Attleborough reprinted in John Daggett, *Sketch of the History of Attleborough from its Settlement to the Present Time* (Boston, 1894 [orig. publ. Dedham, Mass., 1834]), 134–45. In his petition of 1832 Hewes indicated several times that he returned to his family at Wrentham but enlisted at Attleborough. The explanation may be that "these lists comprise all the *town* enlistments, not individual enlistments of certain citizens elsewhere in which the town would have no monetary interest" (Daggett, *Sketch of Attleborough*, 143n). The Attleborough evidence, however, corroborates Hewes's claims: (1) The town's units were in the three campaigns Hewes claimed in 1777, 1778, and 1781. (2) Caleb Richardson, the officer Hewes listed twice as his captain, served in the Attleborough militia. He is listed as captain for six tours of duty, the dates of two of which (1778 and 1780) coincide with Hewes's claims (*Mass. Soldiers*, vol. 13, 230). (3) Luke Drury is listed as Lt. Col. Commandant for the service at West Point that Hewes claimed under "Col. Drury" in 1781 (ibid., vol. 4, 987).

4. In his Pension Application Hewes said he went on board the privateer *Diamond* "about two years after the battle of Bunker Hill," adding, "sometime in the month of April." This would have made it in 1777. But the two vessels whose names he remembered as prizes were taken in Oct. and Dec. 1776. If it was a three months' voyage, as Hewes remembered, this would have meant the *Diamond* sailed about Sept. 1776. See below, n. 15.

5. The clerk wrote that Hewes "enlisted as a volunteer on board of a privateer"; he "volunteered into a company of militia"; "he again volunteered into a company of militia"; but finally, "he enlisted . . . into a company of militia" (Pension Application). Hewes also told Hawkes that in "a hot press for men to go and recapture Penobscot" from the British "I volunteered to go with a Mr. Saltonstall, who was to be the commander

of the expedition, which for some cause, however, failed" (*Retrospect*, 72). This was the naval expedition of July–Aug. 1779, led by Capt. Dudley Saltonstall, which ended in disaster.

6. Robert A. Gross, *The Minutemen and Their World* (New York, 1976), 149.

7. John Shy, *A People Numerous and Armed: Reflections on the Military Struggle for American Independence* (New York, 1976), 171.

8. John Resch to author, May 29, 1980, based on research cited in Chapter 11, n. 13.

9. Gross, *Minutemen*, 151.

10. For example, see the petition of Sylvanus Wood of Woburn, Mass., in Dann, ed., *Revolution Remembered*, 8.

11. Hawkes, *Retrospect*, 62–63.

12. The phrase and analysis are from Lemisch, "Jack Tar Goes A'Privateering" (unpubl. MS). I am indebted to Christopher McKee for sharing his unrivaled knowledge of naval sources.

13. Gardner Weld Allen, *Massachusetts Privateers of the Revolution* (Mass. Hist. Soc., *Collections* 77 [Boston, 1927]): 716–17; James Warren to Samuel Adams, Aug. 15, 1776, in Henry Steele Commager and Richard B. Morris, eds., *The Spirit of 'Seventy-Six: The Story of the American Revolution as Told by Participants*, vol. 2 (New York, 1958), 965; Abigail Adams to John Adams, Sept. 29, 1776, in L. H. Butterfield et al., eds., *Adams Family Correspondence*, vol. 2 (Cambridge, Mass., 1963), 135.

14. Nash, *Urban Crucible*, chaps. 3, 7.

15. Hawkes, *Retrospect*, 64–67; Thatcher, *Memoir of Hewes*, 220–26. William P. Sheffield verifies Hewes's recollections of the vessel, commander (Thomas Stacey), owner (John Brown), and the names of the captured prizes: the *Live Oak*, listed as taken in Dec. 1776, and the *Mary and Joseph*, listed as taken Oct. 1776 (but by the *Montgomery* under Stacey) (*Privateersmen of Newport* [Newport, R.I., 1883], 64). [Jay Coughtry has shared with me evidence confirming that Hewes sailed on the *Diamond*. The Moses Brown Papers, Brown University Library, has "A List of Peoples Names . . . Going in the Ship Diamond Second Cruise" (n.d.), which enumerates Thomas Stacy, Captain and George Hews as a crew member. In 1835, when Hewes stopped in Providence on his way to Boston, he visited Moses Brown, then a venerable Quaker merchant.]

16. Hawkes, *Retrospect*, 67–72; Thatcher, *Memoir of Hewes*, 227–37. Hewes's recollections of the details of this voyage are verified in Louis F. Middlebrook, *History of Maritime Connecticut during the American Revolution* (Salem, Mass., 1925), vol. 1, 44, 51–52, 65, vol. 2, 285–86, 303–4, 306–10, 313–16. Hewes is not on the crew list, I conclude, because Capt. Smedley, who did not give him his wages, eliminated his name (ibid., vol. 1, 70–73). For other vivid details of the encounters of the *Defence*

verifying Hewes, see the diary of a sailor on the accompanying ship
Cromwell in Samuel W. Boardman [ed.], *Log-Book of Timothy Board-*
man. Kept on Board the Privateer Oliver Cromwell . . . (Albany, N.Y.,
1885), entries Apr. 7–30, 1778. For additional verification see the petition
of Abel Woodworth, also on the *Cromwell*, in Dann, ed., *Revolution*
Remembered, 319–320. See also Gardner W. Allen, *A Naval History of the*
American Revolution, vol. 1 (New York, 1913), 321–23.

17. Hawkes, *Retrospect*, 71–72. Ira Dye has very kindly checked for Hewes
    in the computerized naval records of the Continental Congress, 1774–
    1789, Nat'l Archs., but without success.
18. Hawkes, *Retrospect*, 68.
19. Ibid., 65, 68.
20. Thatcher, *Memoir of Hewes*, 216–20. Hewes did not tell this story to
    Hawkes, who reported Hewes as saying, "I went on shore at a safe place,
    and repaired straitway to my family at Wrentham" (*Retrospect*, 61).
    Thatcher elicited the story as he did several others about famous people.
    For the Washingtons at Cambridge see Douglas Southall Freeman,
    George Washington: A Biography, vol. 3 (New York, 1951), 405, 477, 580–
    81. Hewes spoke of being in Boston nine weeks, which means his escape
    would have been late Aug. or early Sept., about the time Washington
    was considering an attack on Boston. Martha Washington did not arrive
    until Dec. 11, 1775. Thatcher reported one other encounter with a famous
    man during the war, an episode at the Newport Island action, Aug. 1778,
    in which Hewes claimed he rescued James Otis, who was "roaming
    about the lines in one of his unhappy spells of derangement" (*Memoir*
    of Hewes, 238). I have not been able to prove or disprove this incident.
21. Hawkes, *Retrospect*, 73–74; Thatcher, *Memoir of Hewes*, 237–40.
22. For shoemakers as officers see Don Higginbotham, *The American War*
    of Independence: Military Attitudes, Policies, and Practice, 1763–1789 (New
    York, 1971), 400, and Shy, *People Numerous and Armed*, 163–79. For shoe-
    maker officers mending shoes see the Baroness von Riedesel's comments
    cited in Forbes, *Paul Revere*, 336.
23. Hawkes, *Retrospect*, 74–75; Daggett, *Sketch of Attleborough*, 128; Jonathan
    Smith, "How Massachusetts Raised Her Troops in the Revolution,"
    Mass. Hist. Soc., *Proceedings* 55 (1921): 345–70.
24. Thatcher, *Memoir of Hewes*, 242–43. How much Hewes made can only
    be guessed: in privateering, very little on his first voyage, nothing on his
    second. For militia duty in 1777 Attleborough paid £3 a month plus a £2
    bounty; in 1778, £2 8s. a month and £5 a month bonus (Daggett, *Sketch*
    of Attleborough, 124, 126). Thus if Hewes served nine months, he might
    have earned £27 in pay and perhaps the same as a bounty. As a resident
    of Wrentham he might have been attracted to Attleborough by extra

pay for nonresidents. Had he wanted to make money from land service he could have enlisted in the Continental army; in 1778 Attleborough was offering £30 a month plus a bounty of £30 for army enlistments.

10. Family Man

1. Hawkes, *Retrospect*, 74–75; James G. Wilson, "The Last Survivor of the Boston Tea Party," *American Historical Register*, n.s., 1 (1897); 5, hereafter cited as Wilson, "Last Survivor." See Ira Dye, "Early American Merchant Seafarers," American Philosophical Society, *Proceedings* 120 (1976): 331–60. After 1796 the federal government issued protection certificates to merchant seamen who requested them. Dye has generously checked for Hewes in abstracts of the surviving certificates, but without success. Providence, however, was not checked.

2. See a will of Joseph Hewes [1796] summarized in Putnam, comp., *Joshua Hewes*, 327–38, and in Bristol County Northern District Registry of Deeds Record Book, two conveyances dated Mar. 18, 1797, in Book 76, p. 126, and Sept. 10, 1810, in Book 91, p. 453, copies of which were kindly provided by Alfred Florence, Assistant Register of Deeds, Bristol County, Taunton, Mass.

3. Jordan D. Fiore, *Wrentham, 1673–1973: A History* (Wrentham, Mass., 1973), 136–40.

4. Kulikoff, "Progress of Inequality," *William and Mary Quarterly*, 3rd ser., 28 (1971): 402. "By 1790, 45 per cent of the taxpayers in town in 1780 had disappeared from tax lists." Of 2,225 individuals on the assessors' books in 1780, 1,000 were missing in 1790. The rate of persistence was only 42 percent for those paying no rent, and 52 percent for those paying from £1 to £20, but 66 percent for those paying from £100 to £199, and 74 percent for those paying over £200 (ibid., 401–2).

5. Hawkes, *Retrospect*, 72.

6. U.S. Bureau of the Census, *Heads of Families at the First Census of the United States Taken in the Year 1790: Massachusetts* (Washington, D.C., 1908), Wrentham, 210, lists a George Hewes; Laraine Welch, comp., *Massachusetts 1800 Census* (Bountiful, Utah, 1973), Norfolk County, 174, lists George R. L. Hewes; Ronald Jackson et al., *Massachusetts 1810 Census Index* (Bountiful, Utah, 1976), does not list Hewes. Anne Lehane Howard, a title examiner, of Quincy, Mass., finds no record of Hewes buying or selling real estate in Suffolk or Norfolk counties in the Suffolk Co. Registry of Deeds, 1695–1899.

7. The Wrentham tax records, incomplete and in disarray, were examined at the Assessor's Office, Wrentham, with the cooperation of Lois McKennson, Assessor, by Gregory Kaster and Patricia Reeve. Hewes is

listed only as a poll rateable for 1791, 1792, 1794, 1796, and 1797; he does not appear in the other available tax lists for 1780, 1798, 1799, and 1817. Daniel Scott Smith helped interpret these data. Kaster did not find Hewes in "Massachusetts Direct Tax of 1798," MS, New England Historical and Genealogical Society, Boston. This was a dwelling tax.

8. One tax list, for 1793, lists Solomon Hewes for £1 4s. under commonwealth real estate assessment and £5 4s. 5d. town tax. He is listed immediately above George R. T. Hewes. This possibly is Solomon his eldest son (1771–1834), who entered his majority in 1792 and would marry in Wrentham in 1794. However, Anne Lehane Howard finds no record of a Solomon Hewes buying or selling property in the Suffolk Co. Registry of Deeds after the death of grandfather Solomon Hewes (1674?–1756).

9. See Bristol County Conveyance, n. 2 above.

10. Putnam, comp., *Joshua Hewes*, 334–35, 353–57, lists nine children, leaving space between Robert and Eleven for three unnamed children, and between Eleven and Fifteen for three more. A relative sent in the names of two "missing" children as Asa and Walter (ibid., Addendum, 601–2). Fifteen was identified as the fifteenth child in a newspaper account (*Providence Journal* reprinted in *Columbian Centinel* [Boston], July 1, 1835). For the significance of child-naming practices see Daniel Scott Smith, "Child Naming Patterns, Kinship Ties, and Change in Family Attitudes in Hingham, Massachusetts, 1641–1880," *Journal of Social History* 18 (1985); 541–66. and Herbert G. Gutman, *The Black Family in Slavery and Freedom, 1750–1925* (New York, 1976), chap. 5.

11. *Vital Records of Wrentham, Massachusetts to the Year 1850*, vol. 2 (Boston, 1910), 321, lists Sarah Hewes, born about 1769, marrying William Morason (*sic*), Nov. 27, 1806. *Vital Records of Attleboro, Massachusetts . . . to 1849* (Salem, Mass., 1934), 456, lists Eliza (*sic*) Hewes, born 1773, marrying Preserved Whipple, "both of Attleboro," Mar. 19, 1795, and Mary Hewes "of Wrentham," born 1777, marrying Abel Jillison of Attleborough, Jan. 21, 1809.

12. The clerk put down that Hewes "resided in Wrentham and Attlebury [*sic*] since the Revolution" (Pension Application, Oct. 16, 1832). The only evidence for Hewes's residence at Attleborough is Elizabeth's marriage record of 1795 (see above, n. 11). The conveyance of the "burying yard," Mar. 10, 1810 (see above, n. 2), lists Hewes as a "cordwainer *of Wrentham.*" I have not conducted a search of the tax records of Attleborough.

13. For the migration from Attleborough see Daggett, *Sketch of Attleborough*, 664–65. John Resch found in a sample of applicants under the 1818 pension law that "a third of the total no longer lived in the regions where their units originated and another 20 per cent appeared to have

moved to a different state within the same region" ("Federal Welfare for Revolutionary War Veterans," *The Social Science Review* 56 [1982]; 172–95). For another veteran who went west see Lemisch, "Life of Andrew Sherburne," sec. XII.

14. Putnam, comp., *Joshua Hewes*, 353–57.

15. Ibid., 339; Wilson, "Last Survivor," 5. Wilson heard the story of the walk out in Otsego County. There S. Crippin, the clerk who endorsed Hewes's pension application at Richfield Springs in 1832, wrote on it: "He was a soldier in the Late War as well as in the Revolution." Hewes himself made no such claim to Hawkes or Thatcher. Hewes's name does not appear on any of the checking lists in the Adams Papers, Mass. Hist. Soc., for either John or John Quincy Adams, kindly checked for me by Malcolm Freiberg.

16. Fiore, *Wrentham*, 100. The War of 1812 pension applications of Eleven and George Fifteen are reported in Putnam, comp., *Joshua Hewes*, 357–58.

11. Veteran

1. Duane Hamilton Hurd, *History of Otsego County, New York* (Philadelphia, 1878), 298–306, *passim*, W. T. Bailey, *Richfield Springs and Vicinity* . . . (New York, 1874), *passim*. I am indebted to Ethylyn Morse Hawkins, local historian, for sharing her knowledge with me, and the following friends of the Hewes family for answering inquiries: Vern Steele of Las Vegas, Nev., and Harry B. Carson of Golden, Colo.

2. Wilson, "Last Survivor," 5.

3. Hawkes, *Retrospect*, 94. "New York State Census for 1820: Otsego County," the handwritten takers' book, 163, lists George R. T. Hewes as living with his wife, and Robert Hewes below him with his family, and, 160, George R. T. F. Hewes, that is, Fifteen. The 1830 census lists only Robert Hewes but with one free white male "of ninety and under one hundred" living with him, confirming Hawkes.

4. For running Hewes down assiduously in the property records, vital records, and newspapers of Otsego County, I am especially indebted to Marion Brophy, Special Collections Librarian, New York State Historical Association, Cooperstown, as well as to Wendell Tripp, Chief of Library Services, and Wayne Wright, Edith R. Empey, and Susan Filupeit of the library staff. Marion Brophy found no record of Hewes's owning property but found Fifteen owning land in Richfield Springs, corroborating Hawkes.

5. Hawkes, *Retrospect*, 77–78, 94; Will of Daniel Hewes, recorded July 16,

1821, Suffolk Co. Probate Court, and Aug. 5, 1822, Record Book 120, 129, for the final sum, $2,904.79, located by Ruth Kennedy.

6. Tombstone, Lakeview Cemetery, Richfield Springs. For Sarah's signature as a mark see the 1797 conveyances above, Chapter 10, n. 2. For the Tea Party see Thatcher, *Memoir of Hewes*, 186, and for Hewes on her age see Hawkes, *Retrospect*, 27.

7. Hawkes, *Retrospect*, 94–97. See also Putnam, comp., *Joshua Hewes*, 353–57. I am grateful to Catherine Wilson of Des Moines, Iowa, a descendant via Solomon, for copies of letters by Virgil Hammond Hewes, George's grandson.

8. Hawkes, *Retrospect*, 94–96, 114. See also Putnam, comp., *Joshua Hewes*, for a story from "a near relative" that Hewes walked 10 miles to visit ex-President John Quincy Adams to ask for help on his pension, possibly a variant of the story about Hewes's walk to ex-President John Adams to get into the navy. For the laws see Resch, "Poverty, the Elderly and Federal Welfare," 1–7. Resch clarified a number of points for me. See also Robert George Bodenger, "Soldiers' Bonuses: A History of Veterans' Benefits in the United States, 1776–1967" (Ph.D. diss., Pennsylvania State University, 1971), 26–42, and Lemisch, "Life of Andrew Sherburne," secs. XII, XIII, for one veteran's long bitter battle for his pension.

9. Hawkes, *Retrospect*, 114; Pension Application. The clerk disallowed the three months on the *Diamond*, probably because it was a privateer, but allowed the seven months and fifteen days on the *Defence*, also a privateer but officially a ship of war in the Connecticut navy, under a naval officer.

10. Wilson, "Last Survivor," 5–6.

11. *Freeman's Journal* (Cooperstown, N.Y.), July 13, 1829; Hawkes, *Retrospect*, 90.

12. Cooper's occasional residence in Cooperstown, 1816–1840, may be established from James F. Beard, *Letters and Journals of James Fenimore Cooper* (Cambridge, Mass., 1960–1964), vols. 1–4, *passim*. Beard kindly answered my inquiry about Cooper's sources. See Cooper, *The Spy: A Tale of the Neutral Ground* (New York, 1821), and *Ned Meyers; or, a Life Before the Mast* (Philadelphia, 1843); and Thomas Philbrick, *James Fenimore Cooper and the Development of American Sea Fiction* (Cambridge, Mass., 1961), chaps. 2, 4.

13. Hawkes, *Retrospect*, 77–80.

14. Wilson repeated a tale that Hewes had attended the laying of the cornerstone of the Bunker Hill Monument in Boston in 1825 ("Last Survivor," 6). Hewes said nothing of this to Hawkes or Thatcher, and Hawkes

said he "had made but one visit," that of 1821 (*Retrospect*, 76). Wilson's tale mixed images of the 1821 and 1835 trips. *Freeman's Jour.*, May 30, June 27, July 11, 1825, and *Cherry Valley Gazette* (N.Y.), June 28, Aug. 9, 1825, say nothing of Hewes in reports of the observance. Benson J. Lossing garbled the story further by claiming that Hewes was at the ceremony for the *completion* of the monument, June 17, 1843, three years after his death (*Pictorial Field-Book of the Revolution; or, Illustrations by Pen and Pencil*. . . , vol. 1 [New York, 1851], 501–2).

15. Wilson, "Last Survivor," 6. Marion Brophy reports that "there are no Methodist church records for the 1830s or 1840s in Richfield unless they are hidden in an attic somewhere. The local officials instituted a search and found nothing" (letter to the author, July 17, 1978).

16. Wilson, "Last Survivor," 6; Hawkes, *Retrospect*, 93–94. He was not a total abstainer; Hawkes indicated that he used "stimulating liquors" when needed.

17. The clerk wrote on Hewes's petition for a pension that there was "no clergyman residing in his neighborhood whose testimony he can obtain pursuant to the instructions from the War department" (see above, n. 9).

18. Paul G. Faler, *Mechanics and Manufacturers in the Early Industrial Revolution: Lynn, Massachussets, 1780–1860* (Albany, 1981), chap. 2; Charles G. Steffen, *The Mechanics of Baltimore: Workers and Politics in the Age of Revolution, 1763–1812* (Urbana, Ill., 1984), chap. 12; Barbara M. Tucker, "Our Good Methodists: The Church, the Factory, and the Working Class in Ante-Bellum Webster, Massachusetts," *Maryland Historian* 8 (1977): 26–37.

19. Bailey, *Richfield Springs*, 148. For the character of early western Methodism see Frank Baker, *From Wesley to Asbury: Studies in Early American Methodism* (Durham, N.C., 1976), chap. 11, esp. 195–97, and George Peck, *Early Methodism within the Bounds of the Old Genesee Conference from 1788 to 1828*. . . (New York, 1860), passim.

12. Hero

1. Auguste Levasseur, *Lafayette in America in 1824 and 1825*, vol. 2 (Philadelphia, 1829), 202–206; Kammen, *Season of Youth*, 21, 26, 120; Oliver Wendell Holmes, *Complete Poems* (Boston, 1836).

2. Joseph Buckingham, *Annals of the Massachusetts Charitable Mechanics Association* (Boston, 1853), 202, reporting a toast at a dinner for Lafayette in 1825; shoemaker toast, 1826, in Kammen, *Season of Youth*, 44–45; Seth Luther, *An Address to the Working-Men of New-England*. . . *Delivered in Boston* . . . (Boston, 1832), 27. For documents of Boston labor organizations, 1825–1835, see John R. Commons et al., eds., *A Documentary His-*

tory of American Industrial Society, vol. 6 (Cleveland, Ohio, 1910), 98, 73–100.

3. *Columbian Centinel*, July 1, 9, 1835; *Evening Mercantile Journal*, July 1, 8, 1835; *American Traveller* (Boston), July 28, 1835. I am indebted to Helen Callahan for making a search of the Boston newspapers for July 1835.

4. *Evening Mercantile Journal*, July 8, 1835; *American Traveller*, July 7, 1835.

5. *Boston Courier*, July 22, 1835; *Providence Journal*, reprinted in *Columbian Centinel*, July 1, 1835.

6. Putnam, comp., *Joshua Hewes*, 362–63, 439, reported this as an oil by Charles Palmer of Richfield Springs, done Jan. 1836 on a board 2'1" × 2'6", in the possession of David Hewes, Robert Hewes's son. Wilson reprints this, "redrawn from a photograph by Mr. Sidney Waldman" ("Last Survivor," 3). I have been unable to locate painting, photograph, or drawing. Hawkes's *Retrospect* has a drawing in the frontispiece, which could have been made from life, and Thatcher's *Memoir of Hewes* has still another drawing, most likely copied from the Cole portrait. Sometime after Hewes's death there was a second printing of Hawkes's *Retrospect* with a new frontispiece drawing of Hewes and 16 illustrations of events of the Revolution, copied from other engravings.

7. Lossing, *Pictorial Field-Book*, 499n, 501–2; with numerous inaccuracies repeated in *Appletons' Cyclopedia of American Biography*, ed. James Grant Wilson and John Fiske, vol. 3 (New York, 1887), 190; William Cullen Bryant and Sidney Howard Gay, *A Popular History of the United States*, vol. 3 (New York, 1883), 374; Henry C. Watson, *The Yankee Tea Party* (Philadelphia, 1851), Drake, *Tea Leaves*, cxv; Samuel Adams Drake, *Old Landmarks and Historic Personages of Boston* (Boston, 1873), 269–70, 282–83; Bailey, *Richfield Springs*, 98–99. Esther Forbes is the only modern historian to have used the memoirs extensively.

8. Putnam, comp., *Joshua Hewes*, 353–58, 601–2. I am indebted to the registrar general of the Daughters of the American Revolution for providing me with copies of five applications by Hewes's descendents.

9. The end of the century had "an obsession with transplanting Revolutionary heroes to more suitable graves" (Kammen, *Season of Youth*, 65).

10. David Kennison, who died in Chicago in 1848, seemingly was the last survivor (see Lossing, *Pictorial Field-Book*, 501–2).

11. *American Traveller*, July 28, 1835, wrote of the portrait that "it is an admirable likeness—everything about it—the coloring, expression &c. even to the cane, are true to life." The Bostonian Society acquired the portrait in 1885, according to an article by D. T. V. Hustoon, its secretary (*Boston Weekly Transcript*, Jan. 26, 1886). For Cole (1803–1858) see William Dunlap, *History of the Rise and Progress of the Arts of Design in the United States*, vol. 3 (New York, 1834), 136, who said that the Hewes por-

trait was "among the best of his portraits." The dating of the portrait is confirmed by Mary Leen, Librarian, Bostonian Society (letter to the author, Aug. 16, 1977).
12. Hawkes, *Retrospect*, 91, citing a toast of July 4, 1833.

Part Two: When Did They Start Calling It the Boston Tea Party?

1. C. Vann Woodward, Preface to *The Strange Career of Jim Crow* (New York, 1955); Michael Kammen, *A Season of Youth: The American Revolution and the Historical Imagination* (New York, 1975); Eric Hobsbawm and Terrence Ranger, eds., *The Invention of Tradition* (Cambridge, Eng., 1983).

1. Taming the Revolution

1. *Peter Oliver's Origin and Progress of the American Rebellion: A Tory View*, ed. Douglass Adair and John A. Schutz (San Marino, Calif., 1961), 65. Pauline Maier, *From Resistance to Rebellion: Colonial Radicals and the Development of American Opposition to Britain, 1765–1776* (New York, 1972), quotations at 123–24; my analysis draws on my Ms. in progress, "In the Streets of Boston: The Common People and the Shaping of the American Revolution."
2. Pauline Maier, "Popular Uprisings and Civil Authority in Eighteenth Century America," *William and Mary Quarterly* 27 (1970): 3–35; Lemisch, "Jack Tar in the Streets"; Lax and Pencak, "The Knowles Riot"; Marcus Rediker, "A Motley Crew of Rebels: Sailors, Slaves and the Coming of the American Revolution," in *The Transforming Hand of Revolution*, ed. Ronald Hoffman and Peter Albert (Charlottesville, 1996), 155–98.
3. Young, "Popes Day, Tar and Feathers and Coronet Joyce Jun." (Ms.); Francis Cogliano, "No King, No Popery: Anti-Popery in New England, 1745–1791" (Ph.D. diss., Boston University, 1993), chaps. 1 and 2 [published Westport, Conn., 1996].
4. Dirk Hoerder, *Crowd Action in Revolutionary Massachusetts, 1765–1780* (New York, 1977), remains the most reliable guide to crowd events; Oliver, *Origin and Progress*; Anderson, "Ebenezer McIntosh."
5. Young, "English Plebeian Culture and Eighteenth Century American Radicalism," in *The Origins of Anglo-American Radicalism*, ed. Margaret Jacob and James Jacob (London, 1984; New Jersey, 1991), 185–213; Hoerder, "Boston Leaders and Boston Crowds, 1765–1776" in *The Amer-*

ican Revolution: Explorations in the History of American Radicalism, ed. Alfred Young (Dekalb, Ill., 1976), 233–71.

6. Hiller Zobel, *The Boston Massacre* (New York, 1970), in conjunction with Lemisch, "Radical Plot in Boston," and Maier, "Revolutionary Violence."

7. L. Kinvin Wroth and Hiller B. Zobel, eds., *Legal Papers of John Adams* (Cambridge, Mass., 1965), vol. 3 for the trials; for a comparison of the depictions of the event by Paul Revere and Alonzo Chappel, see Alfred Young, Terry Fife, and Mary Janzen, *We the People: Voices and Images of the New Nation* (Philadelphia, 1993), 30–31.

8. Kurt Ritter, "Rhetoric and Ritual in the American Revolution: The Boston Massacre Commemorations, 1771–1783" (Ph.D diss., Indiana University, 1974).

9. Bernard Bailyn, *The Ordeal of Thomas Hutchinson* (Cambridge, Mass., 1974), 383–408, for the historiography; Philip Davidson, *Propaganda and the American Revolution, 1763–1783* (Chapel Hill, N.C., 1941), chaps. 14–17.

10. Nash, *The Urban Crucible: Social Change, Political Consciousness, and the Origins of the American Revolution* (Cambridge, Mass., 1979), chap. 13.

11. Robert Blair St. George, *Conversing by Signs: Poetics of Implication in Colonial New England Culture* (Chapel Hill, N.C., 1998), chap. 3, "Attacking Houses."

2. The Destruction of the Tea

1. Benjamin Labaree, *The Boston Tea Party*, (New York, 1964), remains the standard source, and Hoerder, *Crowd Action*, the best account of the crowd. Recent works that shed light on the politics and ideology of the action are John W. Tyler, *Smugglers and Patriots: Boston Merchants and the Advent of the American Revolution* (Boston, 1986); Charles W. Akers, *The Divine Politician: Samuel Cooper and the American Revolution in Boston* (Boston, 1982); and Richard Bushman, *King and People in Provincial Massachusetts* (Chapel Hill, N.C., 1985).

2. The first list to appear in print in Thatcher, *Memoir of Hewes* (1835), had 56 names; by the time Drake published *Tea Leaves* (1884) there were 113 claimants. Claimants accepted by the Boston Tea Party Chapter of the Daughters of the American Revolution number 170. Scholars, using different lists and sources, have come up with roughly similar proportions of occupations and social classes. Hunt, in "The Crowd and the American Revolution," using a list of 102 and identifying 76 men, finds 17 boys and apprentices, 39 artisans, 4 town officials, and 16 merchants;

Hoerder, *Crowd Action*, working with a list of 123, and using the Boston Tax List of 1771, finds 14 out-of-towners, 16 apprentices, and only 34 who can be identified on the tax list. Of these 34, one-third held no property, one-third small property, one-sixth up to £100 and a further one-sixth over £100. George Quintal, Jr., Historian and Genealogist for the Arnold Expedition Historical Society [Colburn House, Arnold Rd., Pittston, Maine 04345], the most recent scholar to analyze the data, in a work in progress has identified additional claimants to produce a list of 201. Of 88 whose occupations he can identify, he tentatively finds 14 apprentices, 47 artisans, and 15 merchants. In addition he identifies 2 unskilled laborers, 2 mariners, 3 merchant's clerks, 4 in service-trades, 5 farmers, and 7 professionals. Quintal is attempting to establish a scale of credibility to the claims for participation.

3. Pauline Maier, *The Old Revolutionaries: Political Lives in the Age of Samuel Adams* (New York, 1980), chap. 3; L. H. Butterfield et al., eds., *Diary and Autobiography of John Adams* (Cambridge, Mass., 1961), vol. 2, 85–87.

4. I draw on E. P. Thompson, *Customs in Common* (New York, 1993), chap. 8, "Rough Music"; for surveys of European scholarship, Peter Burke, *Popular Culture in Early Modern Europe* (New York, 1978), and Samuel Kinser, *Carnival, American Style: Mardi Gras at New Orleans and Mobile* (Chicago, 1990), chap. 1.

5. Mercy Otis Warren, *History of the Rise, Progress and Termination of the American Revolution*, 2 vols. (Boston, 1805), chap. 4; Rodris Roth, "Tea Drinking in Eighteenth Century America: Its Etiquette and Equipage" *United States National Museum Bulletin* 225 (Washington, D.C., 1961): 61–91, conveniently reprinted in Robert Blair St. George, ed., *Material Life in America, 1600–1800* (Boston, 1990), 439–62; David S. Shields, *Civil Tongues and Polite Letters in British America* (Chapel Hill, N.C., 1997), chap. 4, "Tea Tables and Salons."

6. Philip Deloria, *Playing Indian* (New Haven, 1998), chap. 1; Alan Taylor, *Liberty Men and Great Proprietors: The Revolutionary Settlement on the Maine Frontier, 1760–1820* (Chapel Hill, N.C., 1990).

7. Clarence S. Brigham, *Paul Revere's Engravings* (New York, 1969), plates 35, 67, 69.

8. Gillian B. Anderson, ed., *Freedom's Voice in Poetry and Song: An Inventory of Political and Patriotic Lyrics in Colonial American Newspapers, 1773–1783*, Part II, "Songbook" (Wilmington, Del., 1977); Frank Moore, ed., *Songs and Ballads of the American Revolution* (New York, 1855).

9. T. H. Breen, "'Baubles of Britain': The American and Consumer Revolutions of the Eighteenth Century," in *Of Consuming Interests: The Style*

of Life in the Eighteenth Century, ed. Cary Carson, Ronald Hoffman, and Peter J. Albert (Charlottesville, Va., 1994), 474–81.
10. Daniel L. Schachter, *Searching for Memory: The Brain, the Mind, and the Past* (Cambridge, Mass., 1996), 195–201, 283–84 (flashbulb memory); David W. Conroy, Epilogue to *In Public Houses: Drink and the Revolution of Authority in Colonial Massachusets* (Chapel Hill, N.C., 1995).
11. John Adams to Hezikiah Niles, May 10, 1819, in *Army and Navy Chronicle* I (1835). Reminiscences are in Francis Drake, *Tea Leaves* (Boston, 1884), passim, and in John Harris, *The Boston Tea Party. The Trigger of Our Revolution* (Boston, 1973), originally a special supplement to the *Boston Globe.* See also two reminiscences cited above, Chapter 6, nn. 3 and 5.
12. For graphics, see Elizabeth Carroll Reilly, *A Dictionary of Colonial American Printers' Ornaments and Illustrations* (Worcester, 1975), 227–31; Cresswell, ed., *The American Revolution in Drawings and Prints: A Checklist of 1765–1790 Graphics in the Library of Congress* (Washington, D.C., 1975), chap. 2, "Events"; American Antiquarian Society, Catalog of Engravings and Prints (CAEP), a computerized catalog; Young et al., *We the People,* 30–31 (Revere), 42–43 (Doolittle), 62–65 (powderhorns).

3. Taming the Memory of the Revolution, 1783–1820

1. See Young, "Plebeian Culture," for the transmission of festive forms from England to the colonies; "Pope's Day, Tar and Feathers and Coronet Joyce, Jun.," for the transmission during the revolutionary era; and "Artisans on Parade: Measuring Mechanic Consciousness in Boston" (Paper delivered at Conference on Festive Culture, Philadelphia, 1996) for festive celebration after the Revolution. On the end of Pope's Day, see Cogliano, "No King, No Popery," chaps. 4–8.
2. Len Travers, *Celebrating the Fourth: Independence Day and the Rites of Nationalism in the Early Republic* (Amherst, Mass., 1997), passim, and "Hurrah for the Fourth: Patriotism, Politics and Independence Day in Federalist Boston, 1783–1818," *Essex Institute Historical Collections* 125 (1989): 129–61; Simon Newman, *Parades and the Politics of the Street: Festive Culture in the Early American Republic* (Philadelphia, 1997), chap. 3; David Waldstreicher, *In the Midst of Perpetual Fetes: The Making of American Nationalism, 1776–1820* (Chapel Hill, N.C., 1997), chaps. 1–3; *Boston Town Records, 1718–1783* (Boston, 1895), 304–5. Susan G. Davis, *Parades and Power: Street Theatre in Nineteenth-Century Philadelphia* (Berkeley, 1988).

3. Timothy Dwight, *Travels in New England and New York,* ed. Barbara Solomon, 4 vols. (Cambridge, Mass., 1969), vol. 1, 368.

4. Travers, *Celebrating the Fourth,* 157–69.

5. Young, *The Democratic Republicans of New York: The Origins, 1788–1797* (Chapel Hill, N.C., 1967), chap. 18; Newman, *Parades and Politics,* chap. 4.

6. "Communication," *Independent Chronicle,* Sept. 17, 1795; "Brief History of the Rise and Progress of the Recent Mobs and Riots," *Columbian Centinel,* Oct. 31, 1796.

7. William W. Wheildon, *Sentry, or Beacon Hill; The Beacon and the Monument of 1635 and 1790* (Concord, 1877); Harold and James Kirker, *Bulfinch's Boston, 1787–1817* (New York, 1964).

8. Justin Winsor, ed., *Memorial History of Boston,* 4 vols. (Boston, 1881), IV, 27–29, 64–65; *Independent Chronicle,* July 9, 1823. The tablets were later mounted within the State House, and still later, in 1898, on a half-size replica of the monument that today stands behind the building.

9. Ronald P. Formisano, *The Transformation of Political Culture: Massachusetts Parties, 1790s–1840s* (New York, 1983), chap. 3.

10. William V. Wells, *The Life and Public Services of Samuel Adams* (Boston, 1865), III, 376–79 (Sullivan), 290 (house); Maier, *The Old Revolutionaries,* chap. 1, "Samuel Adams"; John Adams to Joseph Ward, June 6, 1809, reprinted in Young, *We the People,* 191; Adams to William Tudor, June 5, 1817, cited in Maier, "Samuel Adams," 7. Portraits of Adams and Hancock by John Singleton Copley were hung in Faneuil Hall between 1833 and 1837. In 1833, Abel Bowen, *Bowen's Picture of Boston* (Boston 1833), 71, mentioned two other paintings in the Hall and no others, but in an oration in 1837 Wendell Phillips referred to the Adams and Hancock portraits on the wall. Phillips, *Speeches, Lectures and Letters* (Boston, 1864), 1–10.

11. *Independent Chronicle,* July 9, 1823; Young, "Mechanics on Parade"; Bowen, *Bowen's Picture of Boston,* 68, 281 (statue); Hosmer, *Presence of the Past,* 106 (statue); David Hackett Fischer, *The Revolution of American Conservatism: The Federalist Party in the Era of Jeffersonian Democracy* (New York, 1965), 123 (parade).

12. Higginson cited in Formisano, *Transformation of Political Culture,* 60.

13. "The Soliloquy Of the Boston Tree of Liberty," *Massachusetts Gazette,* Feb. 22, 1776; Samuel Adams Drake, *Old Landmarks and Historic Personages of Boston,* (Boston, 1873), chap. 14; "The Original Liberty Hall," Boston *Transcript,* Nov. 15, 1891, Scrapbook Collection, Bostonian Society.

14. Walter Muir Whitehill, *Boston: A Topographical History* 2nd ed. (Cambridge, Mass., 1968), chaps. 3, 4; Bowen, *Bowen's Picture of Boston,* 76

(Old State House); Lynn Betlock, Emily Curran, Jane Schwerdtfeger, and Ellen Weiner, *Old South: An Architectural History of the Old South Meeting House* (Boston, 1995): The granite tablet is now mounted within the building in the offices of the Old South Association.

15. Whitehill, *Boston: A Topographical History*, 113 (North End churches); Bowen, Bowen's *Picture of Boston*, 243–45; Caleb Snow, *A History of Boston* (Boston, 1825 2nd ed., 1828).

16. Michael Holleran, *Boston's "Changeful Times": Origins of Preservation and Planning in America* (Baltimore, 1998), chap. 4; Len Tucker, *The Massachusetts Historical Society: A Bicentennial History, 1791–1991* (Boston, 1996), 55–56. The president was James Savage (1841–55).

4. Merchants, Mill Owners, and Master Mechanics

1. St. George, *Conversing by Signs*, chap. 3; Alan Kulikoff, "The Progress of Inequality in Revolutionary Boston," *William and Mary Quartrly* 28 (1971): 375–414. The place of death of claimants to the Tea Party is a useful index of migration. George Quintal (see Chapter 2, n. 2), working with a list of 201 claimants, identified the place of death for 147, of which 90 were in Massachusetts, 35 in other New England states, and 22 outside New England. Of the 90 who died in Massachusetts, only 44 died in Boston.

2. David Van Tassel, *Recording America's Past: An Interpretation of the Development of Historical Studies in America, 1607–1884* (Chicago, 1960); Caleb Bingham, *The Columbian Orator*, 6th ed. (Boston, 1804), *American Preceptor* 32nd ed. (Boston, 1807) Noah Webster *An American Selection of Lessons in Reading and Speaking*, 14th ed. (Hartford, 1801); McGuffy's *Eclectic Reader* (Cincinnati, 1837) carries on the same tradition; see Elliott Gorn, *The McGuffy Readers* (Boston, 1998).

3. Rosemarie Zagarri, *A Woman's Dilemma: Mercy Otis Warren and the American Revolution* (Wheeling, Ill., 1995), 148–49 (Warren); for creative literature, see Sacvan Bercovitch, ed., *The Cambridge History of American Literature* (New York, 1995), vol. 1 (1590–1820), 539–694, especially "Chronology of Important Texts," 695 ff.

4. Tucker, *Massachussets Historical Society*, chaps. 1–3.

5. David Wilson, *United Irishmen, United States: Immigrant Radicals in the Early Republic* (Ithaca, 1998), 103–10; Young, *Masquerade: The Life and Times of Deborah Sampson Gannett, Continental Soldier* (New York, Knopf, forthcoming).

6. Frederic Jaher, *The Urban Establishment: Upper Strata in Boston, New York, Charleston, Chicago and Los Angeles* (Urbana, Ill., 1982), chap. 2, quotation at 21; George W. Piersen, *Tocqueville and Beaumont in America*

(New York, 1918), 364–65; Oliver Wendell Holmes, *Elsie Venner* (Boston, 1861), chap. 1, cited in Thomas H. O'Connor, *Bibles, Brahamins and Bosses: A Short History of Boston* (Boston, 1991), 84.

7. Harlow E. Sheidley, "Sectional Nationalism: The Culture and Politics of the Massachusetts Conservative Elite, 1815–1836" (Ph.D. diss., University of Connecticut, 1990) [published Boston, 1998].

8. Samuel Eliot Morison, *The Life and Letters of Harrison Gray Otis, 1765–1845: The Urbane Federalist*, 2 vols. (Boston, 1913); William Tudor, *The Life of James Otis* (Boston, 1823); Robert McCaughey, *Josiah Quincy, 1772–1864: The Last Federalist* (Cambridge, Mass., 1974), chap. 1; Josiah Quincy, *Memoir of The Life of Josiah Quincy Jun. of Massachusetts* (Boston, 1825); Quincy "An Address . . . July 4, 1816" in Quincy, *A Municipal History of the Town and City of Boston* (Boston, 1852), 429; Fischer, *Revolution of American Conservatism*, chap. 2, 272–74.

9. Kirker, *Bulfinch's Boston*; Whitehill, *Boston: A Topographical History*, chap. 4.

10. Robert F. Dalzell, Jr., *Enterprising Elite: The Boston Associates and the World They Made* (New York, 1987); François Weil, "Capitalism and Industrialization in New England, 1815–1845, *Journal of American History* 84 (1998): 1334–54; *Bowen's Picture of Boston* lists the banks and companies. For other analyses of the Boston elite of this era, see Ronald Story, *The Forging of an Aristocracy: Harvard and the Boston Upper Class, 1800–1825* (Middletown, Conn., 1980), chap. 1; Edward Pessen, *Riches, Class, and Power Before the Civil War* (Lexington, Mass., 1973); E. Digby Baltzell, *Puritan Boston and Quaker Philadelphia: Two Protestant Elites . . . The Spirit of Class Authority and Leadership* (New York, 1979). For ideology, see Linda Kerber, *Federalists in Dissent: Imagery and Ideology in Jeffersonian America* (Ithaca, 1970), chaps. 1, 6.

11. "A Mechanic," *The Democrat*, Oct. 24, 1804; Young, "Artisans and the Constitution" (Merrill Jensen Lecture, University of Wisconsin, 1996); Young, "The Framers of the Constitution and the 'Genius of the People,'" *Radical History Review* 42 (1988): 7–47; Young, "Conservatives, the Constitution and 'The Spirit of Accommodation,'" in *How Democratic Is the Constitution?*, ed. Robert Goldwin and William Schambra (Washington, D.C., 1980), 117–47.

12. Fischer, *Revolution of American Conservatism*, 253.

13. Gary Kornblith, "From Artisans to Businessmen: Master Mechanics in New England, 1789–1850" (Ph.D. diss., Princeton University, 1983), chaps. 2, 3, 12; Joseph T. Buckingham, *Annals of the Massachussetts Charitable Mechanics Association* (Boston, 1853).

14. Forbes, *Paul Revere*; Robert Dubuque, "The Painter and the Portrait: John Singleton Copley's Portrait of Paul Revere," *The Revere House Ga-*

zette 17 (1989): 1–5; Susan Rather, "Carpenter, Tailor, Shoemaker, Artist: Copley and Portrait Painting around 1770," *Art Bulletin* 79 (1997): 269–90.

15. Edmund S. Morgan, ed., *Paul Revere's Three Accounts of His Famous Ride* (Boston, 1968); [Paul Revere Memorial Association] *Paul Revere—Artisan, Businessman, and Patriot: The Man Behind the Myth* (Boston, 1988), chap. 1 by Patrick Leehey.

16. David Hackett Fischer, *Paul Revere's Ride* (New York, 1994), 327–44, Appendix, "Historiography: Myths After the Midnight Ride"; Jane Triber, *A True Republican: The Life of Paul Revere* (Boston, 1998).

5. The Discovery of the Veterans, 1825

1. Everett cited in Sarah Purcell, "Sealed with Blood: National Identity and Public Memory of the Revolutionary War, 1775–1815" (Ph.D. diss., Brown University, 1997), chap. 3.

2. The following library catalogs of imprints arranged by city and dates were searched for Boston for the years 1823–24: New York Public Library, Boston Public Library, Boston Athenaeum, Massachussets Historical Society.

3. Sheidley, "Sectional Nationalism," chap. 6; Peter Linebaugh, "Jubilating: Or, How the Atlantic Working Class Used the Biblical Jubilee Against Capitalism, with Some Success," *Radical History Review* 50 (1991): 143–80, a religious dimension of jubilee unexplored for the American jubilees of the Revolution.

4. John Resch, *Suffering Soldiers: Revolutionary War Veterans, Moral Sentiment, and Political Culture* (Amherst, Mass., 1999), chaps. 1, 4.

5. *Niles Weekly Register*, Apr. 18, June 27, 1818, cited in Resch, "Politics and Public Culture: The Revolutionary War Pension Act of 1818," *Journal of the Early Republic* 8 (1988): 139–58, at 152.

6. Purcell, "Sealed with Blood," chap. 5 (the number of narratives); J. Todd White and Charles H. Lesser, eds., *Fighters for Independence* . . . (Chicago, 1977), lists the memoirs in sec. 3; Joseph Martin, *A Narrative of Some of the Dangers and Sufferings of a Revolutionary Soldier* (Hallowell, Me., 1830); Taylor, *Liberty Men*, 247–49 (on Martin).

7. Van Tassel, *Recording America's Past*, 90–93; Salma Hale, *History of the United States . . . to 1815* (New York, 1822); Charles Goodrich, *History of the United States* (Boston, 1823); Noah Webster, *History of the United States* (New Haven, 1832); Emma Willard, *History of the United States* (New York, 1828); *DAB*, s.v. "Samuel Goodrich."

8. Caleb Snow, *History of Boston* . . . (Boston, 1825); Robin Carver, *History of Boston* (1834) and *Stories About Boston* . . . (Boston, 1833); Alden Brad-

ford, *History of Massachussets*, 3 vols. (Boston, 1822–29); Thomas Hutchinson, *The History of the Colony and Province of Massachusetts Bay*, 3 vols. (Boston, 1828); Carolyn L. Karcher, *The First Woman in the Republic: A Cultural Biography of Lydia Maria Child* (Durham, N.C., 1994), 40–45.

9. Purcell, "Sealed with Blood," chap. 5.

10. My account leans on Purcell, "Sealed with Blood," chap. 5, and Sheidley, "Sectional Nationalism," 346–56; Marian Klamkin, *The Return of Lafayette, 1814–1825* (New York, 1975) chaps. 5, 20.

11. Robert Remini, *Daniel Webster* (New York, 1997), (Demosthnes); Daniel Walker Howe, *The Political Culture of the American Whigs* (Chicago, 1979), 210–225 (spokesman); Webster, *Address . . . Bunker Hill . . .* (Boston, 1825); Sheidley, "Sectional Nationalism," 353 (Appleton).

12. The works cited in Chapter 3, n. 13, and for the building: "The Old Liberty Tree," *Boston Daily Evening Transcript*, Feb. 19, 1850, and "Report of the Boston Landmarks Commission on the Potential Designation of the Liberty Tree Building (March 5, 1985), typescript.

13. Pauline Maier, *American Scripture: Making the Declaration of Independence* (New York, 1997), chap. 4., citing *North American Review* at 177.

14. Oliver Wendell Holmes, *The Complete Poetical Works of Oliver Wendell Holmes* (Boston, 1908), 4–5; Lincoln (1838) cited in Kammen, *Season of Youth*, 30.

15. Formisano, *Transformation of Political Culture*, 60 (carted about); Sheidley, "Sectional Nationalism," 328 (Everett).

6. Claiming the Revolution

1. *Boston Daily Advocate*, July 7, 1834; *DAB*, s.v. "Benjamin Franklin Hallett."

2. Frederick Robinson, *An Oration Delivered before the Trades' Union of Boston and Vicinity . . .* (Boston, 1834).

3. Christopher Tomlins, *Law, Labor and Ideology in the Early American Republic* (Cambridge, Eng., 1993), chap. 6, at 182; Lisa Lubow, "Artisans in Transition: Early Capitalist Development and the Carpenters of Boston, 1787–1837" (Ph.D. diss., UCLA, 1987), 494–549.

4. Formisano, *Transformation of Political Culture*, chap. 10; Arthur Schlesinger, Jr., *The Age of Jackson* (Boston, 1945), chap. 11; Edward Pessen, *Most Uncommon Jacksonians: The Radical Leaders of the Early Labor Movement* (Albany, N.Y., 1967).

5. Philip Foner, ed., *We the Other People: Alternative Declarations of Independence by Labor Groups, Farmers, Woman's Rights Advocates, and Blacks, 1829–1975* (Urbana, Ill., 1976); Bruce Laurie, *Artisans into Workers: Labor*

in Nineteenth Century America (New York, 1989), chap. 2; quotation from Laurie, "The Revolution Revisited: Americans Celebrate the Fourth of July, 1788–1850" (Paper, Milan Group in Early American History, 1988).

6. Waldstreicher, *In the Midst of Perpetual Fetes,* chap. 6; Shane White, "'It Was a Proud Day': African Americans, Festivals and Parades in the North, 1741–1834," *Journal of American History* 81 (1994–95): 13–50.

7. Pessen, *Most Uncommon Jacksonians,* 87–90, and passim.; Louis Hartz, "Seth Luther: The Story of a Working Class Rebel," *New England Quarterly* 13 (1940): 401–18; Schlesinger, *Age of Jackson,* 149–51; Seth Luther, *An Address to the Working Men of New England . . .* 2nd ed. (New York, 1833).

8. Frederick Robinson, *An Oration Delivered before the Trades' Unions of Boston . . .* (Boston, 1834); Tomlins, *Labor, Law and Ideology,* 191–92; Schlesinger, *Age of Jackson,* 167–68.

9. For the documents, John R. Commons et al., eds., *Documentary History of American Industrial Society,* 10 vols. (New York, 1910), vol. 5, 73–99.

10. Theophilus Fisk, *Capital Against Labor: An Address Delivered at Julien Hall before the Mechanics of Boston . . . May 20, 1835* (Boston, 1835), sometimes listed in finding aids as an address delivered July 4, 1835, which I was not able to locate; Pessen, *Uncommon Jacksonians,* 91–93.

11. Commons, *History of Labor,* vol. 1, 387 (the height); Pessen, *Uncommon Jacksonians,* 39 (turning point); Kornblith, "Artisans to Businessmen," 516 (speaker); *Boston Evening Traveller,* Feb. 18, 1834, cited in Thomas Dublin, *Women at Work: The Transformation of Work and Community in Lowell, Massachusetts, 1826–1860* (New York, 1979), 89–93.

12. Theodore M. Hammett, "Two Mobs of Jacksonian Boston: Ideology and Interest," *Journal of American History* 62 (1976): 845–68; Ray Allen Billington, *The Protestant Crusade, 1800–1860* (New York, 1938).

13. David Grimsted, "Rioting in Its Jacksonian Setting," *American Historical Review* 77 (1972): 361–97, quotations at 362, 374; Hammett, "Two Mobs," 853.

14. Thatcher cited in Tomlins, *Law, Labor, and Ideology,* 193–94; Parsons cited in Schlesinger, *Age of Jackson,* 166; Roger Lane, *Policing the City: Boston, 1822–1885* (New York, 1971), chap. 3, 85.

15. David Walker, *Walker's Appeal in Four Articles . . . Written in Boston, September 28, 1829* (Boston, 1830), reprinted in Herbert Aptheker, *One Continual Cry* (New York, 1965); Donald Jacobs, "William Lloyd Garrison's *Liberator* and Boston's Blacks, 1830–1865," *New England Quarterly* 44 (1971): 261; Carolyn Karcher, ed., *A Lydia Maria Child Reader* (Durham, N.C., 1997), 136–37.

16. Morison, *Life of Otis* ("best people"); James B. Stewart, "Boston Aboli-

tionists and the Atlantic World, 1820–1861," in *Courage and Conscience Black and White Abolitionists in Boston*, ed. Donald Jacobs (Boston, 1993), 112–13; Hammett, "Two Mobs," 865–66.
17. Garrison, "Triumph of Mobocracy in Boston," *Liberator,* Nov. 7, 1835.
18. George Ticknor Curtis, *The True Uses of American Revolutionary History* (Boston, 1841).
19. Tomlins, *Law, Labor and Ideology,* 198 (spasmodic war); Windsor, ed., *Memorial History of Boston*, vol. 3, 382 (Mayor Lyman); Karcher, *First Women in the Republic,* 227–28 (Lydia Maria Child).

7. The Recovery of the Tea Party

1. *Boston Evening Traveller,* July 1835, reprinted in *Army and Navy Chronicle*, Aug. 15, 1835.
2. I conducted a search of the following major library catalogs under the subjects "Boston Tea Party," "Tea Party," and "Tea," and by title: Newberry Library, Library of Congress, New York Public Library, American Antiquarian Society, and a search of the major guides to American imprints, namely, Evans, Shaw-Shoemaker, and Sabin. Subsequent searches of Online Computer Library Center (OCLC) and Research Libraries Information Network (RLIN) electronic catalogs turned up no new titles.
3. Hallett, "To Whom it May Concern," Oct. 2, 1834, in *On Our Own Ground: The Complete Writings of William Apess, a Pequot,* ed. Barry O'Donnell (Amherst, Mass., 1992), 167, and for the event, xiii–xxxviii; Jill Lepore, *The Name of War: King Philip's War and the Origins of American Identity* (New York, 1998), 215–20.
4. Wendell Phillips, "The Boston Mob," in Phillips, *Speeches,* 2–3.
5. I sampled but did not comb patriotic orations for Boston, a huge field, because in the nature of the genre, the language of lawyers, ministers, and educated speakers on commemorative occasions was usually ornate, if not pretentious. Cf. Kenneth Cmiel, *Democratic Eloquence: The Fight over Popular Speech in Nineteenth-Century America* (New York, 1990), chaps. 1, 2. Patriotic plays, a better register of vernacular English, might reveal the term.
6. For the songs about the event at the time, see Chapter 2, n. 8. I tracked nineteenth-century songs in Bernard E. Wilson, *The Newberry Collection of Early American Printed Sheet Music,* 3 vols. (Boston, 1983), the Driscoll Collection of 50,000 songs in sheet music. I tracked printed songs in D. W. Krummel, *Bibliographic Inventory of Early Music in the Newberry Library* (Boston, 1977) and examined the following songsters: *The Democratic Songster* (Baltimore, 1794); *The National Songster* (Phila-

delphia, 1808); *The Republican Harmonist* (Boston, 1801), and *Patriotic and Amatory Songster* (Boston, 1810).

7. "The Tea Tax: A Yankee Comic Song" by Mr. Andrews (Boston, 1834), misdated by Krummel as 1827.

8. For prints contemporary with the event, see Chapter 2, n. 12. For nineteenth-century prints, I have searched Catalog of American Engravings and Prints (CAEP), the American Antiquarian Society computerized index in progress, and the prints collections at the American Antiquarian Society, the Boston Athenaeum, the Bostonian Society, and the Library of Congress. The first three American engravings of the event I have found are in Charles Goodrich, *History of the United States* (Hartford, 1833) ("Destruction of the Tea in Boston Harbor"), in Robin Carver, *History of Boston* (Boston, 1834), and in *Peter Parley's Magazine* (1835) ("Throwing the Tea Overboard").

9. Boston *Morning Post*, July 9, 1835; Thatcher, *Memoir of Hewes*, 261–62, identified nine individuals, besides Hewes, who were alive in 1835. He identified Hewes as "one of the last survivors." George Quintal, using his data bank of 201 claimants, finds that 25 were alive in July 1835, when Hewes was represented as "the last survivor" and at least 10 were still alive in November 1840, when Hewes died. Of the 25 at least 5 died in Boston or a suburb. Of all these, the only person I know of who made a public claim to be "the last survivor" was David Kennison, whose assertion that he had been at the tea party is itself not credible. See Young et al., *We the People*, 207, based on Albert G. Overton, "David Kennison and the Chicago Sting" (typescript, 1980), Chicago Historical Society Library.

10. Jane C. Nylander, *Our Own Snug Fireside: Images of the New England Home, 1760–1860* (New York, 1993), 240–47; Sargent's painting is reproduced on page 241; Robert Roberts, *The House Servant's Directory: or, a Monitor for Private Families Comprising Hints on the Arrangement and Performance of Servant Work*, ed. Graham R. Hodges (Boston, 1827; New York, 1997).

11. Waldstreicher, *In the Midst of Perpetual Fetes*, reprints the broadside with analysis, 326–27; Eric Lott, *Love and Theft: Blackface Minstrelsy and the American Working Class* (New York, 1993); William J. Mahar, "'Backside Albany' and Early American Minstrelsy . . ." *American Music* 6 (1988): 1–27.

12. David Grimsted, *American Mobbing, 1828–1861: Toward Civil War* (New York, 1998), chap. 1, which the author kindly let me read in MS.

13. Roth, "Tea Drinking in Eighteenth-Century America," 450–51; Frank Luther Mott, *Golden Multitudes: The Story of Best Sellers in the United States* (New York, 1947), 99 (an American success).

14. "Tea Party," *Oxford English Dictionary on Historical Principles*; "Boston Tea Party" in Eric Partridge, *A Dictionary of Slang* (1937; 8th ed., 1984); *Random House Dictionary of American Slang*, vol. 1, has no entries; *Dictionary of American Regional English* (Cambridge, Mass. 1985), vol. 1, has no entries.
15. See Part I, Chapter 9.
16. Deloria, *Playing Indian*, 62–65; Lepore, *In The Name of War*, chap. 8.

8. The Appropriation of the Shoemaker

1. *American Traveller*, July, 1835. [Probably July 1] Reprinted in "The Centennarian Patriot," [Washington] *Army and Navy Chronicle* 1 (July 16 1835): 231.
2. See *Boston Advocate, Columbian Centinel, Boston Transcript*, July 1–10, 1835, for advance notices and reports of the celebration.
3. The fullest report is in the *Evening Gazette*, reprinted in the *Columbian Centinel*, July 8, 1835.
4. James S. Loring, *The One Hundred Boston Orators . . .* (Boston, 1853), 551 (Smith biography); "A Citizen of Massachusetts" [J. V. Smith] *Memoirs of Andrew Jackson* (Boston, 1828); Smith, *Oration Delivered in South Boston, July 4, 1835* (Boston, 1835), quotations at 9, 13–14; Putnam, *Lieutenant Joshua Hewes*, 351, says Richard Brooke Hewes "held a position in the Custom House"; *Register of All Officers and Agents . . . in the Service of the United States* (Washington, D.C., 1829–37) lists Robert B. Hewes as an inspector for 1829, 1831, 1835, and 1837, who, I think, can be taken as the same Hewes. N. Hawthorne is listed for 1839, when the Democratic Party leader George Bancroft was chief.
5. *DAB*, s.v., "Abbott Lawrence"; Dalzell, *Enterprising Elite*, passim; Schlesinger, *Age of Jackson*, 422 ("guiding genius"); *The Life of Davy Crockett by Himself*, originally published 1834–36 (New York, 1955), chap. 21 (visit to Lowell); for the Whig convention of 1840, see the print on the song "Freeman's Quick Step Dedicated to the Delegates of the Bunker Hill Whig Convention of 1840," by George Hews (Boston Athenaeum Collection).
6. *The Atlas*, July 6, 1835.
7. Smith, *Address*, 25–26.
8. *American Traveller*, July 28, 1835 (portrait in Athenaeum); The newspaper alone reports the portrait in the Athenaeum Gallery, but while the *Boston Athenaeum Art Exhibition Index, 1827–1874* (Boston 1980) does not, "it is entirely possible that the painting was brought in—informally, so to speak—and hung," especially if Abbott Lawrence, a prominent shareholder, was involved (Hina Hirayama, Art Department, to Alfred Young, Sept. 18, 1998); Carver, *History of Boston*, 85 ("fashionable re-

sort"); National Portrait Gallery (Washington, D.C.) for a catalog of Cole's portraits; Andrew Oliver et al., *Portraits in the Massachusetts Historical Society* (Boston, 1988), 31–32 (John Davis). A note in the curatorial file for the Hewes portrait, Bostonian Society, reports that Cole "painted the picture in the interest of H. W. Sellers of Philadelphia," who would be Horace Wells Sellers, a descendant, and that the Society purchased it in 1885 from Henry M. Hewes of Medford, Mass.

9. Thatcher, *Memoir of Hewes*, 132.

10. Taylor, *Liberty Men*, 49 (Bowdoin), 193 (Sheriff Samuel Thatcher); Nehemiah Cleaveland, *History of Bowdoin College* (Boston, 1882), passim; *DAB*, s.v. "Thatcher, Benjamin Bussey" (prominent authors).

11. For Thatcher's conservatism *The Colonizationist and Journal of Freedom*, 128–30, 133–37, 358–60, 377–82; Thatcher, *Preface to Indian Biography . . .* , 2 vols. (New York, 1832); *Indian Traits*, 2 vols. (New York, 1833), vol. 1, 20–21.

12. Boston *Advocate*, July 7, 1834 (Thatcher's hymn) and for the reports on Hewes's doings after July 4, 1835: Boston *Advocate*, July 6; *Evening Mercantile Journal*, July 8; *American Traveller*, July 28, Aug. 28; *Boston Courier*, July 22; *Daily Evening Transcript*, July 24, 25, 29, 31, Aug 25, 27; *Atlas*, July 29, 30.

13. Neal Doubleday, ed., *Hawthorne: Tales of His Native Land* (Boston, 1962), 142, claims Hawthorne read Hutchinson; "My Kinsman, Major Molineux" was first printed in *The Token for 1832* (Boston, 1831).

14. Vernon Louis Parrington, *Main Currents of American Thought*, 3 vols. (New York, 1927–30), vol. 2, 439–41; *The Complete Poetical Works of Henry Wadsworth Longfellow* (Boston, 1882), 220, 234.

15. Thatcher, *Memoir of Hewes*, 195–97. The appearance of and reaction to Thatcher's book have eluded me. *Daily Atlas*, July 29, 1835, reported a memoir "now in press" which "will be published in a few days." *Daily Evening Transcript*, July, 29, 1835, an evening paper, reported that Hewes's relatives proposed to prepare a memoir, criticizing the book mentioned in the *Atlas* as "an imposition on the public." The *Atlas*, July 30, then reported "news of a second memoir which claims to be more authentic" and withdrew from the quarrel. I found no reports of a biography appearing in these papers over August. In his appendix, Thatcher published an article from *American Traveller*, Aug. 28, 1835, which leads me to believe that the book appeared some time in the fall of 1835.

16. Previously, I assumed Hawkes was a resident of New York City, where the book was published, and was unable to identify him. On a hunch I found him in S. C. Hutchins, ed., *Civil List . . . of the Colony and State of New York* (Albany, 1869) which lists all governmental officeholders. The federal censuses for 1820 and 1830 identify James Hawks in the town of Richfield; *Otsego Herald*, Mar. 8, 1819 identifies James Hawks as a

Republican candidate; *Biographical Directory of the American Congresses, 1774–1961* (Washington, D.C., 1961) writes up James Hawkes as a member of the 17th Congress, 1821–23. The Hewes memoir is attributed to James Hawkes on the basis of the copyright on the reverse of the title page. A search by librarians at New York State Historical Association, Cooperstown, has not produced any further biographical information.

9. Into History

1. Tucker, *Massachusetts Historical Society*, 89.
2. See Chapter 7, n. 9.
3. David Grimsted to Alfred Young, July 14, 1998; Grimsted, *American Mobbing*; Richards, *Gentlemen of Property and Standing*, 68 (Philadelphia), 98 (Cincinnati).
4. Taylor, *Liberty Men*, chap. 7; Taylor, "Agrarian Independence: Northern Land Rioters after the Revolution," in Young, ed., *Beyond the American Revolution*, 221–45.
5. J. Reeve Huston, "Land and Freedom: The Antirent Wars, Jacksonian Politics, and the Contest over Free Labor in New York, 1785–1865" (Ph.D. diss., Yale University, 1994), chap. 6; Henry Christman, *Tin Horns and Calico* (New York, 1945), 74 (Boughton), 122, 128, 251, 324.
6. Harry T. Peters, *Currier and Ives: Printmakers to the American Republic* (New York, 1942), 11; Jane C. Bland, *Currier and Ives: A Manual for Collectors* (New York, 1931), 309–10.
7. Russell Nye, *George Bancroft: Brahmin Rebel* (New York, 1945), chaps. 4, 6; Schlesinger, *Age of Jackson*, chap. 13.
8. George Bancroft, *History of the United States from the Discovery of the Continent*, 10 vols. (1834–1874), vol. 5, chap. 6.
9. The celebrations are reported fully in *Boston Evening Transcript*, Dec. 17, 1873; *Boston Daily Advertiser*, Dec. 16, 17, 1873; *New York Times*, Dec. 17, 1873; the illustrations are in *Frank Leslie's Illustrated News-Paper*, Jan. 3, 1874, and *Harper's Bazaar*, Jan. 10, 1874.
10. Robert C. Winthrop, *Addresses and Speeches on Various Occasions from 1869 to 1879* (Boston, 1896), 286–97.
11. Tucker, *Massachusetts Historical Society*, 144–146; Mass. Hist. Soc. *Proceedings* 13 (1873–1875), 151–215; *Daily Advertiser*, Dec. 17, 1873 (the relics); Holmes, *Songs of Many Seasons, 1862–1874* (Boston, 1875), 31–35.
12. *Boston Evening Transcript*, July 8, 1876; Winthrop, *Addresses and Speeches*, 378–425; Kammen, *Mystic Chords of Memory*, chap. 5 (centennial).
13. Holleran, *Boston's "Changeful Times,"* chap. 4; Phillips, *Speeches, Lectures, and Letters* (Boston, 1900), 232–42, also in *Old South Leaflets*, No. 202, with excerpts from other speeches.

14. Holloran, *Boston's "Changeful Times,"* chap. 4; [State Street Trust Company] *Boston's Story in Inscriptions* (Boston, 1908).
15. Mass. Hist. Soc. *Proceedings* 2nd ser., 3 (1886–87); 313–18; Tucker, *Massachusetts Historical Society*, 155–58; Dale Freeman, "The Crispus Attucks Monument Dedication," *Historical Journal of Massachusetts* 25 (1997): 125–37.
16. See the books listed in Part I, Chapter 12, n. 7 above.
17. Edward Pierce, "Recollections as a Source of History," Mass. Hist. Soc. *Proceedings* 30 (1895–96): 475–80; *DAB*, s.v. "Pierce, Edward."

Afterword

1. *Boston Globe*, Dec. 17, 1973; Dec. 16 (NOW); Dec. 18 (*Beaver II*); for the contest at the Bicentennial of the Battles of Lexington and Concord, see Edward T. Linenthal, *Sacred Ground: Americans and their Battlefields* (Urbana, Ill., 1993), chap. 1.
2. Howard Zinn, *You Can't Be Neutral on a Moving Train: A Personal History of Our Times* (Boston, 1994), chap. 11 at 142.
3. *Boston Globe*, Apr. 16, 1998.
4. J. Anthony Lukas, *Common Ground: A Turbulent Decade in the Lives of Three American Families* (New York, 1985), 315–16; Michael Musuraca, "The 'Celebration Begins at Midnight': Irish Immigrants and the Celebration of Bunker Hill Day," *Labor's Heritage* (July, 1990), 48–62.
5. *Boston Globe*, Nov. 22, 1998; *Boston Herald*, Dec. 11, 1998; *The Broadside* [National Park Service Newsletter] 4 (1998), p. 5; "The Boston Freedom Award Program" (Boston Duck Tours, typescript, March 1999). In 1964, the Massachusetts state legislature established August 14 as "Liberty Tree Day." In 1997 and 1998, the day was commemorated in a ceremony at the elms on the Boston Common at which the effigies of 1765 were hung and the historian David Hackett Fischer spoke, an event sponsored by Mass ReLeaf, a division of the Massachusetts Department of Environmental Management. In 1999, a number of proposals were under consideration for the Liberty Tree site. Chinatown Main Street proposed a Liberty Tree Park to be landscaped by an elm tree and beacons. Others proposed adding the site to the Freedom Trail and a museum. "Boston 2000" announced a Boston Freedom Award initiated and funded by Andrew Wilson, founder of Boston Duck Tours, "to honor a person who exemplifies the special courage, passion, and determination of those who gathered, debated and celebrated at the site of Boston's Liberty Tree." (Conversations of the author with David H. Fischer, Edith Makra, Antonio Lorenzo, Irene Thai, and Andrew Wilson, October 1998–March 1999.)
6. Marty Carlock, *A Guide to Public Art in Boston* (Boston, 1993), pas-

sim; Susan Wilson, *Boston Sites and Insights: A Multicultural Guide to Fifty Historic Landmarks in and Around Boston* (Boston, 1994), 185–212 (Black Heritage Trail); 212–18 (Women's Heritage Trail); Martin Blatt, Thomas Brown, and Donald Yacovone, eds., *Hope and Glory: Essays on the Legacy of the 54th Massachusetts Regiment* (Amherst, Mass., forthcoming).

7. Old South Meeting House Association, *Tea Is Brewing: A Guide for Teachers* (Boston, 1990); *The Dial* 10 (Spring, 1998): 3.

8. Mike Wallace, *Mickey Mouse History and Other Essays on American Memory* (Philadelphia, 1996), 3–32, 133–74; for the old Colonial Williamsburg; Richard Handler and Eric Gable, *The New History in an Old Museum: Creating the Past at Colonial Williamsburg* (Durham, N.C., 1997) for the efforts to broaden historical interpretation.

9. David Dixon of Goody/Clancy consultants, *The Freedom Trail: Foundations for a Renewed Vision* (Boston, 1995) and *The Freedom Trail: A Framework for the Future* (Boston, 1996), reports prepared for Boston National Historical Park; quotation from the 1996 report, p. 6. The sites are variously controlled by not-for-profit associations, city and state governments, and the National Park Service. In 1974 Congress created the Boston National Historical Park under the supervision of the National Park Service. The Park Service was responsible for the exhibit in the Old State House, planned in the late 1980s and opened in 1992.

10. For the preservation of the Revere house, see Holleran, *Boston's "Changeful Times,"* chap. 9; for current interpretation, see Paul Revere Memorial Association, *Paul Revere—Artisan, Businessman, and Patriot; The Revere House Gazette,* a newsletter, passim, and Wilson, *Boston Sites and Insights,* 20–25.

11. Paul Staiti, "Character and Class," in *John Singleton Copley in America,* ed. Carrie Rebora et al. (New York, 1995), 53–78 and 162–324, for the catalog of portraits.

12. National Park Service, *Boston and the American Revolution* (Washington, 1998), contains Barbara Clark Smith, "A Revolutionary Era," 3–73, and Susan Wilson, "Travels in Historic Boston," 75–92; "Tea Party Etiquette," a video written by Josh Brown and produced by Stephen Brier (American Social History Project, Graduate School, City University of New York, 1984).

13. Wendell Phillips, Address, Mar. 5, 1858, in Phillips, *Addresses,* 72–78.

14. Robert R. Livingston to William Duer, June 12, 1777, cited in Young, *Democratic Republicans of New York,* 15.

Acknowledgments

For Part One, I repeat the following from my original essay: "This essay would not have been possible without the help of a large number of scholars, librarians and descendants and friends of the Hewes family. I acknowledge each of these scholars at the relevant point in the notes. I wish to express my special appreciation to three scholars who read and commented on the essay in several drafts: Jesse Lemisch, Gary Nash, and Lawrence W. Towner. Michael Kammen and James Henretta also offered valuable reactions to an early draft. My debt to Jesse Lemisch is large; he helped me to work out problems too numerous to mention and provided a pioneering example of a biography of an ordinary person in 'The American Revolution and the American Dream: A Life of Andrew Sherburne, a Pensioner of the Navy of the Revolution' (Columbia University Seminar on Early American History and Culture, 1975), to be published in his *The American Revolution and American Dream*. I have also profited from the criticism of colleagues at the Conference on The 'New' Labor History and the New England Working Class, Smith College, 1979; the Graduate Colloquium, Northern Illinois University; and the Newberry Library Seminar in Early American History.

Research for the essay was completed on a Newberry Library–National Endowment for the Humanities Fellowship." Michael McGiffert's rigor as editor of the *William and Mary Quarterly* was matched by his enthusiasm; he was a true enabler.

After the essay was published I received helpful critiques from members of the Princeton University Seminar, including Rhys Isaac, John Murrin, and Sean Wilentz. Jay Coughtry sent me confirmation that Hewes sailed out of Providence on the *Diamond* and David Ingram added to my knowledge about Hewes's father, but I received no corrections or additional information from other scholars. By serendipity I met my first living descendant of Hewes in Paris, Thomas Hewes, a physician (who has a home in Rhode Island), and a second, Carolyn Damon Andrews of New Braintree, Massachusetts. I was relieved—and a bit disappointed—that there was no other family lore about Hewes and no caches of family "papers" thus far.

The essay in Part Two covers such a wide span of time and so many subjects that it literally would not have been possible without the help of a large number of historians, researchers, librarians, curators, and other keepers of the past, who do history in the many historical institutions of Boston.

Josh Brown and Stephen Brier unknowingly planted the seed: Josh as art director and Steve as director of the American Social History Project, City University of New York, wrote and produced the imaginative video *Tea Party Etiquette* (1984) around the tension between Hewes's memory and his biographer Thatcher's version of the Revolution.

At the National Park Service Boston National Historical Park, Martin Blatt, chief of cultural resources, provided me with leads into many subjects and introductions to numerous keepers of the past. This project would not have been possible without his assistance. Park Service rangers Michael Bradford and John Manson guided me through various Boston sites, and Matt Greif, a storehouse of knowledge about Boston history, tracked events in obscure sources, opening up new vistas for the memory of the Revolution. Pat Leehey, director of research for the Paul Revere Memorial Association, guided me through the North End.

I had research assistance from Michael Fertik and Scott Hovey, who read newspapers of the 1830s attentively, and from Paul Uek, who searched for graphics with customary skill. A large number of scholars generously shared with me their research in progress or on the verge of publication: Robert E. Cray, Jr. (on the contested memory of the Revolution in New York), Philip Deloria (on "playing Indian"), James Green (on landmarks in labor history), David Grimsted (on antebellum rioting), J. Reeve Huston and Thomas Humphrey (on Hudson Valley agrarian protest), Benjamin Irvin (on tarring and feathering), Sarah J. Purcell (on the postwar memory of the Revolution), George Quintal (on tea party participants), John Resch (on veterans), Charles Chauncey Wells (on Boston burial grounds), and Elizabeth Young (on the memory of the Civil War).

Other scholars who patiently answered my queries, sent me material, or pointed my search in useful directions are David Blight, David H. Fischer, Elliot Gorn, James Grossman, Greg Kaster, Bruce Laurie, Staughton Lynd, Brendan McConville, Pauline Maier, Lucy Murphy, James O'Brien, Elizabeth Reilly, Paul Staiti, Len Travers, Susan Wilson, Peter Wood, Conrad Wright, Donald Yacovone, and Howard Zinn.

At the Newberry Library, my base of operations, the late David Thackery and John Aubrey were creative guides. Librarians, curators, and museum and site personnel who went out of their way to help me were, at the American Antiquarian Society: Georgia

Barnhill; at the Boston Athenaeum: Sally Pierce and Hina Hirayma; at Boston Duck Tours: Andrew Wilson; at the Boston Public Library: Henry Scannell and R. Eugene Zepp; at the Bostonian Society: Douglas Southard, Steven Hill, Kerry Ackerman, and Susan J. Goganian; at the Boston Museum of Fine Arts: Carol Troyen; at the Massachusetts Historical Society: William Fowler, Jennifer Tolpa, and Suzy Nunes; at the National Portrait Gallery: Patricia H. Svoboda; at the New York State Historical Association: Wayne Wright; at the Old South Meeting House: Emily Curran and Jill Sanderson; at the Paul Revere Memorial Association: Pat Leehey; and at the Tea Party Ship and Museum: Renee Meyer.

I received valuable criticism of the second essay at the Newberry Seminar in Early American History and the Boston Area Seminar in Early American History at the Massachusetts Historical Society. Wayne Franklin's undergraduate seminar at the American Antiquarian Society on "Memory and the American Revolution" helped me think through my views, as did the audience for my lecture at the Society in 1996, for which John Hench was my host. Ronald Grele, director of the Columbia University Oral History Research Office, conducted a one-person seminar for me on the scholarship of memory, and Daniel Schacter invited me to an enlightening interdisciplinary conference on memory at Harvard University sponsored by the "Mind/Brain Initiative." The stimulating Milan Group in Early United States History responded to my early thoughts on the memory of the Revolution at its 1992 symposium.

I extend my warm appreciation to scholars who gave me tough, insightful readings of several drafts of this essay: Jesse Lemisch, David Waldstreicher, and Matt Greif, who saved me from many errors. Scholars who read one draft or another and gave me the benefit of their expertise include Martin Blatt, Ronald P. Formisano, Louis P. Hutchins, Pat Leehey, and Christopher Tomlins. Needless to say, none of the many scholars I have mentioned is responsible for the errors that remain, much less for my interpretations and opinions.

At Beacon Press I owe a special debt of gratitude to Deb Chasman, editorial director, who had a vision of what this book might be and whose enthusiasm and editorial suggestions made it possible, and to Amy Blair, who gave the essay an astute reading. Linda Howe was a demanding and skillful editor. My old friends Robin and Robert Cohen were warm, welcoming hosts on my many trips to Boston, as were Elizabeth and Jerry Reilly on my trips to Worcester.

Index